CHOICE WORDS

CHOICE WORDS

WRITERS ON ABORTION

Edited by Annie Finch

Haymarket Books
Chicago, Illinois

Published in 2020 by
Haymarket Books
P.O. Box 180165
Chicago, IL 60618
773-583-7884
www.haymarketbooks.org
info@haymarketbooks.org

ISBN: 978-1-64259-148-4

Distributed to the trade in the US through Consortium Book Sales and Distri-
bution (www.cbsd.com) and internationally through Ingram Publisher Services
International (www.ingramcontent.com).

This book was published with the generous support of Lannan Foundation
and Wallace Action Fund.

Special discounts are available for bulk purchases by organizations and institu-
tions. Please email orders@haymarketbooks.org for more information.

Cover design by Abby Weintraub.

Printed in Canada.

Library of Congress Cataloging-in-Publication data is available.

For my sister

Mary Dabney Baker Finch (1952–2018)
with sorrow that your
secret youthful abortion
wounded you and
many others

CONTENTS

MIND

BODY

HEART

WILL

FOREWORD

Katha Pollitt

Women have been ending pregnancies for thousands of years, but it's hard to think of many classic poems or stories in which abortion makes an appearance, and most of what exists was written by men who disapproved of it. Think of T. S. Eliot's *The Waste Land*, in which working-class women in a pub gossip crudely about a friend who took pills to "bring it off," or Hemingway's "Hills Like White Elephants," in which an aimless expatriate tries to persuade his sweet, passive girlfriend into an abortion she clearly doesn't want. With few exceptions, abortion figures in men's writings as a symbol—of modern alienation, of a larger sterility.

It took women writers to give the subject both bloody realism and emotional and social complexity. Even before the women's liberation movement of the 1960s and 1970s, women wrote about abortion as simultaneously a personal experience and something more general: a necessary form of self-defense against poverty, stigma, exhaustion, crushing social expectations, one's own sheer fertility, and brutal men.

The experience of abortion is something millions of women share, but there is no universal abortion experience, because every woman is different. Nearly every kind of abortion you can imagine is represented here. Abortions legal and illegal, safe and dangerous, and fatal; abortions despite the wishes of others and abortions at the behest—the compulsion—of others; abortion as a claiming of self and abortion as an abnegation of self. There is abortion as tragedy, and also abortion as an occasion for wry comedy, as in Vi Khi Nao's "An Avocado Is Going to Have an Abortion":

> An avocado is going to have an abortion. What is the grapefruit going
> to do about it? It hasn't gotten it pregnant. Certainly not.

In "First Response," Desiree Cooper captures the multiplicity of abortion, and also its ubiquity:

> Joyce didn't have sex until she was married eight years later. Trish went back to work like nothing ever happened. We made a donation every anniversary. We were pregnant with memory for the rest of our lives. We never thought about it again.

In the popular imagination, abortion is the rejection of motherhood— women who have abortions are coldhearted "career women," child-haters, feckless sluts. In real life, the majority—about 60 percent—of American women who have abortions are already mothers. It's not surprising, but it is important, that in these pages we find abortion most often placed in the context of motherhood, especially for Black writers. Georgia Douglas Johnson's abortion poem is "Motherhood"; Gwendolyn Brooks's is called "the mother." In "the lost baby poem," Lucille Clifton writes:

> if i am ever less than a mountain
> for your definite brothers and sisters
> let the rivers pour over my head

There is one kind of abortion you won't find here, though, and that is the mythical one of anti-abortion propaganda: the frivolous abortion for no good reason, the abortion of sluttish, worthless women who just can't be bothered, the abortion for "convenience." As Marge Piercy writes in her poem brilliantly titled "Right to Life,"

> I am not your cornfield,
> not your uranium mine, not your calf
> for fattening, not your cow for milking.
> You may not use me as your factory.
> Priests and legislators do not hold
> shares in my womb or my mind.
> This is my body. If I give it to you
> I want it back. My life
> is a nonnegotiable demand.

Abortion is always serious. As serious as birth.

INTRODUCTION

Annie Finch

I had an abortion in 1999. Searching for literature to help me absorb my experience, I realized that I had rarely read anything about abortion (and I have a PhD in literature). I was astounded to discover that there was no major literary anthology about one of the most profound experiences in my life and that of millions of others. A physical, psychological, moral, spiritual, political, and cultural reality that navigates questions of life and death, abortion should be one of the great themes of literature.

Choice Words is the result of the twenty-year search that grew out of this initial sense of shock and loss. As I put out calls for poetry, novels, short stories, and drama and reached out to writers and scholars for recommendations and leads, I discovered that major writers had indeed written about the subject, but that much of the literature was hard to find, unpublished, or buried within larger literary works. The project was dispiriting at times, and I had nearly given up when a traumatic presidential election and an enraging Supreme Court appointment renewed my energy to complete the book.

Over the years, the anthology grew to encompass lyric and narrative poems, plays, short stories, tweets, memoirs, flash fiction, rituals, journals, and excerpts from novels. Here are writings that invoke grief, defiance, fear, shame, desperation, love, awe, tenderness, sorrow, regret, compassion, hope, despair, resolve, rage, triumph, relief, and peace. Here are writers from the sixteenth through twenty-first centuries, across ethnicities, cultures, genders and sexualities, including U.S. writers of diverse backgrounds and voices from Bulgaria, China, England, Finland, India, Iran, Ireland, Kenya, Northern Ireland, Pakistan, Romania, Saudi Arabia, Scotland, South Africa, Sudan, and Syria, sharing how class, patriarchy,

1

race and ethnicity, wealth, poverty, and faith traditions impact our understanding and experience of abortion.

Choice Words includes courageous, iconic texts that speak out ahead of their time, such as Blandiana's "The Children's Crusade"; Brooks's "the mother"; Clifton's "Lost Baby Poem"; Lamb's *What Have You Done for Me Lately?*; Piercy's "Right to Life"; Saleh's "A Million Women Are Your Mother"; and Wollstonecraft's *Maria: or, The Wrongs of Woman*. Some of the pieces included are moving first-person accounts ranging from contemporary high schoolers in Pakistan to feminist legends such as Audre Lorde and Gloria Steinem. Others express the imaginative literary vision of major writers such as Margaret Atwood, Ruth Prawer Jhabvala, Ursula LeGuin, Gloria Naylor, Joyce Carol Oates, Anne Sexton, Ntozake Shange, Leslie Marmon Silko, Edith Södergran, Amy Tan, Mo Yan, and so many more.

The powerful literary writing in *Choice Words* depicts the collective courage of our struggle to gain back reproductive freedom and make clear that bodily autonomy is necessary to human freedom and integrity. They describe the tragic emotional and physical toll of cultural, political, and religious attempts to force us to have children, to force us to have abortions, or to surround our reproductive choices with shame, silence, and isolation. These are the words we need to learn from now.

ORGANIZATION OF THE BOOK

Choice Words is organized into five sections: "Mind," "Body," "Heart," "Will," and "Spirit." "Mind" focuses on how people make the often agonizing decision to terminate a pregnancy, and how we carry the weight of that decision alone in times and cultures where abortion is not openly spoken of: the oppression of silence. From Debra Bruce's tale of a young woman harassed out of her decision by protesters to Gloria Naylor's portrait of poverty and domestic conflict from *The Women of Brewster Place* to Lindy West's contemporary account of a matter-of-fact choice, this section offers graphic evidence that the final say on abortion needs to rest only with the person whose womb holds the embryo, since regardless of others' influence, this is the mind, body, heart, will, and spirit that will live with the decision forever. As Caitlin McDonnell writes, "However painful the decision-making process, however fraught it is with ambivalence and paradox, it is ours."

"Body" focuses on the physical experience of abortion, universal and yet so different across times and cultures, starting with the heroine seeking an abortifacient "herb in the merry green wood" in the sixteenth-century English ballad "Tam Lin." From Shirley Geok-lin Lim's description of a dehumanizing abortion among "long silent rows" of cots in the 1970s to Ruth Prawer Jhabvala's account of a peaceful abortion provided through massage by midwives in India, these writings demonstrate not only the reality of abortion but also its flexibility; abortion is so varied that we are free to reimagine its traditions for ourselves, however we need it to be.

"Heart" centers on the profound emotional aspects of abortion, opening with Gwendolyn Brooks's haunting poem "the mother" with its unforgettable line "abortions will not let you forget." Here is the grief of unprocessed emotions, as in Diane di Prima's "Brass Furnace Going Out: Song, After an Abortion" and Zofia Nałkowska's tragic portrait of a Polish woman in 1935 suffering from depression after an isolated, traumatic abortion. And here is the loneliness of keeping silent in polite society, depicted in an unforgettably scathing satire by Dorothy Parker. Many of the writings in this section also bring to life the love of those caring people who help us through abortions. Here are supportive friends, the fraught bond between mother and daughter in Ursula K. Le Guin's "Standing Ground," and Judith Arcana's tender depiction of the courageous and compassionate abortion activists who helped people find illegal abortions in the days before Roe vs. Wade.

"Will" addresses the personal and political power inherent in our ability to give life, and the courage and determination that the exercise of choice can require even where it is legal and culturally acceptable. Many of these pieces show women reclaiming moral authority over death and life within our own bodies, as a birthright that naturally arises from our reproductive capacities—whether it is Alexis Quinlan brazenly putting reproductive freedom into the terms of an army slogan from the late twentieth century, "be all you can be," or Edith Södergran, a hundred years earlier, claiming the same right in more clandestine terms. This section includes Audre Lorde's solitary, secretive abortion in Brooklyn in the 1950s and Marge

Piercy's magnetic rant "Right to Life," opening with the memorable lines "A woman is not a pear tree/Thrusting her fruit in mindless fecundity/Into the world. . ."; Kathy Acker's classic of experimental literature "Don Quixote's Abortion," which envisions the heroine as a brave knight with a green hospital gown as armor; and Ntozake Shange's riveting portrayal of a woman's determination to rid herself of a traumatic pregnancy at all costs.

"Spirit" closes the book with poems, essays, and dramatic ritual ceremonies that place abortion in a spiritual framework. A common theme in this section is the shame and confusion many experience in trying to understand their relationship with abortion in the context of patriarchal religions. Madame X, a Victorian midwife in Kate Manning's novel, describes her ethics of abortion in the only way possible for her as a Christian ("it was never alive"). On the other hand, Leslie Marmon Silko and Margaret Atwood portray the spiritually healing power of nature to women at this vulnerable time. Like Deborah Maia's and Ginette Paris's pieces elsewhere in the book, the rituals in this section show that the relation between abortion and feminist spirituality is reciprocal: the need to come to terms with abortion can spur women to reclaim the thread of women's spiritual wisdom, and an existing connection with women-centered spirituality can offer a context for abortion in which both life and death are held sacred.*

Patterns and Common Themes

We count on writers to illuminate our feelings, to help us claim and integrate the unacknowledged parts of ourselves and the aspects of others that feel alien or threatening, and to play out the complexities and paradoxes of our thoughts. That is one reason literature has such a vital role to play in the conversation about abortion right now. The political arguments have been made repeatedly; in some ways there is nothing else left to say, and yet so much more needs to be said. The voices in this book bring exact insight, body-knowledge, compassion, strength of will, and intuitive blessing to bear. They don't provide simple answers, but they do offer patterns:

---

* Mary Condren's brilliant book on the origins of patriarchy in Ireland, *The Serpent and the Goddess*, offers a stunning case history of such connections.

Abortion as an act of love

In a perceptive and forward-thinking essay, the philosopher Soran Reader points out that mothers choose abortion as a loving act of caretaking, whether for existing children or for the child they choose not to have.* That our current social structure surrounds abortion with the opposite stereotype shows the gulf between women and those who make the laws and precepts. Yet if the many accounts of violence suffered by women in this book at the hands of government and religion incite anger and grief, note the glimmers of light emerging from the shadows, the premonitions of the way it could be better. The remarkable pieces by Ruth Prawer Jhabvala, Deborah Maia, and Hanna Neuschwander, for example, show with courage and tenderness that it is possible to support empowering and respectful abortion amid loving community.

Abortion as a normal human activity

Though suspicion and discomfort about women and about death combine into a toxic cloud around the act of abortion, the harrowing experiences described in some of the pieces in this book are caused not by abortion itself but by its control, compulsion, criminalization, censoring, or condemnation. Whether the outcome is unnecessary death, as in the contributions by Langston Hughes and Amy Tan, or the shame and alienation caused by enforced silence, as in Soniah Kamal's "The Scarlet A," it is the loss of sovereignty over the truth of one's own body that haunts and destroys. The great diversity of this book's perspectives shows that reproductive choices are uniquely individual and complex—and should therefore never be legislated by anyone for another. Abortion is normal; violent control over it is not.

Abortion as symbol and archetype

Like death and birth, abortion has huge symbolic power that can enlarge a writer's canvas. For some writers in this book, abortion is not so much the topic as a way of talking about a different topic; for example, a connection

---

* Soran Reader, "Abortion, Killing, and Maternal Moral Authority," *Hypatia* 23, no. 1 (Jan–March 2008): 136–139.

between putting oneself ahead of a pregnancy and moving to the center stage of one's own life is evident in numerous contributions including those by Rita Mae Brown, Angelique Imani Rodriguez, and Lindy West. The abortion in Ulrica Hume's "Lizard" can be seen, on one level, as setting in motion a deeper transformation within the character that may be the real theme of the story. As Katha Pollitt points out in her foreword, male writers have often used abortion as a symbol for sterility and alienation. Langston Hughes's "Cora, Unashamed" can be seen to continue this tradition, though in a way made more nuanced and complex through issues of race. In Amy Tan's excerpt from *The Hundred Secret Senses* the choice to have an abortion seems to have mythic resonance as it calls in destructive forces beyond the bounds of realistic expectation. Pat Falk has written about her poem in this book that "the images of [Barbara Jane's] death, dismemberment—desecration—have become, in my mind, a metaphor for the female principle that has been de-formed, denied, devalued in women and men, in myself."

Only freedom is nonviolent—and freedom depends on justice

There is violence in anything that forces reproductive choices against a person's will. Jennifer Hanratty's Twitter stream, like Hanna Neuschwander's essay, shares the pain that women who need to abort much-wanted babies for medical reasons suffer from anti-abortion laws or bias. One surprise that many readers may find in this book is that, while in the U.S. and most of Europe we think of the freedom to *have* an abortion as a basic liberty, there are, as the pieces by Linda Ashok, Shikha Malaviya, Manisha Sharma, and Mo Yan make clear, millions of women struggling desperately *not* to have abortions—usually of female babies. Choice is only possible when there is reproductive justice, and writings by Ai, Gloria Naylor, Saniyya Saleh, and numerous others here demonstrate over and over how differences based on poverty, wealth, politics, ethnicity, class, religion, marital status, age, geography, or nationality unjustly restrict reproductive freedom. Yet for all the dazzling variety of differences that patriarchy exploits to justify imposing reproductive injustice, the cross-cultural truth-telling in this book exposes core similarities among the injustices themselves—for example, between the situations faced by the protagonists in Amy Tan's *The Kitchen God's Wife* and Mary

Wollstonecraft's *Maria: or, The Wrongs of Woman*. To recognize such widespread patterns can be as bracing and illuminating as it is horrifying.

Reproductive freedom can be emotionally complex

While this book assumes that access to safe, legal abortion is a fundamental human right, I chose to include many poignant expressions of grief and regret over the choice to terminate a pregnancy, or ambivalence about the ethical and spiritual nature of abortion, by writers including Lucille Clifton, Teri Cross Davis, and Farideh Hassanzadeh-Mostafavi. There is no contradiction here. The fact that we may have negative emotions about a particular abortion doesn't mean that abortion is wrong. As Caitlin McDonnell points out, the possibility of negative feelings is part of the responsibility of choice.

Feelings about an abortion can evolve

The aftermath of abortion is as various as the experience itself, and recovery can be a dynamic and changing process. As Ava Torre-Bueno's valuable book *Peace After Abortion* explains, the need some of us feel for emotional healing after an abortion may offer a doorway to confronting other, far older wounds that have nothing to do with abortion. Several contributors told me of the peace of mind they found in writing about an abortion thirty, forty, or even fifty years later; some felt that this anthology gave them permission to write about it for the first time. Abortion stories that need to be told don't give up. But by contrast, some of the writings describe moving on nearly immediately—with a flirtatious dance in a lesbian bar, a glass of wine in Bulgaria, or a pastrami sandwich in Greenwich village.

The role of connection and support

Many of these writings portray the crucial importance of a caring supporter: the daughter in Ursula K. LeGuin's "Standing Ground," Miz Lewis in Audre Lorde's *Zami*, the soon-to-be-lover in Rita Mae Brown's *RubyFruit Jungle*, the doctor in Gloria Steinem's memoir, Spirit Mother in Deborah

Maia's *Self-Ritual for Invoking Release of Spirit Life in the Womb*, the friend in Sholeh Wolpé's "Jewel of Tehran." On the other hand, the absence of such support can be wrenching, as satirized in Dorothy Parker's brutally funny story or expressed in the mother's harshness in Deborah Hauser's "Hail Mary" or the loneliness in the words of Kenyan teenagers in "She Did Not Tell Her Mother." One subtle, sad discernible truth is that the patriarchy's wounding of women and gender non-conforming people resonates down through the generations, compromising our ability to tend and cherish one other during our life-and-death moments.

Vision for the Role of This Book

My vision for the role of *Choice Words* takes the form of three concentric circles: individual experience, collective understanding, and social change. On the individual level, I hope the book will be helpful to people who are dealing with abortion in their own lives or who seek to understand it more deeply, offering compassion, support, companionship, and insight. No matter where you are on this issue, may this book bring you closer to understanding that people who have abortions are full human beings. If you are reading this book in a reproductive health clinic waiting room (thanks to the nearly five hundred backers who supported a Kickstarter campaign to donate copies to clinics), even if you have only a few minutes, here's hoping you will open the book to some words, perhaps by Leyla Josephine, Busisiwe Mahlangu, or Marge Piercy, that will focus your mind, soothe your heart, or strengthen your will.

On the level of collective understanding, I envision *Choice Words* as a source of knowledge and illumination within and between cultures and literatures. Even those who don't normally read much literature will find a wealth of human connection in these pages—stories about lives that matter to us, poems that express feelings we need to understand more deeply, plays and essays that lay out urgent new ways of contextualizing our lives and thoughts. As for literature, when contributors to this book respond to male texts—Kathy Acker to Cervantes, Joanna C. Valente to Richard Brautigan—or illuminate the role of abortion in the imaginations of women writers we thought we knew—Lesley Wheeler on Edna

St. Vincent Millay, Yesenia Montilla on Anne Sexton—they reshape literary tradition in unprecedented ways.

Choice Words is, like any anthology, only a beginning. I felt this deeply during the editing process, when my prolonged and diligent hunt for literature from some writers whose perspectives badly need to be heard—including imprisoned and transgender writers—yielded nothing. As Gillian Branstetter of the National Center for Transgender Equality told me, "stigma and silence make it difficult for any person to talk about their abortion, and it is frequently worse for people who feel excluded from the conversation—including transgender men and nonbinary people. That is just why their stories are so important." Readers who want to learn more about abortion in the trans community will find information and support at local Planned Parenthoods, the Planned Parenthood Federation, the National Partnership for Women and Families, the Center for Reproductive Rights, the Abortion Access Fund, and the National Center for Transgender Equality. I hope this book will inspire future editors to continue in these directions and numerous others.

On the level of social justice and reproductive rights, I hope this book will provide a focal point for community organizing and activism. Many are beginning to recognize that control of sexual and reproductive autonomy is integrally related to other forms of authoritarianism and exploitation. *Choice Words* can be used as a topic for book club discussions as we take the first step towards change, raising awareness; it can be used as a source text for abortion healing circles and consciousness-raising groups as we take the next step towards change, healing ourselves; and it can be used as the focus of community discussions across ideological lines or as a source of readings performed at fundraisers as we move forward together into action.

Conclusion

I write these words sitting in the main reading room in the Library of Congress at a profoundly challenging time for reproductive rights in the U.S. and in many other parts of our planet. Yet I am heartened and moved by the continuity of this chorus of literary voices across eras and continents. Today's circumstances are driving new voices to speak up without hesitation or shame about the central importance of reproductive justice for human rights all over the world. To bring the power of literature to bear on the topic of abortion at this hinge time in the resurgence of our full and complete human rights has been my privilege and my joy.

Editor's Note: While I share in the widespread condemnation of recent inolerant statements by Ana Blandiana, I chose to include her work here in view of the historical importance of her contribution to the literature of abortion.

It is also important to note that because of the breadth of times and locations represented in this anthology, some of the language in these literary works may sound outdated or biased to contemporary readers.

MIND

YOU ARE HERE

Cin Salach

Oh land of the free and home of the brave
how much courage does it take
to hurl lies threats boasts
at those who do not agree with those who do not agree?

How much more courage would it take
to hold each other in each other's arms
reminding ourselves *we're all made of flesh*
whispering into each other's lives
I disagree with you but I love you.
I disagree with you but I respect you.
I disagree with you but I will not ram my sign down your throat
so your voice is silenced and only mine is heard.

listen to me listen to me listen to me listen to me listen to me
listen to you listen to you listen to you listen to you listen to you
listen to me listen to you listen to me listen to you

This chorus of voices, let's call them ideas
let's call them demands
let's call them rights and wrongs, lefts and rights
this chorus of voices, let's call them ours
and sing at the top of our lungs
You belong to me you beautiful opinion you
and I shall name you Freedom.

When does life begin? All the time.
With every breath, things start over.
At what moment does conception become reality

become flesh become mine?
Would I need a stopwatch to know?
A so, so, so precise way of measuring time
counting down to the last millisecond 3 2 1 1 1
push breathe push breathe push
Congratulations, it's a life all right. *Mine.*

This is America. If you can't stand the freedom
get out of the country.

FIRST RESPONSE

Desiree Cooper

The moment we read the stick, some of us buckled on the bathroom floor. Having only bled once, we thought it was impossible. Having bled forever, we shook our graying heads and thought, "This is no miracle." Susan, who at fourteen still slept with her favorite doll, bit back the tears and started packing her bags. We knew our mothers would not believe us. Abby bought a ticket to New York to secretly take care of it.

We locked ourselves in the bathroom sobbing while the kids banged on the door: "Mommy, please come out." For some of us, three healthy children were enough. For others, a special-needs child was one too many. One day, we would have many children. One day, decades later, we would still be child free.

The ultrasound technician drew in a deep breath and did not let it out. We feared a perfect baby. Undecided, we waited too long. Decisive, we were instantly clear about what to do. We were happy about it until we weren't.

We borrowed cash from our friends so that it wouldn't show on the insurance bill. We had no insurance. We had insurance, but the D & C was covered only for miscarriages. Brittany's college roommates threw her a "baby shower" with vodka served in sippy cups. Our aunts said, "You're lucky you won't be butchered in someone's basement like I was."

Lynne was dropped off by her stepfather, along with her suitcase and her cat. We called in sick at the firm even though it was tax season. Mary's boyfriend slapped her and pushed her out of the car. "You better have dinner ready tonight. And your fat ass better not still be pregnant."

The bus. A cab. The heat. A bike. The snow. The traffic. We were late, but we made it. We were two hours early because we couldn't sit at home alone.

In the waiting room, we would not return a gaze. Our men held us tightly. Jan nervously fiddled with a ring from her make-believe fiancé.

We were by ourselves and puffy-faced. Diane was already showing—every time, she seemed to show a few weeks earlier. One couple argued with the receptionist. They had driven from another state, but didn't know about the twenty-four-hour waiting period. Some of us let the tears river while others slumped in pink chairs and listened to our iPods. We were horrified to be with these people. Full of shame, we fingered a rosary. Full of anger, we cursed God.

"Relax," the kind nurse held our hands as the doctor readied. "You're going to be fine."

We wondered if anything would be fine again. Annie quaked; the doctor took off his mask and said, "I'm not doing this. You're not ready." We listened to the vacuum. We didn't know what hit us. When the room went silent, we rose up in wonder; it had been so easy. The nausea was over at last. For Kita, the nausea from the chemo would go on. We wondered if we would ever forgive ourselves. We didn't need anybody's forgiveness.

Every recliner in the recovery room was full. It was over; we looked up. Many smiled compassionately. Some felt theirs was the only good reason. Liz, who still had three AP exams, didn't know who she was anymore. We wanted to hold hands. We wanted to get the hell away from these losers. We wanted to cocoon in our beds. We longed for our mothers.

Some lovers promised: "We'll try again when I get a job." Cindy wouldn't have to cancel her Paris vacation. Carrie forgot to ask if she could hustle that night. We realized how much our husbands loved us. Jenna had to wait until child protective services came to pick her up. We were relieved that our grandchildren wouldn't see our swelling stomachs.

Joyce didn't have sex until she was married eight years later. Trish went back to work like nothing ever happened. We made a donation every anniversary. We were pregnant with memory for the rest of our lives. We never thought about it again.

FROM *THE WOMEN OF BREWSTER PLACE*

Gloria Naylor

"I lost my job today," he shot at her, as if she had been the cause.

The water was turning cloudy in the rice pot, and the force of the stream from the faucet caused scummy bubbles to rise to the surface. These broke and sprayed tiny, starchy particles onto the dirty surface. Each bubble that broke seemed to increase the volume of the dogged whispers she had been ignoring for the last few months. She poured the dirty water off the rice to destroy and silence them, then watched with a malicious joy as they disappeared down the drain.

"So now, how in hell I'm gonna make it with no money, huh? And another brat comin' here, huh?"

The second change of water was slightly clearer, but the starch-speckled bubbles were still there, and this time there was no way to pretend deafness to their message. She had stood at that sink countless times before, washing rice, and she knew the water was never going to be totally clear. She couldn't stand there forever—her fingers were getting cold, and the rest of the dinner had to be fixed, and Serena would be waking up soon and wanting attention. Feverishly she poured the water off and tried again.

"I'm fuckin' sick of never getting ahead. Babies and bills, that's all you good for."

The bubbles were almost transparent now, but when they broke they left light trails of starch on top of the water that curled around her fingers. She knew it would be useless to try again. Defeated, Ciel placed the wet pot on the burner, and the flames leaped up bright red and orange, turning the water droplets clinging on the outside into steam.

Turning to him, she silently acquiesced. "All right, Eugene, what do you want me to do?"

He wasn't going to let her off so easily. "Hey, baby, look, I don't care what you do. I just can't have all these hassles on me right now, ya know?"

"I'll get a job. I don't mind, but I've got no one to keep Serena, and you don't want Mattie watching her."

"Mattie—no way. That fat bitch'll turn the kid against me. She hates my ass, and you know it."

"No, she doesn't, Eugene." Ciel remembered throwing that at Mattie once. "You hate him, don't you?" "Naw, honey," and she had cupped both hands on Ciel's face. "Maybe I just loves you too much."

"I don't give a damn what you say—she ain't minding my kid."

"Well, look, after the baby comes, they can tie my tubes—I don't care." She swallowed hard to keep down the lie.

"And what the hell we gonna feed it when it gets here, huh—air? With two kids and you on my back, I ain't never gonna have nothin'." He came and grabbed her by the shoulders and was shouting into her face. "Nothin', do you hear me, nothin'!"

"Nothing to it, Mrs. Turner." The face over hers was as calm and antiseptic as the room she lay in.

"Please, relax. I'm going to give you a local anesthetic and then perform a simple D & C, or what you'd call a scraping to clean out the uterus. Then you'll rest here for about an hour and be on your way. There won't even be much bleeding." The voice droned on in its practiced monologue, peppered with sterile kindness.

Ciel was not listening. It was important that she keep herself completely isolated from these surroundings. All the activities of the past week of her life were balled up and jammed on the right side of her brain, as if belonging to another woman. And when she had endured this one last thing for her, she would push it up there, too, and then one day give it all to her—Ciel wanted no part of it.

The next few days Ciel found it difficult to connect herself up again with her own world. Everything seemed to have taken on new textures and colors. When she washed the dishes, the plates felt peculiar in her hands, and she was more conscious of their smoothness and the heat of the water. There was a disturbing split second between someone talking to her and the words penetrating sufficiently to elicit a response. Her neighbors left her presence with a slight frown of puzzlement, and Eugene could be heard mumbling, "Moody bitch."

She became terribly possessive of Serena. She refused to leave her alone, even with Eugene. The little girl went everywhere with Ciel, toddling along on plump, uncertain legs. When someone asked to hold or play with her, Ciel sat nearby, watching every move. She found herself walking into the bedroom several times when the child napped to see if she was still breathing. Each time she chided herself for this unreasonable foolishness, but within the next few minutes some strange force still drove her back.

MOTHERHOOD

Georgia Douglas Johnson

Don't knock on my door, little child,
I cannot let you in,
You know not what a world this is
Of cruelty and sin.
Wait in the still eternity
Until I come to you.
The world is cruel, cruel, child,
I cannot let you in!

Don't knock at my heart, little one,
I cannot bear the pain
Of turning deaf ears to your call,
Time and time again.
You do not know the monster men
Inhabiting the earth.
Be still, be still, my precious child,
I cannot give you birth!

(AMBER)

Debra Bruce

A girl holds her baby on a hint of hip.
She'd never known that word before—*injunction*—
until the lady outside the clinic stepped
as carefully as counting and did not come
too close or shout, but she spoke to the core
of the girl going in, whose name she didn't know,
(Amber)—volunteers in pink at the door.
Then Amber—just a few more steps to go—

walked away. Now she yanks a pillow
under her boyfriend's head—didn't he promise
he'd babysit although it's not even his,
until he gets a job? And then the girl,
just like the lady said, will find a way.
She hasn't seen the lady since that day.

FROM *THE KITCHEN GOD'S WIFE*

Amy Tan

One day, perhaps six months after Yiku had been born, the servant girl came to me, telling me she had to leave. She was fourteen years old, a small girl, always obedient, so Hulan had no reason to scold her. When I asked why she wanted to leave, she excused herself and said she was not a good enough worker.

That was the Chinese way, to use yourself as an excuse, to say you are unworthy, when really you mean you are worth more. I could guess why she was unhappy. Over the last few months, Hulan had started asking the girl to do lots of little tasks that turned into big ones. And that poor girl, who never knew how to refuse anyone, soon had twice as much work for the same amount of money I paid her.

I did not want to lose her. So I told her, "You are an excellent servant, never lazy, deserving of even more money, I think."

She shook her head. She insisted she was unworthy. I said, "I have praised you often, don't you remember?"

She nodded.

And then I thought maybe Hulan had been treating her in a mean way, scolding her behind my back, and now this girl couldn't take it anymore. Oh, I was mad! "Has someone else been causing you problems?" I said to the girl. "Someone is giving you trouble, am I right? Don't be afraid, tell me."

She began to cry, nodding her head without looking at me.

"Someone is making it hard for you to work here? Is this so?"

She nodded again, more tears. And then she told me who. "*Tai-tai*, he is not well, very sick. I know this. So I am not blaming your husband."

"Blame? What is your meaning for bringing up this word?" I said. It was summertime, but a chill rushed over my body and I ordered the girl to speak. I listened from a faraway place as the servant girl begged me to forgive her, slapped her own face twice, and confessed she was the one who was wrong. She said she was the one who was weak for letting him touch her. She cried and prayed for me to not say anything to my husband.

And now I don't remember exactly how I got all her words out, how I pulled them out, one by one. But that afternoon I found out that my husband had started to put his hands on her while I was in the hospital, that she had struggled each time, and each time he had raped her. She did not say "rape," of course. A girl that young and innocent, how could she know such a word? She knew only how to blame herself.

I had to ask her many times: The bruise on her face that she claimed was her own clumsiness—was that the time he had tried once before? The times she claimed to be ill, always in the morning—was that after it happened?

Each time the girl confessed something, she cried and slapped her own face. I finally told her to stop hitting herself. I patted her arm and told her I would settle this problem for her.

Her face became scared. "What will you do, *tai-tai*?"

I said, "This is not your worry anymore." And then I felt so tired and confused I went upstairs to Yiku's room. I sat in a chair and watched my baby daughter sleeping, so peaceful in her bed.

What an evil man! How could I have known such an evil man existed on this earth! Last year's accident had taught him nothing!

And then I thought, "What will people think when they find out? What will they think of me—if I take sides against my husband and defend a servant girl instead?" I imagined Hulan scolding me, accusing me of seeing only the worst in everything and everybody. I saw others criticizing me for not managing my house better. I could imagine people laughing—a husband who chases after a servant girl because his own wife is not enough—the classic old story!

And then I thought to myself, "What he did was wrong, maybe it was a crime, but not a big one. Many men did those kinds of things with servants. And who would believe a servant girl?" My husband would say she lied, of course he would. He would claim that the girl seduced him, a big hero. Or he would say she had already slept with many pilots. He could say anything.

And what would I gain by accusing my husband? I would get a big fight from him in return, pitiful looks from Hulan and Jiaguo, all that shame. So what would it matter if I tried to help that girl? What would I gain? Only trouble in my own bed. And then what would I lose? I could not even begin to imagine that.

I sat down and remembered a saying Old Aunt used to tell me whenever I complained that I had been wrongly accused: "Don't strike a flea on a tiger's head." Don't settle one trouble only to make a bigger one.

So I decided to say nothing, do nothing. I made myself blind. I made myself deaf. I let myself become just like Hulan and Jiaguo, that time they said nothing when Wen Fu slapped me.

I gave the servant girl three months' wages. I wrote her a good recommendation. She went away, I don't know where. I think she was grateful she could quietly leave. And when Wen Fu asked two days later where the servant girl was, I said, "That girl? Oh, she got an offer from her mother to marry a village boy. So I sent her home."

Several weeks later I heard the servant girl was dead. Hulan told me while I was nursing Yiku. She said the girl had gone to someone else's house to work. And one morning, after the girl knew she was pregnant, she used the old country way. She took a piece of straw from a broom, poked her womb until she began to bleed, but the bleeding never stopped.

"So stupid to use a piece of straw like that," said Hulan. "And the family who took her in—oyo!—so mad that she brought a ghost on them. Lucky for us she didn't die in our house."

While Hulan talked, I felt strange, as if I were feeling that slap to my face all over again, everyone in the room looking down on me, saying this was my fault. I could see that girl lying on the floor, her blood spilled all around, people lamenting only that she had left a big mess behind.

Of course, Hulan didn't know it was Wen Fu who got that girl in trouble. Or maybe she knew and wasn't saying anything. Still, how could she think this way! Criticizing a helpless servant girl, congratulating us for being rid of her before she turned into a ghost. Why was she not thinking of her own sister, the one who died almost the same way? And I was just as bad, because I had become almost like Hulan: no sympathy, only relief that I had avoided troubles for myself.

After Hulan left, I picked up Yiku and went upstairs. I told her, "Don't be like me. You see how helpless I am. Don't be like me."

When Wen Fu came home that night, I showed him my anger for the first time. I had waited until after the evening meal, after late rounds of tea and card games, gossip and laughter. "That little servant girl, you remember her," I said when we were up in our room. "Today she died."

Wen Fu was taking his shoes off. "My slippers, where are they?"

I could hear Hulan and Jiaguo, still talking downstairs in the kitchen. I closed the door to our room. I repeated what I had said, louder this time. "The servant girl is dead." And when he continued to ask for his slippers, I added, "She died trying to get rid of your baby, you fool!"

He stood up. "What's your meaning? Whose lies have you been listening to?" he said. He leaned toward me, staring, one eye droopy, the other large and wide open. I did not look down. I stared back at him, so strong. I had a new feeling, like having a secret weapon.

And suddenly—*whang!*—he knocked over a chair. He cursed. He was shouting at me. "Who are you to accuse me?"

Yiku was now crying in the next room, a scared kind of crying. I started to go toward her room, but Wen Fu shouted for me to stop. I did not listen, and I went to her and saw she was standing up in her crib, reaching with one arm to be comforted. I picked her up and soothed her. Wen Fu followed me, still shouting, knocking things over, but I was not afraid. This time he did not scare me. I put Yiku back in her crib.

"I know what happened!" I shouted back. "You pushed that girl down, ruined her life, who knows how many others. And now I'm telling you, you do your dirty business somewhere else. In the streets, I don't care, only not in my bed anymore."

He raised his fist. I did not look away or cover myself. "Hit me, I still won't change!" I shouted. "Hero, big hero! The only one you can scare is a baby."

He looked surprised. He looked toward Yiku standing behind me in her crib. She was crying hard. He put his hand down. He walked over to the crib very fast. And I thought he was sorry that he had made her cry. I thought he was going to pick her up and say he was sorry. And then, before I could even think to stop him, he slapped her—*kwah!*—hit her hard on the face, so hard half of her face turned red. "Quiet!" he shouted.

Her eyes were pinched closed. Her mouth was open, but no sounds came out. She could not breathe. So much pain! I can still see that look on her face, hurting worse than any slap to my own.

I rushed over to Yiku, but Wen Fu pushed me away and I fell. And then I heard her cry again. Her breath finally came back! And she cried even louder, higher. *Kwah!* Wen Fu hit her again—*kwah!*—again and again. And by the time I could get to my feet and push my body in between, I saw Yiku had rolled up into a little ball. She was making small animal sounds. And I was crying and begging Wen Fu, "Forgive me! I was wrong! Forgive me!"

After that, every time Yiku saw her father come into the room, she fell down and curled herself up small, just like the first time. She sucked her fingers, making little sounds. This is true, only six months old, and she had learned not to cry. Can you imagine—a baby who learned to be that scared before she even knew how to crawl away?

She became a strange baby. She never looked at people's faces. She pulled out hair from one side of her head. She banged her head on the wall. She waved her hands in front of her face and laughed. And when she learned how to walk, she stood on her toes, like a ballerina dancer. She tiptoed quickly across the floor, as if she could lift herself up into the air with each step. But each time she saw her father come into the room, she fell back down again, same as when she was a baby. She did not cry. She spoke no words, only the outside shapes of them, like the voice of a ghost.

Her voice sang up and down, high and pretty, sounding the way I often called to her, "Yiku, look at me, look at me." And then her voice would become harsh, grunting the same way Wen Fu shouted, "Yiku, stupid thing. Go away!" Those were the only sounds she knew how to make.

She was strange all the time. I was worried, so worried. But Hulan kept telling me, "When she's older, she'll change. Now she's just nervous. Everyone's the same way. When the war is over, she'll change. You'll see."

I wanted to believe her. Why wouldn't I? I had never raised a baby. I didn't want to think my baby had lost her mind. I kept thinking the war would soon be over, then Yiku would get better. I believed that, one hope leading to the other.

THE END

Sharon Olds

We decided to have the abortion, became
killers together. The period that came
changed nothing. They were dead, that young couple
who had been for life.
As we talked of it in bed, the crash
was not a surprise. We went to the window,
looked at the crushed cars and the gleaming
curved shears of glass as if we had
done it. Cops pulled the bodies out
Bloody as births from the small, smoking
aperture of the door, laid them
on the hill, covered them with blankets that soaked
through. Blood
began to pour
down my legs into my slippers. I stood
where I was until they shot the bound
form into the black hole
of the ambulance and stood the other one
up, a bandage covering its head,
stained where the eyes had been.
The next morning I had to kneel
an hour on that floor, to clean up my blood,
rubbing with wet cloths at those glittering
translucent spots, as one has to soak
a long time to deglaze the pan
when the feast is over.

A MILLION WOMEN ARE YOUR MOTHER

Saniyya Saleh

O forest that my body has set on fire,
come close,
disregard what can't be disregarded,
whisper your hidden rustle
into my mouth, into my ears,
and into my pores;
reveal your rebellion
and blossom
in the perforated dome
of a collapsing body.
Isn't winter harsh? Aren't time and snow,
rain and storms, too?
But oh, how beautiful they are
as they go away.
I didn't know that forgetfulness has legs,
yet it comes and goes like an unruly horse
waiting for the bronze-colored rose to fall
from the top of the branches.
If the rose falls on the horse's back,
the horse will fly away with it;
if it falls between its legs,
the horse will kick it.
O forest that has blossomed in my body,
don't be afraid.
I've hidden my soul in you
or between two cracks as strong as armies
(although armies don't know us and don't care).
Plunge your head into me,
penetrate me

until our bones almost intertwine.
Let us be next to each other,
interlaced like the heart's duality.
Touch me as God would touch the clay
and I will turn into a human being in a flash.
How can I escape, Sweetheart,
when my heart's fire runs in all directions,
in speech and in silence,
so that you may be born a million times
in ages of greater strangeness.
O my blond forest, unite your fear
and mine strongly;
let your bones enter the tunnel of my bones,
then pull the remainder of your body in
and enter.
There will be long, narrow passages
in front of you, and Truth lies in the narrowest.
Take care and don't forget that you're going there
to scream,
to reject,
and not to bend.
Behold, the ghosts of the world are advancing,
so hide
and steal a look from the cracks of windows
or keyholes.
Whenever a god passes, applaud him
or climb on the edges of trucks
and shout: the moon's blood is from his blood
and its flesh is from his fabric.
But when will you come
so that I may tell you secretly
who the real god is?
The harsh rain was singing a military march
and shooting its bullets at the roots.
(How were you born in the midst of that fight?)

O God, command the valley
to take us to the original fountain,
and the mountain to take us to the real summit.
If the great darkness flees from the whip
and Truth lies flat on the executioner's floor
and the alphabet turns into unfair laws
and the poets turn into dust on the tables,
I will fold up my time and hide it in my bosom.
And if I see my shadow, I will think I am crawling
in order to gnaw on the dry bread of famine.
But two feet of stone can't walk.
Behold, noon is like hard concrete
and the spears of ice cut through the limbs.
Souls that taste like bread are crunched by the air.
A million women are your mother, my little one,
and they untie the string
of the horizon for you so that
death may become temporary, like sleep.
Let us dig up the slaves and bondsmen,
and let us bury the masters of hunger;
and fountains have opened their white mouth
and sent forth their tragic call.
(How terrible giving up the soul is!)
Yet the fountains leave geranium
and damascene roses in their trace.
What angry power is it
that tears out the fetuses from our wombs?
Let that flood
weave the bed of our loneliness.
What will its beast do upon stumbling
while the winter, like an eagle,
beats it with its wings?
In its body are millions of waves,
a chronic eagerness for the earth,
while the drowning mariners

come out of the gates of Time's water
with a sharper vision,
the lines of their ribs visible on their back,
and they say:
the forests that have entered the sea
will bear leaves again
because their heart does not die.
Thus, when Time locks its door to everyone,
I will enter the train of death, pleased;
I will hold the string of absence and pull it,
and my imaginary self will come,
my self that was born of the wombs of mirrors
with their frightening and obscure words.
But frightened bodies secrete what will save them,
and, behold, the door of peace opens
between Paradise and the Earth.
Life alone can take us away and return us.
Death has perished
and worms have become extinct.
The human stone is split so that
new generations will be born.
As for me,
I will withhold the eggs of reproduction
in my womb
to live thus as virgins,
so that spring may not be pressed
by force into the spray of bullets.

Translated from the Arabic by Issa J. Boullata

"OH YEAH, BECAUSE YOU COULD CHOOSE NOT TO" FROM *NOW FOR THE NORTH*

Emily DeDakis

This monologue was written as part of Three's Theatre Company's production Now for the North *in Belfast, Northern Ireland. As of 2019, choosing to end a pregnancy in Northern Ireland is illegal in almost every circumstance.*

I'm babysitting tonight.
You're off to the cinema one last time before they tear it down.
You won't tell me who your date is—even when I beg:
You know him, I know you know him, just . . . lemme see how it goes.
Fair enough, ok, ok.
I tell you, you look pretty.
Wow, Mommy, your dress, she says. She actually gasps. (She's two.)
You fancy the walk so you leave before dinner.
I run through possibilities in my head while I fix macaroni and cheese:
That weird bartender with the 'stache? Kyle the Virtuous? Finn? Benji?
None seem right. I doubt you'd take the punt.
You're not picky; you just know yourself.
After dinner she orchestrates T. Rex attacks on the dollhouse while I do the washing up.
We share melty chocolate buttons & watch the CBeebies bedtime story:
"The Dinosaur That Pooped a Planet."
She looks up at me very solemnly & says, *This is amazing.*
You bought her foam letters that stick to the side of the bath.
I spell silly words: PING. DROOP. MINGER.
She won't tip her head back so I can rinse the shampoo. She will not.
It won't get in your face if you—look, if you just—
You're only making things hard for yourself, girl.
It's me saying it, kneeling by the bath, but I hear your mum saying it too—

The night you told her & she cried down the phone at you.

You told me right when I came over. I was the first one there.

You opened cans of G & T & sat staring at yours. Shit, I wasn't thinking.

An emergency urban family summit. Gradually everyone arrived:

Greg & Sam holding hands, looking wise.

Helen with buns. Flora all righteous fire.

Ollie late, of course—even for this.

Sara was in London but Helen got her on FaceTime.

We're all here for you.

Everyone said it at the door, over the shoulder of the hug, like paying a toll.

No matter what, we all said.

It was clear pretty quick that everyone meant the same what, called the same shot.

They were Googling, doing the math.

Someone started a collection right there on the coffee table.

I saw you stare at the pile of notes & I knew it—I know what you're like.

Suddenly I was Ned Stark at a small council meeting, it's just my mouth wouldn't open.

It seemed like something you needed to say, that you'd decided.

For them it's a given—

Because you said he was an eejit, weeks ago, just two dates in—

You unmatched him, deleted him off WhatsApp, blocked him on Insta—

Because there was nothing to the thing with him & that left you on your own again,

Because of the placards you wrote & the lunch breaks you spent in the street,

Because you cared enough to be out there

Surely it's a given?

He said it too when you told him, before he demanded the paternity test:

You talked a great game about being a feminist, didn't you? And now this.

Because who in their right mind would choose to alone?

It's the kind of thing that happens when you don't have a choice—

& she was your choice.

You named her, on the opening page of a lined spiral-bound notebook—your first journal.

You were twelve. You couldn't spell but you were already writing to her.

Because being in love with him never mattered. You already loved her.
And for all that knowing, all that love, it was still a choice. A hard one.
You were bricking it. Your doubts were our doubts:
What's going to happen? Who's paying for nappies? How do I keep both
of us alive? Forever?
You're only making things hard for yourself, girl.
It's not like any of us could really imagine, not then anyway.
Even now, I mean, what do I—?
I don't always know myself.
I remember us outside City Hall
placards made from Sharpies & inside-out cereal boxes
us adamant at not being forced & railroaded, the other side insisting that
life is life is life.
Two kids walked by us—they were seventeen, maybe less—
One said to the other, *What's happening?*
And the other said, *It's a pro-abortion thing*
And I said, *Actually it's a pro-choice thing*
And both of them were quiet for a second, thinking
And one said, *Oh yeah because you could choose not to have one*
And you said, *Exactly.*
It's never a given, so how could you make that choice for someone else?
How do you even make that choice?
[*Pause. Distracted for a moment, she taps a rhythm on her belly*]
Sure, you know yourself
You stay quiet for a second, thinking
You kneel by a bathtub, &
I just hope I
[*She smiles & shakes her head, sheepish*]
I dunno.

FROM *THE MILLSTONE*

Margaret Drabble

It took me some time to realize that I was pregnant: the possibility had of course crossed my mind fairly early on, but I had dismissed it as being too ridiculous and unlikely a symptom of my sense of doom to be worth serious attention. When I was finally obliged to acknowledge my condition, I was for the first time in my life completely at a loss. I remember the moment quite well: I was sitting at my usual desk in the British Museum looking up something on Sir Walter Raleigh, when out of the blue came the sudden suspicion, which hardened instantly as ever into a certainty. I got out my diary and started feverishly checking on dates, which was difficult as I never make a note of anything, let alone of trivial things like the workings of my guts. In the end, however, after much hard memory work, I sorted it out and convinced myself that it must be so. I sat there, and I could see my hands trembling on the desk. And for the first time the prospect before me seemed so appalling that even I, doom-suspecting and creating as I have always been, could not look at it. It was an unfamiliar sensation, the blankness that occupied my mind instead of the usual profuse images of disaster. I remained in the state for some five minutes before, wearily, I set my imagination to work. What it produced for me was very nasty. Gin, psychiatrists, hospitals, accidents, village maidens drowned in duck ponds, tears, pain, humiliations. Nothing, at that stage, resembling a baby. These shocking forebodings occupied me for a half hour or more, and I began to think that I would have to get up and go, or to go out and have a cup of coffee or something. But it was an hour before my usual time for departure, and I could not do it. I so often wanted not to do my full three hours, and had so often resisted the lure of company or distraction in order to complete them, that now I felt myself compelled to sit there, staring at the poems of Sir Walter Raleigh, in a mockery of attention. Except that after some time I found myself really attending: my mind, bent from its true obsession with what seemed at first intolerable strain, began to revert almost of its own accord to its more accustomed preoccupations, and by the end of the morning I had covered exactly as much ground as I had planned. It gave me much satisfaction, this fact. Much self-satisfaction. And as I walked down the road to meet Lydia for lunch, I discovered another source of satisfaction: now, at least, I would be compelled to see George. I had an excuse, now, for seeing him.

Later that afternoon I realized that I was going to see George now less than ever. It took some time for the full complexity of the situation to sink in. When I realize the implications of my deceit, it became apparent that I was going to have to keep the whole thing to myself. I could not face the prospect of speculation, anyone's speculation. So I decided to get on with it by myself as best I could. I have already recounted my ludicrous attempt with the gin: after this I got in touch with a Cambridge friend of mine who had had an abortion, and asked for the address and details, which I obtained. I rang the number once, but it was engaged. After that I went no further. I do not like to look back on those first months, before anyone but me knew what was happening: it seems too much like a nightmare, like a hallucination, and I kept waking up each morning and thinking it must be a dream, the kind of dream that my nonconformist guilt might be expected to project: I even wondered if all the symptoms for which I suffered might not be purely psychological. In the end it was the fear of being made a fool of by my subconscious that drove me to the doctor.

Seeing the doctor was not as simple an operation as one might have supposed. To begin with, I did not know which doctor to see. It was so many years since I had been unwell that I did not know how to set about it; in fact, I had not been unwell since I had become an adult. I had never had to do it on my own. The only doctor I knew was our old family doctor, who lives near our old but now abandoned family residence in Putney, and he was clearly unsuitable. I supposed that I ought to go to the nearest GP, but how was I to know who he was, or where he lived? Living within two minutes' walk of Harley Street as I did, I was terrified that I might walk into some private waiting room by accident, and be charged fifty guineas for what I might and ought to get for nothing. Being my parents' daughter, the thought outraged me morally as well as financially. On the other hand, it did not seem a good plan to pick a surgery so evidently seedy that it could not exist but on the National Health: though this was in fact what I did. I passed one day, in the small road off George Street, after visiting an exhibition by a very distant friend, the brass plaque on the front door that said Dr. H. E. Moffett. There was a globular light over the door, with surgery painted all in black letters. It was not the kind of door behind which anyone could be charged fifty guineas, and I made a note of the surgery hours and resolved to return the next day at five-thirty.

I visited the doctor the next day. That visit was a revelation: it was an initiation into a new way of life, a way that was thenceforth to be mine forever. An initiation into reality, if you like. The surgery opened at five-thirty, and I made an appointment there. Promptly: I arrived at about twenty-eight minutes to six, thinking that I was in plenty of time, and would have to wait hardly at all. But when I opened that shabby varnished door, I found the waiting room overflowing with waiting patients, patiently waiting.

THE ABORTION I DIDN'T WANT

Caitlin McDonnell

I'm lying on a table at a women's health clinic being held down by three young clinicians while a doctor performs the procedure. There are tapestries and Georgia O'Keeffe prints on the walls. I can't move or see what's beneath my knees. My body resists; I do not want this. The hands restrain me until it's done.

"You're not pregnant anymore," the doctor says, and then leaves the room.

A cold wind of grief blows through me. My body feels empty, like a dried rind. X drives me home in silence. I lie on the bed and pull thick blankets over me, trying to turn off the resounding emotional pain. He leaves the house and goes on a walk. I take a pill to help me numb. It will be years before I begin to process this day.

Every abortion is a story. It might be mundane or dramatic, involve great sacrifice or great relief. Too often these stories live only in whispers between trusted comrades or tucked away in journals. Abortion is just one example of how women have grown accustomed to living with stories that never get told publicly. Mine is a story of an abortion I didn't want but chose to go through with anyway. It's a grief I live with. It's my grief. I wouldn't have it any other way.

* * *

I'd sung along with Fiona Apple the whole way on my drive across country to move in with X. *I'm going to make a mistake/I'm going to do it on purpose.*

We barely knew each other. He was a rising literary star. I was a poetry fellow at an art colony where he did a reading and we struck up an intense long-distance connection. He was starting a new teaching job in a new city and proposed I come with him when my fellowship ended.

But I soon felt trapped at the walled-in college campus and struggled to find work. We argued about how to clean, whether to have a faux bear-skin rug, how to play Scrabble, what to eat, whether marriage mattered, and how we might raise a child. When I told him my news, he said he needed to take a walk. When he returned, he looked at me with a defiant distance in his eyes.

"This is the worst thing I'm going to do in my whole life, but no part of me wants to take this journey with you." It felt like someone was reading a horrible line from a play. I wanted to hand him a different line, and tried to, for weeks, months. I was in the kind of love with him that shocks the system with its compelling wrongness. We were in a standoff.

In the midst of it all, we named the fetus Malachai. I pictured a boy who was a combination of us both. X looked at me sideways and said we weren't going to have a baby just because it would be "a cool color." I was paralyzed by indecision, sleepy with denial and hormones. I made termination appointments and cancelled them for one reason after another. I had the flu. I had the wrong insurance.

"How do you think you're going to do it," he kept asking. "How?"

I kept finding ways to defer my decision. A Kaiser clinic didn't understand what "strabismus" was in my medical history. It wasn't until being told I'd passed the date when a chemical abortion could be induced that I felt real fear. It is the kind of choice nature makes for you if you don't make it yourself.

During my intake at the women's clinic, I told them that I didn't think I could say I wanted an abortion but that I thought they should do it anyway. Understandably, they didn't know what to do with me. They took me into a room and counseled. "Are you sure? Have you explored all your options?" I told them I had.

They left me alone and argued among themselves. I just kept repeating my outrageous statement. At one point they tried to send me home.

* * *

"We think you should think more about it," a clinician said. I was firm. I wasn't leaving. But I couldn't say I wanted it. Every alternative they offered made me shake my head no. I couldn't say anything more affirmative than "You should do it."

I needed to end my pregnancy—and not think about being an arbiter of life and death, at least not that day. I asked them to hold me down because I was afraid my body might resist. What they did for me that day was heroic and kind.

I think I'm not alone in feeling that to truly wrap my head around the enormousness of the choice that day was too much. The inevitability of this abortion felt bigger than me, and I needed to experience it as a great wave coming over me rather than as something I was doing.

The wave was a slow one. "When will I feel better?" I asked my friend from my bed cocoon after the procedure.

"Not until you have a baby," she answered, from her own experience.

I believe life begins at conception, but that doesn't change the fact that women have dominion over the life inside their own. I grieved because I wanted a child. Maybe if I'd been less in love with X, or had a better job, or had more money saved, then I would have done something different. I had more resources than some, less than others.

The woman who had been my therapist through my adolescence and my parents' troubled divorce said, "Sometimes it's the ultimate act of generosity."

If I had remained pregnant, I'd have been bringing into the world a child with a dearth of stability and a father who'd stated clearly that he didn't want him. I think I probably would have made it work somehow, but my wanting a child at that point was not compatible with the reality of my circumstances and it would have tied me irrevocably to a man I didn't trust.

The distinction between grief and regret is an important one. I wanted to be a mother and knew I was terminating a potential life. When I did get pregnant again, years later, grief gave the experience an added gravity. Each ultrasound reminded me of Malachai. Each concern sent me down a spiral of thinking that I might somehow be punished, or that I had lost my one chance.

Did I make a choice? I now see that I did, despite my efforts to shroud it. Do I regret my actions? That's a trickier question.

I had beers with my friend Gabe in San Francisco a couple of months after the abortion, and he counseled me not to be afraid of the word "regret." We all live with regrets, as death lives alongside life. Every meaningful relationship has regret in its DNA. It doesn't mean we're doing the wrong things.

Merritt Tierce wrote last year in her incisive *New York Times* opinion piece, "This Is What an Abortion Looks Like," that we need to stop categorizing abortions as justified or unjustified according to the amount of suffering a woman contends with. She argued that the personal contexts, the stories surrounding the abortion, are not relevant until we grant "each woman the right to make and do with her body what she will."

Tierce is right in cautioning us against using the stories to justify the choice, but what if we all start telling them anyway, in all their great variance of comedy and pain, until they are a normalized part of the human experience?

In 1984, my aunt, Kathleen McDonnell, a feminist who lives and writes in Canada, wrote a book called *Not an Easy Choice* in which she explores the silence women have to live with after an abortion if they feel grief. Any expression of sadness is pounced on as regret by abortion opponents. Women deserve both the complexity of the decisions that affect their bodies and the fundamental right to make them.

I didn't want my abortion, but if I could close my eyes and return to that table, I would do the same thing. However painful the decision-making process, however fraught it is with ambivalence and paradox, it is ours. We aren't simple. Some choices take years to understand. My abortion opened up the scope of my life in a way I couldn't see clearly that day, and for that I am grateful.

I now have the most amazing daughter in the world. She knows she has always been wanted. I accept the sadness that accompanies the choices I've made, both by seizing my agency and by ducking it. I live with the grief of my abortion in the same way I live with the grief of many paths not taken. They are all part of the story that got me here.

FREE AND SAFE ABORTION

Ana Gabriela Rivera

I'm curious to know the meaning
Of the difference between legality and illegality
For centuries past
My sisters who give birth,
My sisters who also decide not to give birth
Have not been stopped by these laws,
They've only put us in danger

We join together so we can better understand ourselves
Because out there
Nobody wants to inform us.
Not the lawyers, not the doctors, not the scientists
All the experts
Want to make decisions about my body,
Outlawing ancestral practices

Today, September 28th
I lift up my voice
I let out a shout to reach the ears of pastors and priests
I put forward a demand for justice to the clowns who govern us
I demand that my decision be respected
That my right to make decisions about the right time be respected
That the spaces in which i walk be respected
Because letting us interrupt a pregnancy
Does not obligate anyone to do it
Because sex education is not blasphemy
Because there's no reason that my knowing about my body has to
impede you.
But if it is blasphemy and if it does impede you:

Today I do not care!
Because my sisters' deaths have no justification!

Today, September 28
I shout for all of those who have died trying to carry out an abortion
In secret
For those who have been forced to be mothers against their will.
For those victims of your judgement, victims of violence masked
As tradition,
For the women who do not know how to use contraceptives to
Make decisions about their own time.

Translated by Sarah Leister

MERELY BY WILDERNESS

Molly Peacock

The breasts enlarge, and a sweet white discharge
coats the vaginal lips. The nipples itch.
A five-week fetus in the uterus,
as the larger share of a large soft pear,
soaks quietly there. Should I run directly
and insist that he marry me? Resist
is what we do. It is this: I'm in what
I never thought I could be caught in,
and it's a strong net, a roomy deluxe net,
the size of civilization. To shun
this little baby—how can I? Maybe
I could go it alone, fix up a home
for us, never ask why inside the lie
we'd not look beyond, so not ask beyond:
a poor scratch—castle with a beat-in door.
I can't do this alone, yet I am so alone
no one, not even this child inside me, even
the me I was, can feel the wild cold buzz
that presses me into this place, bleakness
that will break me, except I cannot be
broken merely by wilderness, I can only
be lost.

FROM *MARIA: OR, THE WRONGS OF WOMAN*

Mary Wollstonecraft

Maria, the novel's narrator, is an educated upper-class woman whose husband has taken away her child and imprisoned her in an insane asylum in order to control her. There she makes friends with one of the asylum staff members, Jemima, who tells her the story below.

"At sixteen, I suddenly grew tall, and something like comeliness appeared on a Sunday, when I had time to wash my face, and put on clean clothes. My master had once or twice caught hold of me in the passage; but I instinctively avoided his disgusting caresses. One day however, when the family were at a Methodist meeting, he contrived to be alone in the house with me, and by blows—yes; blows and menaces, compelled me to submit to his ferocious desire; and, to avoid my mistress's fury, I was obliged in future to comply, and skulk to my loft at his command, in spite of increasing loathing.

"The anguish which was now pent up in my bosom, seemed to open a new world to me: I began to extend my thoughts beyond myself, and grieve for human misery, till I discovered, with horror—ah! what horror!—that I was with child. I know not why I felt a mixed sensation of despair and tenderness, excepting that, ever called a bastard, a bastard appeared to me an object of the greatest compassion in creation.

"I communicated this dreadful circumstance to my master, who was almost equally alarmed at the intelligence; for he feared his wife, and public censure at the meeting. After some weeks of deliberation had elapsed, I in continual fear that my altered shape would be noticed, my master gave me a medicine in a phial, which he desired me to take, telling me, without any circumlocution, for what purpose it was designed. I burst into tears, I thought it was killing myself—yet was such a self as I worth preserving? He cursed me for a fool, and left me to my own reflections. I could not resolve to take this infernal potion; but I wrapped it up in an old gown, and hid it in a corner of my box.

"Nobody yet suspected me, because they had been accustomed to view me as a creature of another species. But the threatening storm at last broke over my devoted head—never shall I forget it! One Sunday evening when I was left, as usual, to take care of the house, my master came home intoxicated, and I became the prey of his brutal appetite. His extreme intoxication made him forget his customary caution, and my mistress entered and found us in a situation that could not have been more hateful to her than me. Her husband was 'pot-valiant,' he feared her not at the moment, nor had he then much reason, for she instantly turned the whole force of her anger another way. She tore off my cap, scratched, kicked, and buffeted me, till she had exhausted her strength, declaring, as she rested her arm, 'that I had wheedled her husband from her.—But, could anything better be expected from a wretch, whom she had taken into her house out of pure charity?' What a torrent of abuse rushed out till, almost breathless, she concluded with saying, that I was born a strumpet; it ran in my blood, and nothing good could come to those who harbored me.

"My situation was, of course, discovered, and she declared that I should not stay another night under the same roof with an honest family. I was therefore pushed out of doors, and my trumpery thrown after me, when it had been contemptuously examined in the passage, lest I should have stolen anything.

"Behold me then in the street, utterly destitute! Whither could I creep for shelter? To my father's roof I had no claim, when not pursued by shame—now I shrunk back as from death, from my mother's cruel re-proaches, my father's execrations. I could not endure to hear him curse the day I was born, though life had been a curse to me. Of death I thought, but with a confused emotion of terror, as I stood leaning my head on a post, and starting at every footstep, lest it should be my mistress coming to tear my heart out. One of the boys of the shop passing by, heard my tale, and immediately repaired to his master, to give him a description of my situation; and he touched the right key—the scandal it would give rise to, if I were left to repeat my tale to every inquirer. This plea came home to his reason, who had been sobered by his wife's rage, the fury of which fell on him when I was out of her reach, and he sent the boy to me with half-a-guinea, desiring him to conduct me to a house where beggars and other wretches, the refuse of society, nightly lodged.

"This night was spent in a state of stupefaction, or desperation. I detested mankind, and abhorred myself.

"In the morning I ventured out, to throw myself in my master's way, at his usual hour of going abroad. I approached him, he damned me for a b——, declared I had disturbed the peace of the family, and that he had sworn to his wife, 'never to take any more notice of me.' He left me; but, instantly returning, he told me that he should speak to his friend, a parish-officer, to get a nurse for the brat I laid to him; and advised me, if I wished to keep out of the house of correction, not to make free with his name.

"I hurried back to my hole, and, rage giving place to despair, sought for the potion that was to procure abortion, and swallowed it, with a wish that it might destroy me, at the same time that it stopped the sensations of newborn life, which I felt with indescribable emotion. My head turned 'round, my heart grew sick, and in the horrors of approaching dissolution, mental anguish was swallowed up. The effect of the medicine was violent, and I was confined to my bed several days; but, youth and a strong constitution prevailing, I once more crawled out, to ask myself the cruel question, 'Whither I should go?' I had but two shillings left in my pocket, the rest had been expended, by a poor woman who slept in the same room, to pay for my lodging, and purchase the necessaries of which she partook.

"With this wretch I went into the neighboring streets to beg, and my disconsolate appearance drew a few pence from the idle, enabling me still to command a bed; till, recovering from my illness, and taught to put on my rags to the best advantage, I was accosted from different motives, and yielded to the desire of the brutes I met, with the same detestation that I had felt for my still more brutal master."

CORA, UNASHAMED

Langston Hughes

I.

Melton was one of those miserable in-between little places, not large enough to be a town, nor small enough to be a village—that is, a village in the rural, charming sense of the world. Melton had no charm about it. It was merely a nondescript collection of houses and buildings in a region of farms—one of those sad American places with sidewalks, but no paved streets; electric lights, but no sewage; a station, but no trains that stopped, save a jerky local, morning and evening. And it was 150 miles from any city at all—even Sioux City.

Cora Jenkins was one of the least of the citizens of Melton. She was what the people referred to when they wanted to be polite, as a Negress, and when they wanted to be rude, as a nigger—sometimes adding the word "wench" for no good reason, for Cora was usually an inoffensive soul, except that she sometimes cussed.

She had been in Melton for forty years. Born there. Would die there probably. She worked for the Studevants, who treated her like a dog. She stood it. Had to stand it; or work for poorer white folks who would treat her worse; or go jobless. Cora was like a tree—once rooted, she stood, in spite of storms and strife, wind, and rocks, in the earth.

She was the Studevants' maid of all work—washing, ironing, cooking, scrubbing, taking care of kids, nursing old folks, making fires, carrying water.

Cora, bake three cakes for Mary's birthday tomorrow night. You, Cora, give Rover a bath in that tar soap I bought. Cora, take Ma some Jell-O, and don't let her have even a taste of that raisin pie. She'll keep us up all night if you do. Cora, iron my stockings. Cora, come here. . . Cora, put. . . Cora. . . Cora. . . Cora! Cora!

And Cora would answer, "Yes, m'am."

The Studevants thought they owned her, and they were probably right: they did. There was something about the teeth in the trap of economic circumstance that kept her in their power practically all her life—in the Studevant kitchen, cooking; in the Studevant parlor, sweeping; in the Studevant backyard, hanging clothes.

You want to know how that could be? How a trap could close so tightly? Here is the outline:

Cora was the oldest of a family of eight children—the Jenkins niggers. The only Negroes in Melton, thank God! Where they came from originally—that is, the old folks—God knows. The kids were born there. The old folks are still there now: Pa drives a junk wagon. The old woman ails around the house, ails and quarrels. Seven kids are gone. Only Cora remains. Cora simply couldn't go, with nobody else to help take care of Ma. And before that she couldn't go, with nobody to see her brothers and sisters through school (she the oldest, and Ma ailing). And before that— well, somebody had to help Ma look after one baby behind another that kept on coming.

As a child Cora had no playtime. She always had a little brother, or a little sister in her arms. Bad, crying, bratty babies, hungry and mean. In the eighth grade she quit school and went to work with the Studevants.

After that, she ate better. Half day's work at first, helping Ma at home the rest of the time. Then full days, bringing home her pay to feed her father's children. The old man was rather a drunkard. What little money he made from closet-cleaning, ash-hauling, and junk-dealing he spent mostly on the stuff that makes you forget you have eight kids.

He passed the evenings telling long, comical lies to the white riff-raff of the town, and drinking licker. When his horse died, Cora's money went for a new one to haul her Pa and his rickety wagon around. When the mortgage money came due, Cora's wages kept the man from taking the roof from over their heads. When Pa got in jail, Cora borrowed ten dollars from Mrs. Studevant and got him out.

Cora stinted, and Cora saved, and wore the Studevants' old clothes, and ate the Studevants' leftover food, and brought her pay home. Brothers and sisters grew up. The boys, lonesome, went away, as far as they could from Melton. One by one, the girls left too, mostly in disgrace.

"Ruinin' ma name," Pa Jenkins said, "Ruinin' ma good name! They can't go out berryin' but what they come back in disgrace." There was something about the cream-and-tan Jenkins girls that attracted the white farm hands.

Even Cora the humble, had a lover once. He came to town on a freight train (long ago now), and worked at the livery-stable. (That was before autos got to be so common.) Everybody said he was an IWW.* Cora didn't care. He was the first man and the last she ever remembered wanting. She had never known a colored lover. There weren't any around. That was not her fault.

This white boy, Joe, he always smelt like the horses. He was some kind of foreigner. Had an accent, and yellow hair, big hands, and grey eyes.

It was summer. A few blocks beyond the Studevants' house, meadows and orchards and sweet fields stretched away to the far horizon. At night, stars in the velvet sky. Moon sometimes. Crickets and katydids and lightning bugs. The scent of grass. Cora waiting. That boy, Joe, a cigarette spark far off, whistling in the dark. Love didn't take long—Cora with the scent of the Studevants' supper about her, and a cheap perfume. Joe, big and strong and careless as the horses he took care of, smelling like the stable.

Ma would quarrel because Cora came home late, or because none of the kids had written for three or four weeks, or because Pa was drunk again. Thus, the summer passed, a dream of big hands and grey eyes.

Cora didn't go anywhere to have her child. Nor tried to hide it. When the baby grew big within her, she didn't feel that it was a disgrace. The Studevants told her to go home and stay there. Joe left town. Pa cussed. Ma cried. One April morning the kid was born. She had grey eyes, and Cora called her Josephine, after Joe.

Cora was humble and shameless before the fact of the child. There were no Negroes in Melton to gossip, and she didn't care what the white people said. They were in another world. Of course, she hadn't expected to marry Joe, or keep him. He was of that other world, too. But the child was hers—a living bridge between two worlds. Let people talk.

---

* The Industrial Workers of the World Labor union.

Cora went back to work at the Studevants'—coming home at night to nurse her kid, and quarrel with Ma. About that time, Mrs. Art Studevant had a child, too, and Cora nursed it. The Studevants' little girl was named Jessie. As the two children began to walk and talk, Cora sometimes brought Josephine to play with Jessie—until the Studevants objected, saying she could get her work done better if she left her child at home.

"Yes, m'am," said Cora.

But in a little while they didn't need to tell Cora to leave her child at home, for Josephine died of whooping-cough. One rosy afternoon, Cora saw the little body go down into the ground in a white casket that cost four weeks' wages.

Since Ma was ailing, Pa, smelling of licker, stood with her at the grave. The two of them alone. Cora was not humble before the fact of death. As she turned away from the hole, tears came—but at the same time a stream of curses so violent that they made the grave-tenders look up in startled horror.

She cussed out God for taking away the life that she herself had given. She screamed, "My baby! God damn it! My baby! I bear her and you take her away!" She looked at the sky where the sun was setting and yelled in defiance. Pa was amazed and scared. He pulled her up on his rickety wagon and drove off, clattering down the road between green fields and sweet meadows that stretched away to the far horizon. All through the ugly town Cora wept and cursed, using all the bad words she had learned from Pa in his drunkenness.

The next week she went back to the Studevants. She was gentle and humble in the face of death—she loved their baby. In the afternoons on the back porch, she would pick little Jessie up and rock her to sleep, burying her dark face in the milky smell of the white child's hair.

II.

The years passed. Pa and Ma Jenkins only dried up a little. Old Man Studevant died. The old lady had two strokes. Mrs. Art Studevant and her husband began to look their age, greying hair and sagging stomachs. The children were grown, or nearly so. Kenneth took over the management of the hardware store that Grandpa had left. Jack went off to college. Mary was a teacher. Only Jessie remained a child—her last year in high school. Jessie, nineteen now, and rather slow in her studies, graduating at last. In the fall she would go to Normal.

Cora hated to think about her going away. In her heart she had adopted Jessie. In that big and careless household, it was always Cora who stood like a calm and sheltering tree for Jessie to run to in her troubles. As a child, when Mrs. Art spanked her, as soon as she could, the tears still streaming, Jessie would find her way to the kitchen and Cora. At each school term's end, when Jessie had usually failed in some of her subjects (she quite often failed, being a dull child), it was Cora who saw the report card first with the bad marks on it. Then Cora would devise some way of breaking the news gently to the old folks.

Her mother was always a little ashamed of stupid Jessie, for Mrs. Art was the civic and social leader of Melton, president of the Woman's Club three years straight, and one of the pillars of her church. Mary, the elder, the teacher, would follow with dignity in her footsteps, but Jessie! That child! Spankings in her youth, and scoldings now, did nothing to Jessie's inner being. She remained a plump, dull, freckled girl, placid and strange. Everybody found fault with her but Cora.

In the kitchen Jessie bloomed. She laughed. She talked. She was sometimes even witty. And she learned to cook wonderfully. With Cora, everything seemed so simple—not hard and involved like algebra, or Latin grammar, or the civic problems of Mama's club, or the sermons at church. Nowhere in Melton, nor with anyone, did Jessie feel so comfortable as with Cora in the kitchen. She knew her mother looked down on her as a stupid girl. And with her father there was no bond. He was always too busy buying and selling to bother with the kids. And often he was off in the city. Old, doddering Grandma made Jessie sleepy and sick. Cousin Nora (mother's cousin) was as stiff and prim as a minister's daughter. And Jessie's older brothers and sisters went their ways, seeing Jessie hardly at all, except at the big table at mealtimes.

Like all the unpleasant things in the house, Jessie was left to Cora. And Cora was happy. To have a child to raise, a child the same age as her Josephine would have been, gave her a purpose in life, a warmth inside herself.

It was Cora who nursed and mothered and petted and loved the dull little Jessie through the years. And now Jessie was a young woman, graduating (late) from high school.

But something had happened to Jessie. Cora knew it before Mrs. Art did. Jessie was not too stupid to have a boyfriend. She told Cora about it like a mother. She was afraid to tell Mrs. Art.

Afraid! Afraid! Afraid!

Cora said, "I'll tell her." So, humble and unashamed about life, one afternoon she marched into Mrs. Art's sun porch and announced quite simply, "Jessie's going to have a baby."

Cora smiled, but Mrs. Art stiffened like a bolt. Her mouth went dry. She rose like a soldier. Sat down. Rose again. Walked straight toward the door, turned around, and whispered, "What?"

"Yes, m'am, a baby. She told me. A little child. Its father is Willie Matsoulos, whose folks runs the ice-cream stand on Main. She told me. They want to get married, but Willie ain't here now. He don't know yet about the child."

Cora would have gone on humbly and shamelessly talking about the little unborn had not Mrs. Art fallen into uncontrollable hysterics. Cousin Nora came running from the library, her glasses on a chain. Old Lady Studevant's wheelchair rolled up, doddering and shaking with excitement. Jessie came, when called, red and sweating, but had to go out, for when her mother looked up from the couch and saw her she yelled louder than ever. There was a rush for camphor bottles and water and ice. Crying and praying followed all over the house. Scandalization! Oh, my Lord! Jessie was in trouble.

"She ain't in trouble neither," Cora insisted. "No trouble having a baby you want. I had one."

"Shut up, Cora!"

"Yes, m'am. . . But I had one."

"Hush, I tell you."

"Yes, m'am."

III.

Then it was that Cora began to be shut out. Jessie was confined to her room. That afternoon, when Miss Mary came home from school, the four white women got together behind closed doors in Mrs. Art's bedroom. For once Cora cooked supper in the kitchen without being bothered by an interfering voice. Mr. Studevant was away in Des Moines. Somehow Cora wished he was home. Big and gruff as he was, he had more sense than the women. He'd probably make a shot-gun wedding out of it. But left to Mrs. Art, Jessie would never marry the Greek boy at all. This Cora knew. No man had been found yet good enough for sister Mary to mate with. Mrs. Art had ambitions which didn't include the likes of Greek ice-cream makers' sons.

Jessie was crying when Cora brought her supper up. The Black woman sat down on the bed and lifted the white girl's head in her dark hands. "Don't you mind, honey," Cora said. "Just sit tight, and when the boy comes back I'll tell him how things are. If he loves you he'll marry you. And there ain't no reason why you can't marry, neither—you both white. Even if he is a foreigner, he's a right nice boy."

"He loves me," Jessie said. "I know he does. He said so."

But before the boy came back (or Mr. Studevant either) Mrs. Art and Jessie went to Kansas City. "For an Easter shopping trip," the weekly paper said.

Then spring came in full bloom, and the fields and orchards at the edge of Melton stretched green and beautiful to the far horizon. Cora remembered her own spring, twenty years ago, and a great sympathy and pain welled up in her heart for Jessie, who was the same age that Josephine would have been, had she lived. Sitting on the kitchen porch shelling peas, Cora thought back over her own life—years and years of working for the Studevants; years and years of going home to nobody but Ma and Pa; little Josephine dead; only Jessie to keep her heart warm. And she knew that Jessie was the dearest thing she had in the world. All the time the girl was gone now, she worried.

After ten days, Mrs. Art and her daughter came back. But Jessie was thinner and paler than she'd ever been in her life. There was no light in her eyes at all. Mrs. Art looked a little scared as they got off the train.

"She had an awful attack of indigestion in Kansas City," she told the neighbors and club women. "That's why I stayed away so long, waiting for her to be able to travel. Poor Jessie! She looks healthy, but she's never been a strong child. She's one of the worries of my life." Mrs. Art talked a lot, explained a lot, about how Jessie had eaten the wrong things in Kansas City.

At home, Jessie went to bed. She wouldn't eat. When Cora brought her food up, she whispered, "The baby's gone."

Cora's face went dark. She bit her lips to keep from cursing. She put her arms about Jessie's neck. The girl cried. Her food went untouched.

A week passed. They tried to make Jessie eat then. But the food wouldn't stay on her stomach. Her eyes grew yellow, her tongue white, her heart acted crazy. They called in old Doctor Brown, but within a month (as quick as that) Jessie died.

She never saw the Greek boy any more. Indeed, his father lost his license, "due to several

complaints by the mothers of children, backed by the Woman's Club," that he was selling tainted ice-cream. Mrs. Art Studevant had started a campaign to rid the town of objectionable tradespeople and questionable characters. Greeks were bound to be one or the other. For a while they even closed up Pa Jenkins' favorite bootlegger. Mrs. Studevant thought this would please Cora, but Cora only said, "Pa's been drinkin' so long he just as well keep on." She refused further to remark on her employer's campaign of purity. In the midst of this clean-up Jessie died.

On the day of the funeral, the house was stacked with flowers. (They held the funeral, not at the church, but at home, on account of old Grandma Studevant's infirmities.) All the family dressed in deep mourning. Mrs. Art was prostrate. As the house for the services approached, she revived, however, and ate an omelet, "to help me go through the afternoon."

"And Cora," she said, "cook me a little piece of ham with it. I feel so weak."

"Yes, m'am."

The senior class from the high school came in a body. The Woman's Club came with their badges. The Reverend Doctor McElroy had on his highest collar and longest coat. The choir sat behind the coffin, with a special soloist to sing "He Feedeth His Flocks Like a Shepherd." It was a beautiful spring afternoon, and a beautiful funeral.

Except that Cora was there. Of course, her presence created no comment (she was the family servant), but it was what she did, and how she did it, that has remained the talk of Melton to this day—for Cora was not humble in the face of death.

When the Reverend Doctor McElroy had finished his eulogy, and the senior class had read their memorials, and the songs had been sung, and they were about to allow the relatives and friends to pass around for one last look at Jessie Studevant, Cora got up from her seat by the dining-room door. She said, "Honey, I want to say something." She spoke as if she were addressing Jessie. She approached the coffin and held out her brown hands over the girl's body. Her face moved in agitation. People sat stone-still and there was a long pause. Suddenly she screamed. "They killed you! And for nothin'. . . They killed your child. . . They took you away from here in the springtime of your life, and now you'se gone, gone, gone!"

Folks were paralyzed in their seats.

Cora went on: "They preaches you a pretty sermon and they don't say nothin'. They sings you a song, and they don't say nothin'. But Cora's here, honey, and she's gone tell 'em what they done to you. She's gonna tell 'em why they took you to Kansas City."

A loud scream rent the air. Mrs. Art fell back in her chair, stiff as a board. Cousin Nora and sister Mary sat like stones. The men of the family rushed forward to grab Cora. They stumbled over wreaths and garlands. Before they could reach her, Cora pointed her long fingers at the women in black and said, "They killed you, honey. They killed you and your child. I told 'em you loved it, but they didn't care. They killed it before it was. . ."

A strong hand went around Cora's waist. Another grabbed her arm. The Studevant males half pulled, half pushed her through the aisles of folding chairs, through the crowded dining room, out into the empty kitchen, through the screen door into the backyard. She struggled against them all the way, accusing their women. At the door she sobbed, great tears coming for the love of Jessie.

She sat down on a wash-bench in the backyard, crying. In the parlor she could hear the choir singing weakly. In a few moments she gathered herself together, and went back into the

house. Slowly, she picked up her few belongings from the kitchen and pantry, her aprons and her umbrella, and went off down the alley, home to Ma. Cora never came back to work for the Studevants.

Now she and Ma live from the little garden they raise, and from the junk Pa collects—when they can take by main force a part of his meager earnings before he buys his licker.

Anyhow, on the edge of Melton, the Jenkins niggers, Pa and Ma and Cora, somehow manage to get along.

YOU HAVE NO NAME, NO GRAVE, NO IDENTITY

Manisha Sharma

More girls in India and China are eliminated every year than the number of girls born in the U.S. Over the last decade, six million plus girls were eliminated before birth in India; this is more than the number of Jews killed in the Holocaust by the Nazis.

—Sabu M. George, MA, PhD, and member of India's Campaign Against Sex Selection, 10 September 2013

"Praise be to the goddesses," the curly-haired mother of two boys,
my gynecologist, spoke in code for: *it's a girl, a D & C must be done.*

At dawn for your father's lunch, I seal the lid on hot tomato-tempered dal,
two pale-hued roti discs, crescent-shaped grains of brown rice (a fistful)

sour yogurt (a measured cup). I pack for myself in a wide straw basket:
a cotton sari, blouse, petticoat, a bundle of soft rags for post procedure

drowned under loads of reams of razor-edged pages. Your father
drowned under unexplainable jars of illness, your grandmother.

Your uncle drops me a block from the clinic on the corner of X and Y.

Collapsed on a sterile, sanitary-pad-shaped stretcher, I feel:
my hospital-gowned body sensing cool clinic sheets,
my groggy eyes seeing disappearing green drapes,
my fingers pinching my nose to ward off sharp disinfectant,
my ears hearing stretcher wheels squeaking like rats
chewing away old linen in the luxury of the night.

On my right: white tray on a white table, foggy forceps,
scissors that grow bold and big then shrink like raisins.
I soak every night for your father.
Everything is a blank, an erased memory.

All I know is this:
you will have no name, no grave, no identity, my girl,
you would have been my second child.

FIVE MONTHS VULNERABLE

Burleigh Mutén

Entitlement never entered my mind.
I was pregnant, five months vulnerable,
when a doctor suggested I have an abortion.
This is why we do amniocentesis, he said.

I was pregnant, five months vulnerable,
an extra X chromosome in every cell.
This is why we do amniocentesis, he said.
This fetus will develop breasts in his teens.

An extra X chromosome in every cell.
No real concept of diversity in 1984.
This fetus will develop breasts in his teens.
No words: pangender or transgender.

No real concept of diversity in 1984,
a science-based, legal procedure, that's all.
No words: pangender or transgender.
No social, evidence-based research, just

a science-based, legal procedure, that's all
when a doctor suggested I have an abortion.
No social, evidence-based research, just
entitlement never entered my mind.

FROM *PAST DUE*

Anne Finger

I am walking out the back door and I see a plastic jar of tissue and blood waiting to be sent to the path lab, and in the plastic jar a tiny, perfect white hand; it looks like the hand of a not very realistic doll. Anti-abortion propaganda often shows just a hand or just a foot, because feet and hands develop so much earlier than everything else. The hand looks human, while the heart is still a primitive thump, the brain no bigger than a pea, the whole a white jelly-thing. But it's close, too close not to trouble me.

That flat palm reaching up through a wine-red wash of blood. Why does that stay with me? Surely it isn't looking human that makes us human.

Would I have asked myself these questions ten, twelve years ago? Would they have been doubts that niggled at the edge of my mind, never forming into words? Is it the current political climate that does this?

A few months later, back in San Francisco, I went to another meeting of the Committee to Defend Reproductive Rights. We watched a video, "Silent Scream," purporting to show the scream of a fetus being aborted. Then we talked: about the shift in emphasis from the woman to the embryo/fetus; do we address people's questions about when life begins or does that mean letting the Right set the terms of the debate; how do we talk about the ethics of abortion?

Another disabled woman had joined CDRR. She was blind and had-cerebral palsy. In CDRR, everyone raises their hands and waits for the chair to call on them before they speak. Except for Jaime, who kept talking out of turn, and no one would tell her to raise her hand and wait till she got called on, but they would with anyone else. And I thought: "Fucking liberals."

And then somebody said that life is socially defined, and that the biological definitions of life are not the ultimate ones. When we have that sort of broad-ranging discussion in CDRR, we write with felt-tip markers on butcher paper the boiled-down essence of what we're saying. It's a way of holding together all the disparate views, making sure that ideas don't get lost in the shuffle.

And so someone wrote in blue felt-tip: "Life does not equal the right to live."

Oh, great, I thought. Life is socially defined. Now, who gets to make the definitions and who gets defined out of existence? Disabled people? Jews? Old people?

I wanted to say something then, but I didn't. Because I didn't want to sound like a crank, like a woman with a one-track mind. Because I didn't want to get accused of calling people Nazis.

About the same time, I read an article in *Ms.* on anti-abortion terrorism. It said:

> Joseph Schiedler [a leader of the movement to disrupt abortion clinics] made the extremist claim that abortion is the American Holocaust, the equivalent of the Nazi Holocaust. The irony is that Hitler was anti-choice; he outlawed abortion in Nazi Germany, and one of the key goals of the Third Reich was to force Aryan women to have as many children as possible.

I wrote a letter saying that's only partly true. Abortion was illegal but widely tolerated during the pre-Nazi period of the Weimar Republic. And while the majority of women found abortions impossible to obtain in the Nazi period, Hitler did legalize abortion for women who were carrying fetuses believed to be "defective"—almost always women who were themselves disabled or who had a disabled family member. These women were often forced to have abortions.

One researcher who studied deaf survivors of the Nazi era reported that most of those who underwent abortion were past their fifth month. Obviously, those women who were "defectives" or married to "defectives" tried to hide their pregnancies.

I try to see the faces behind that statistic. I see a deaf woman sitting in a frayed overstuffed chair, crying, her makeup running down her face, in a third-floor flat, waiting for the policeman to come up the stairs, her hand pressed against her belly to feel the last kicks of what should have been her child. Who turned her in: the worker at the deaf social club? Her resentful sister who just joined the Nazi Party?

Sister, we who should remember you have written your memories out of our history.

How do I put these things together? These random facts, not so random:

Nearly 80 percent of all people in the U.S. support abortion in the case of (unspecified) "fetal defect."

When you are pregnant, suddenly everyone is asking you: "How old are you?" (i.e., Are you over thirty-five?)

That health has become the overriding metaphor for what is good in our society. If women have doubts about whether or not they did the right thing in having an abortion, they'll often tell you they had an abortion because they were worried about their health, or about their future child's health.

That the Nazis drew tremendous metaphoric power from their claim to be creating the heilanstaat, the healthy state. The healthy body and a healthy state became one. Genocide began as a cleansing of the defective, disease-ridden dregs.

If abortion is acceptable because a fetus's brain isn't fully developed, and therefore they aren't human, then what is a person with brain damage? Even though I base my beliefs about abortion on women's rights and status, not on that of the fetus within her, plenty of people don't.

I like living in hard places. Well, I'm not so sure I like it: I just seem to find myself there a lot.

ABORTION

Ai

Coming home, I find you still in bed,
but when I pull back the blanket,
I see your stomach is flat as an iron.
You've done it, as you warned me you would
and left the fetus wrapped in wax paper
for me to look at. My son.
Woman, loving you no matter what you do,
what can I say, except that I've heard
the poor have no children, just small people
and there is room only for one man in this house.

FROM *SHRILL: NOTES FROM A LOUD WOMAN*

Lindy West

I'm not sure how I got pregnant—we were careful, mostly—but I don't know, sometimes people just fuck up. I honestly don't remember. Life is life. If I had carried that pregnancy to term and made a half-Mike/half-me human baby, we may have been bound to each other forever, but we would have split up long before the birth. Some people should not be together, and once the stakes are real and kicking and pressing down on your bladder, you can't just pretend shit's fine anymore. Mike made me feel lonely, and being alone with another person is much worse than being alone all by yourself.

I imagine he would have softened, and loved the baby; we would share custody amicably; maybe I'd move into my parents' basement (it's nice!) and get a job writing technical case studies at Microsoft, my side gig at the time; maybe he'd just throw child support at me and move away, but I doubt it. He was a good guy. It could have been a good life.

He didn't want to be in Seattle, though—New England pulled at his guts like a tractor beam. It was all he talked about: flying down running trails at peak foliage; flirting with Amherst girls in Brattleboro bars; keeping one foot always on base, in his glory days when he was happy and thrumming with potential. He wanted to get back there. Though it hurt me at the time (why wasn't I as good as running around in circles in Vermont and sharing growlers of IPA with girls named Blair!?), I wanted that for him too.

As for me, I found out I was pregnant with the part-Mike fetus just three months before I figured out how to stop hating my body for good, five months before I got my first e-mail from a fat girl saying my writing had saved her life, six months before I fell in love with my future husband, eight months before I met my stepdaughters, a year before I moved to Los Angeles to see what the world had for me, eighteen months before

I started working at *Jezebel,* three years before the first time I went on television, four years and ten months before I got married to the best person I've ever met, and just over five years before I turned in this book manuscript.

Everything happened in those five years after my abortion. I became myself. Not by chance, or because an abortion is some mysterious, empowering feminist bloode-magick rite of passage (as many, many—*too many for a movement ostensibly comprising grown-ups*—anti-choicers have accused me of believing), but simply because it was time. A whole bunch of changes—set into motion years, even decades, back—all came together at once, like the tumblers in a lock clicking into place: my body, my work, my voice, my confidence, my power, my determination to demand a life as potent, vibrant, public, and complex as any man's. My abortion wasn't intrinsically significant, but it was my first big, grown-up decision—the first time I asserted unequivocally, "I know the life that I want and this isn't it"; the moment I stopped being a passenger in my own body and grabbed the rudder.

So, I peed on the thingy and those little pink lines showed up all, "LOL, hope u have $600, u fertile betch," and I sat down on my bed and I didn't cry and I said, "Okay, so this is the part of my life when this happens." I didn't tell Mike; I'm not sure why. I have the faintest whiff of a memory that I thought he would be mad at me. Like getting pregnant was my fault. As though my clinginess, my desperate need to be loved, my insistence that we were a "real" couple and not two acquaintances who had grown kind of used to each other, had finally congealed into a hopeful, delusional little bundle and sunk its roots into my uterine wall. A physical manifestation of how pathetic I was. How could I have let that happen? It was so embarrassing. I couldn't tell him. I always felt alone in the relationship anyway; it made sense that I would deal with this alone too.

It didn't occur to me, at the time, that there was anything complicated about obtaining an abortion. This is a trapping of privilege: I grew up middle-class and white in Seattle, I had always had insurance, and, besides, abortion was legal. So, I did what I always did when I needed a common, legal, routine medical procedure—I made an appointment to see my doctor, the same doctor I'd had since I was twelve. She would get this whole implanted embryo mix-up sorted out.

The nurse called my name, showed me in, weighed me, tutted about it, took my blood pressure, looked surprised (fat people can have normal blood, NANCY), and told me to sit on the paper. I waited. My doctor came in. She's older than me, with dark, tightly curled hair, motherly without being overly familiar. "I think I'm pregnant," I said. "Do you want to be pregnant?" she said. "No," I said. "Well, pee in this cup," she said. I peed all over my hand again. "You're pregnant," she said. I nodded, feeling nothing.

I remember being real proud of my chill 'tude in that moment. I was the Fonz of getting abortions. "So, what's the game plan, doc?" I asked, popping the collar of my leather jacket like somebody who probably skateboarded here. "Why don't you go ahead and slip me that RU-486 prescriptsch and I'll just [moonwalks toward exam room door while playing the saxophone]." She stared at me.

"What?" I said, one hundred combs clattering to the floor.

Turns out, THE DOCTOR IS NOT WHERE YOU GET AN ABORTION.

I'd been so sure I could get this taken care of today, handle it today, on my own, and move on with my life—go back to pretending like I had my shit together and my relationship was bearable, even good. Like I was a normal woman that normal men loved. When she told me I had to make an appointment at a different clinic, which probably didn't have any openings for a couple of weeks, and started writing down phone numbers on a Post-it, I crumpled.

"That's stupid," I sobbed, my anxiety getting the better of me. "You're a doctor. This is a doctor's office. Do you not know how to do it?"

"I covered it in medical school, yes," she said, looking concerned in an annoyingly kind way, "but we don't do them here at this clinic."

"Well, why did I even come here? Why didn't they tell me on the phone that this appointment was pointless?"

"You want reception to tell everyone who calls in that we don't do abortions here, no matter what they're calling about?"

"YES," I yelled.

She didn't say anything. I heaved, and cried a little bit more, then a little bit less, in the silence.

"Is there anything else I can do for you right now?" she asked, gently.

"No, I'm fine." I accepted a tissue. "I'm sorry I got upset."

"It's okay. This is a stressful situation. I know." She squeezed my shoulder.

I went home, curled up in bed, and called the clinic (which had some vague mauve nighttime soap name like "Avalon" or "Dynasty" or "Falcon Crest"), still wobbling on the edge of hysteria. Not for all the reasons the forced birth fanatics would like you to think: not because my choice was morally torturous, or because I was ashamed, or because I couldn't stop thinking about the tiny fingernails of our "baby," but because life is fucking hard, man. I wanted someone to love me so much. I did want a baby, eventually. But what I really wanted was a family. Mike wasn't my family. Everything was wrong. I was alone and I was sad and it was just hard.

The woman on the phone told me they could fit me in the following week, and it would be $400 after insurance. It was the beginning of the month, so I had just paid rent. I had about $100 left in my bank account. Payday was in two weeks.

"Can you bill me?" I asked.

"No, we require full payment the day of procedure," she said, brusque from routine but not unkind.

I felt like a stripped wire. My head buzzed and my eyes welled.

"But . . . I don't have that."

"We can push back the appointment if you need more time to get your funds together," she offered.

"But," I said, finally breaking, "I can't be pregnant any more. I need to not be pregnant. I'm not supposed to be pregnant."

I didn't want to wait two more weeks. I didn't want to think about this every day. I didn't want to feel my body change. I didn't want to carry and feed this artifact of my inherent unlovability—this physical proof that any permanent connection to me must be an accident. Men made wanted babies with beautiful women. Men made mistakes with fat chicks. I sobbed so hard I think she was terrified. I sobbed so hard she went to get her boss.

The head of the clinic picked up the phone. She talked to me in a calm, competent voice—like an important businesswoman who is also your mom, which is probably fairly accurate. She talked to me until I started breathing again. She didn't have to. She must have been so busy, and I was wasting her time with my tantrum. Babies having babies.

"We never do this," she sighed, "because typically, once the procedure is done, people don't come back. But if you promise me you'll pay your bill, if you really promise—you can come in next week and we can bill you after the procedure."

I promised, I promised, I promised so hard. Yes, oh my god, yes. Thank you so much. Thank you. Thank you! (And I did pay—as soon as my next paycheck came in. They were so surprised, they sent me a thank-you card.)

I like to think the woman who ran the clinic would have done that for anyone—that there's a quiet web of women like her (like us, I flatter myself) stretching from pole to pole ready to give other women a hand. She helped me even though she didn't have to, and I am forever grateful. But I also wonder what made me sound, to her ears, like someone worth trusting, someone who was safe to take a chance on. I certainly wasn't the neediest person calling her clinic. The fact is, I was getting that abortion no matter what. All I had to do was wait two weeks, or have an awkward conversation I did not want to have with my supportive, liberal, well-to-do mother. Privilege means that it's easy for white women to do each other favors. Privilege means that those of us who need it the least often get the most help.

I don't remember much about the appointment itself. I went in, filled out some stuff on a clipboard, and waited to be called. I remember the waiting room was crowded. Everyone else had somebody with them; none of us made eye contact. I recognized the woman working the front desk— we went to high school together (which should be illegal)*—but she didn't say anything. Maybe that's protocol at the vagina clinic, I thought. Or maybe I just wasn't that memorable as a teenager. Goddammit.

---

* Same goes for you, dildo store cashier. (But thank you for the discount).

Before we got down to business, I had to talk to a counselor. I guess to make sure I wasn't just looking for one of those cavalier partybortions that the religious right is always getting its sackcloth in a bunch over. (Even though, by the way, those are legal too.) She was younger than me, and sweet. She asked me why I hadn't told my "partner," and I cried because he wasn't a partner at all and I still didn't know why I hadn't told him. Everything after that is vague. I think there was a blood test and maybe an ultrasound. The doctor, a brisk, reassuring woman with gray hair in an almost military buzz cut, told me my embryo was about three weeks old, like a tadpole. Then she gave me two pills in a little cardboard billfold and told me to come back in two weeks. The accompanying pamphlet warned that, after I took the second pill, chunks "the size of lemons" might come out. LEMONS. Imagine if we, as a culture, actually talked frankly and openly about abortion. Imagine if people seeking abortions didn't have to be blindsided by the possibility of blood lemons falling out of their vaginas via a pink photocopied flyer. Imagine.

That night, after taking my first pill, as my tadpole detached from the uterine wall, I had to go give a filmmaking prize to my friend and colleague Charles Mudede—make a speech on stage in front of everyone I knew at the Genius Awards, the *Stranger's* annual arts grant. It was surreal. Mike and I went together. We had fun—one of our best nights. There are pictures. I'm glassy-eyed, smiling too big, running on fumes and gallows humor. I remember pulling a friend into a dark corner and confessing that I had an abortion that day. "Did they tell you the thing about the lemons?" she asked. I nodded. "Don't worry," she whispered, hugging me tight. "There aren't going to be lemons."

She paused.

"Probably no lemons."

THE PILL VERSUS THE SPRINGFIELD MINE DISASTER

Joanna C. Valente

for Richard Brautigan

Don't blame me. I only killed
what I could not take care
of.

YOU DON'T KNOW

Judith Arcana

You think I didn't care about that baby,
didn't wonder if we'd like each other
when she turned fourteen;
didn't think he'd follow anywhere
his older brother went.
You think we take them out, like gangsters;
disappear them, like generals.
You don't know how
it works then, do you?
You don't know what
sits on both sides of the scale,
what it means to decide:
what I got and what I gave,
gave that baby I didn't have,
baby who couldn't make me laugh—
applesauce upside down on her head;
couldn't make me cry—
taking his first step right off the porch.
You don't even know that this is not about regret.
You don't know one blessèd, I say blessèd, thing about it.

GHAZAL

Jenna Le

Our grandmas, bless their hearts, their sweet skip-to-my-lou's,
were lying when they said virginity hurts to lose.

Lil' sis, here's what you do so that there'll be no pain:
one finger Sunday, two on Monday, three on Tuesday.

There's stretching regimens that'll help as well. The web
is glad to teach you these when Ma and Moms refuse.

This notion sex must hurt, must come all tangled up
with pregnancy and punishment—that's just their ruse.

Who isn't scared of pain? Pain here, though, is a symbol.
They paid, so now they want you, too, to pay your dues.

I feared the hurt, the pop, the snap, the break. They warn
a girl her hymen rips like paper when she screws.

So, when it was my turn, I sank into my fear.
I let the boy, my fear, and chance do all the choosing.

I could've planned ahead: got on the pill, all that.
But I don't blame myself. What's there to blame? Old news.

We did it in his dorm, but I'm remembering now
that clinic bed, that clink of tools between my shoes.

FROM *WHAT HAVE YOU DONE FOR ME LATELY?*

Myrna Lamb

First performed at New Feminist Repertory Theatre, New York City, March 1969.

Time: whenever.

Place: a space, silent, encapsulated. A man lies with his head angled up and center stage, feet obliquely toward audience. His couching, by all means psychiatric in flavor, should also be astronautic and should incline him acutely so that he almost looks as though he is about to be launched. An almost perpendicular slant board comes to mind or a simple sliding pond or seesaw.

There is a simple desk or table, angled away from the man, and a chair placed toward the desk that will keep the occupants' back toward man in authodox (approximate) psychiatric practice, but will give profile or three-quarter view to audience.

At rise a man in a business suit is situated as delineated. Woman in a simple smock (suggestive of surgical smock) comes on upstage and crosses without looking at man. He does not see her. He sits silently. Some time elapses. A soldier, in a Green Beret outfit, complete with M-1 rifle, comes to stage center. He faces audience.

MAN: Where am I? What have you done to me? Where am I? What have you done to me? Where am I? What have you done to me?

(SOLDIER *stands at attention*)

WOMAN: Are you in pain?

MAN: Yes. I think I am in pain.

WOMAN: Don't you know?

MAN: I haven't been able to consider it fully. The whole procedure . . . strange room—anesthetic—nurses? Sisters in some order?

WOMAN: Nurses. Sisters. In some order. Yes, that would cover it. Yes, anesthetic.

MAN: I don't believe it. I can't believe this nightmare.

WOMAN: Well, that is how many people feel upon learning these things. Of course, most of those people have been considered female. That made a difference, supposedly. We've managed to attach a bit of ovary to the uterus. I don't think it will do any real good, but I will give you a course of hormonal and glandular products to maintain the pregnancy.

MAN: Maintain the pregnancy, indeed! How dare you make that statement to me!

(*Using outreaching arm of* GIRL *and foot leverage,* SOLDIER *flips her over and throws her to floor.*)

WOMAN: I dare. There is a human life involved, after all.

MAN: There is a human life involved? You insane creatures, I'm fully aware that there is a human life involved. My human life. My human life that you have decided to play with for your own despicable purposes, whatever they are.

WOMAN: Do you think you are in the proper frame of mind to judge? My purposes?

(SOLDIER *does pushups with sexual-soldier connotations over outstretched body of* GIRL.)

Your ultimate acceptance of what you now so vociferously reject? The relative importance of your mature and realized life and the incipient potential of the life you carry within you? Your life is certainty involved. But perhaps your life is subsidiary to the life of this barely begun creature which you would seek to deny representation.

MAN: Why should I give this . . . this thing representation?

(SOLDIER *rises and kicks* GIRL *aside. Walks to rifle. Walks around* GIRL, *pacing, right shoulder arms.*)

It is nothing to me. I am not responsible for it or where it is, nor do I wish to be. I have a life, an important life. I have work, important work, work, I might add, that has more than incidental benefit to the entire population of this world—and this—this mushroom which you have visited upon me—in your madness—has no rights, no life, no importance to anyone, certainly not to the world. It has nothing. It has no existence. A little group of cells. A tumor. A parasite. This has been foisted upon me and then I am told that I owe it primary rights to life, that my rights are subsidiary! That is insanity! I do not want this thing in my body. It does not belong there. I want it removed. Immediately. Safely.

WOMAN: Yes, I understand how you feel. But how would it be if every pregnancy brought about in error or ignorance or through some evil or malicious or even well-meaning design were terminated because of the reluctance or the repugnance of the host? Surely the population of the world would be so effectively decimated as to render wholly redundant the mechanisms of lebensraum, of national politics, of hunger as a method, of greed as a motive, of war itself as a method.

(SOLDIER *lunges and stabs at the invisible enemy, accompanying movements with the appropriate battle grunts and cries. There is hatred and despair in the sounds.*)

Surely, if all the unwilling human beings who found motherhood forced upon them through poverty or chance or misstep were to be given the right to choose their lives above all else, the outpouring of acceptance and joy upon the wanted progeny of desired and deliberate pregnancies would eliminate forever those qualities of aggression and deprivation that are so necessary to the progress of society. After all you must realize there are so many women who find themselves pregnant and unmarried, pregnant and unprepared, with work that cannot bear interruption, with no desire to memorialize a casual sexual episode with issue. So many human beings whose incidental fertility victimizes them superfluously in incidents of rape and incestuous attack.

(*Following the lunges, stabs, and grunts,* SOLDIER *slams the rifle against the stage in vertical butt strokes.*)

So many creatures confounded by sexual desire or a compelling need for warmth and attention who find themselves penniless, ill, pitifully young, and pregnant too.

(*Finally* SOLDIER *simply stands, lifts rifle to shoulder.*)

And so many women who with the approval of society, church, and medicine have already produced more children than they can afford economically, psychically, physically. Surely you can see the overwhelming nature of the problem posed by the individual's desire to prevail as articulated by you at this moment. If one plea is valid, then they might all be. So you must learn to accept society's interest in the preservation of the fetus, within you—within all in your condition.

MAN: Do you know that I want to kill you? That is all I feel: the desire to kill you.

(SOLDIER *points rifle at* GIRL's *head.*)

WOMAN: A common reaction. The impregnated often feel the desire to visit violence upon the impregnator or the maintainers of the pregnancy.

POST-ABORTION QUESTIONNAIRE— POWERED BY SURVEYMONKEY

Susan Rich

1. Do you feel reluctant to talk about the subject of abortion?

> In the center of the ceiling a marigold weeps,
> or perhaps it's an old chandelier.
> Inside, there's an interior glow,
> shards illuminated in violet-pink
> and layers of peeling gold leaf.
> Such minds at night unfold.

2. Do you feel guilt or sorrow when discussing your own abortion?

> The cabbage is a blue rose,
> an alchemical strip show. They scream
> when dragged from the earth
> only to be submerged in boiling water.
> The narrative unscrolls from cells
> of what-ifs and hourglass hopes.

3. Have you found yourself either avoiding relationships or becoming overly dependent on them since the abortion?

> If I could unhinge myself from myself,
> attach to bookshelves, sever
> my tongue, I would watch
> as it grew back, rejuvenated
> and ready to speak.

4. Do you have lingering feelings of resentment toward people involved in your abortion (perhaps the baby's father or your parents)?

> One must be careful what one takes
> when one turns away forever:

a Tuareg scarf, two photographs,
untamed thoughts that curse, then lift—
occasionally yes, though mostly not.

5. *Do you tend to think of your life in terms of "before" and "after" the abortion?*

Too scared to speak my name—
not etherized upon the table—
I wore silver stirrups, a blue wrap-around gown.
The young nurse and I held hands—
you're doing great, she cooed.
I remained awake, awakened.

6. *Have you felt a vague sort of emptiness, a deep sense of loss, or had prolonged periods of depression?*

The sky no longer speaks to me directly—
and the beautiful man?
He has dropped through the floorboards
though sometimes he answers emails:
Thank you, our family has survived the Paris bombings.
Sincere condolences on your new president.

7. *Do you sometimes have nightmares, flashbacks, or hallucinations relating to the abortion?*

Never mind, I told myself, *it's only a nightmare.*
But then I remembered I'd barely gone to bed at all.
Then thirty years had passed, now thirty-one.

8. *Have you begun or increased use of drugs or alcohol since the abortion, or do you have an eating disorder?*

First the fog tastes sweet, then sour—
what is identity but forged glamour?
Strong doses of celibacy taken regularly.

9. *Did your relationship to or concept of God, or Karma, or Fate change after your abortion?*

If my own voice falters, tell them

I tried not to live inside the clock
or under the skin of pomegranates.
Does anyone escape her own story—
head-on collision, nor'easter, earthquake,
or the racist seeding of our country?

10. *Has your self-concept or self-esteem changed since your abortion?*

Once I abandoned my car in a forest of red cedar,
let it tumble down the mountain
precipice by itself. In my next diorama there's a friend
at the wheel, and she urges, *let's go on;*
build yourself, like a paint color, an infant's song.

11. *Are you bothered by certain sounds like machinery that makes loud*
noises?

Coffee grinders, vacuum cleaners,
electronic sewing machines—
Also: truck backfires, sparklers,
the sharp scrape of chair legs—
gunfire overhead, handsaws—the evening
news—aren't you?

12. *Is there anything you would like to ask?*

Why does Google Maps allow blind spots;
for example, the city of Zinder, Niger?
Is it possible for one person to photograph each galaxy—
to comprehend this bewilderment of light?

BODY

FROM "TAM LIN"

Anonymous Balladeers

(Scottish, sixteenth century)

Lady Margaret, Lady Margaret, was sewing at her seam.
And she's all dressed in black,
When a thought comes to her head to run into the wood,
To pick flowers to flower her hat, me boys,
To pick flowers to flower her hat.

She's hoisted up her petticoats a bit above her knee
And so nimbly she'd run o'er the plain.
And when she's come to the merry green wood,
She pulled them branches down, down
She pulled them branches down.

And suddenly she spied a fine young man
Stood underneath the tree,
Saying, "How dare you pull them branches down
Without the leave of me, lady,
Without the leave of me?"

She says, "This little wood it is me very own,
Me father give it me.
And I can pull these branches down
Without the leave of thee, young man,
Without the leave of thee."

He's taken her by the lily-white hand
And by the grass-green sleeve
And he's laid her down at the foot of a bush.

He's never once asked her leave, me boys,
He's never once asked her leave.

And when it was done she has turned herself about
To ask her true-love's name.
But she nothing heard and nothing saw
And all the woods grew dim, me boys,
And all the woods grew dim.

There're four and twenty ladies all in the court
Grown red as any rose.
Excepting for young Margaret
And green as glass she goes, any glass,
Yes, green as glass she goes.

Outten spoke the first serving girl,
She lifted her head and smiled,
"I think me lady's loved too long
And now she goes with child, me dears,
Now she goes with child."

And outten spoke the second serving girl
"Oh, ever and alas," said she,
"I think I know a herb in the merry green wood
That'll twine the babe from thee, Lady,
That'll twine the babe from thee."

Lady Margaret, she picked up her silver comb,
Made haste to comb her hair.
She's away to the merry green wood
As fast as she can tear, me boys,
As fast as she can tear.

She hadn't pulled a herb in that merry green wood
A herb but barely one

When by her stood young Tam Lin
Saying, "Margaret, leave it alone, me love,
Margaret, leave it alone."

"Oh no, how can you pull that bitter little herb
The herb that grows so grey
To take away that sweet babe's life
We got in our play, me love,
That we got in our play?"

"Oh tell me the truth, young Tam Lin," she says
"If an earthly man you be."
"I'll tell you no lies, Lady Margaret," he says,
"I was christened the same as thee, me dear,
I was christened the same as thee."

"But as I rode out one cold and bitter day
From off me horse I fell,
And the Queen of Elfland she took me
In yonder green hill to dwell, me dear,
In yonder green hill to dwell."

"But this night it is the Hallow-een
When the Elven Court must ride.
And if you would your true love win
By the old-mill bridge you must bide, me dear,
By the old-mill bridge you must bide."

"And first will come the black horse and then come by the brown
And then race by the white.
But you'll hold me fast and fear me not
And I will not you affright, me love,
I will not you affright."

"And then they will change me all in your arms
Into many a beast sae wild.
But you'll hold me fast and fear me not
I'm the father of your child, you know,
You know that I'm the father of your child."

So, Margaret has taken up her silver comb,
Made haste to comb her hair.
And she's away to the old-mill bridge
As fast as she can tear, me boys,
As fast as she can tear.

And at the dead hour of the night
She heard the harness ring.
And oh, me boys, it chilled her heart
More than any mortal thing, it did,
More than any mortal thing.

And first come by the black horse and then come by the brown
And then race by the white.
And she held it fast and feared it not
And it did not her affright, me boys,
It did not her affright.

The thunder rolled across the sky,
And the stars they blazed like day,
And the Queen of Elfland gave a thrilling cry,
"Oh, young Tam Lin's away, away
Oh, young Tam Lin's away."

And then they have changed him all in her arms
To a lion that roared so wild.
But she held it fast and feared it not,
It was the father of her child, she knew
It was father of her child.

And then they have changed him all in her arms
Into a loathsome snake.
But she held it fast and feared it not,
It was one of God's own make, she knew
It was one of God's own make.

And then they have changed him all in her arms
To a red-hot bar of iron.
But she held it fast and feared it not,
It did to her no harm, me boys
It did to her no harm.

And at last they have changed him all in her arms
It was to a naked man.
And she's flung her mantle over him,
Crying, "Me love I've won, I've won,"
Oh crying, "Me love I've won."

And outten spoke the Queen of Elfland
From the bush wherein she stood,
"I should have tore out your eyes Tam Lin
And put in two eyes of wood, of wood
Put in two eyes of wood."

THE BUSINESS OF MACHINES

Shirley Geok-lin Lim

The woman:
    It moves. I don't want to.
    She would not look into his eyes.
    It was business they
    Were there on together.
The stranger:
    Part your legs. Relax.
    It could have been a stone.
    A splinter curled. The shock
    Of her nature, almost forgotten,
    Showed still pacing, able to kill.
The story:
    It could have been funny.
    Or wicked. His machine took back
    The stone, the splinter, the mess
    On the floor. She was part
    Of a process of numbers.

The women napped on white cots
In long silent rows.

FROM *HEAT AND DUST*

Ruth Prawer Jhabvala

Maji was in the state of *samadhi*. To be in that state means to have reached a higher level of consciousness and to be submerged in its bliss. At such times, Maji is entirely unaware of anything going on around her. She sits on the floor in the lotus pose; her eyes are open but the pupils turned up, her lips slightly parted with the tip of the tongue showing between them. Her breathing is regular and peaceful as in dreamless sleep.

When she woke up—if that's the right expression, which it isn't—she smiled at me in welcome as if nothing at all had occurred. But, as always at such times, she was like a person who has just stepped out of a revivifying bath, or some other medium of renewal. Her cheeks glowed and her eyes shone. She passed her hands upwards over her face as if she felt it flushed and fiery. She has told me that whereas it used to be very difficult for her to make the transition from *samadhi* back to ordinary life, now it is quite easy and effortless.

When I spoke to her about the woman who had so mysteriously followed me, she said, "You see, it has started." Apparently, it wasn't mysterious at all—the woman was a midwife marking me down as a potential client. She must have noticed me before and followed me today to check up on her suspicions. My condition would be perfectly obvious to her by the way I walked and held myself. In a day or two she would probably offer me her services. And now Maji offered me her own again: "This would be a good time," she said, "Eight or nine weeks—it would not be too difficult."

"How would you do it?" I asked, almost in idle curiosity.

She explained that there were several ways, and at this early stage a simple massage, skillfully applied, might do it. "Would you like me to try?" she asked.

I said yes—again I think just out of curiosity. Maji shut the door of her hut. It wasn't a real door but a plank of wood someone had given her. I lay down on the floor, and she loosened the string of my Punjabi trousers. "Don't be afraid," she said. I wasn't, not at all. I lay looking up at the roof which was a sheet of tin, and at the mud walls blackened from her cooking fire. Now, with the only aperture closed, it was quite dark inside and all sorts of smells were sealed in—of dampness, the cow dung used as fuel, and the lentils she had cooked; also of Maji herself. Her only change of clothes hung on the wall, unwashed.

She sat astride me. I couldn't see her clearly in the dark, but she seemed larger than life and made me think of some mythological figure: one of those potent Indian goddesses who hold life and death in one hand and play them like a yo-yo. Her hands passed slowly down my womb, seeking out and pressing certain parts within. She didn't hurt me—on the contrary, her hands seemed to have a kind of soothing quality. They were very, very hot; they are always so, I have felt them often (she is always touching one, as if wanting to transmit something). But today they seemed especially hot, and I thought this might be left over from her *samadhi*, that she was still carrying the waves of energy that had come to her from elsewhere. And, again, I had the feeling of her *transmitting* something to me—not taking away, but giving.

Nevertheless, I suddenly cried out, "No, please stop!" She did so at once. She got off me and took the plank of wood from the door. Light streamed in. I got up and went outside, into that brilliant light. The rain had made everything shining green and wet. Blue tiles glinted on the royal tombs and everywhere there were little hollows of water that caught the light and looked like precious stones scattered over the landscape. The sky shone in patches of monsoon blue through puffs of cloud, and in the distance, more clouds, but of a very dark blue, were piled on each other like weightless mountains.

"Nothing will happen, will it?" I asked Maji anxiously. She had followed me out of the hut and was no longer the dark mythological figure she had been inside but her usual, somewhat bedraggled motherly self. She laughed when I asked that and patted my cheek in reassurance. But I didn't know what she was reassuring me of. Above all I wanted nothing to happen—that her efforts should not prove successful. It was absolutely clear to me now that I wanted my pregnancy and the completely new feeling—of rapture—of which it was the cause.

1923

Satipur also had its slummy lanes, but Khatm had nothing else. The town huddled in the shadow of the Palace walls in a tight knot of dirty alleys with ramshackle houses leaning over them. There were open gutters flowing through the streets. They often overflowed, especially during the rains, and were probably the cause, or one of them, of the frequent epidemics that broke out in Khatm. If it rained rather more heavily, some of the older houses would collapse and bury the people inside them. This happened regularly every year.

It had happened the week before opposite the house to which Olivia was taken. The women attending on her were still talking about it. One of them described how she had stood on the balcony to watch a wedding procession passing below. When the bridegroom rode by, everyone surged forward to see him, and there was so much noise, she said, the band was playing so loudly that, at first, she had not realized what was happening though it was happening before her eyes. She saw the house opposite, which she had known all her life, suddenly cave inwards and disintegrate, and the next moment everything came crashing and flying through the air in a shower of people, bricks, tiles, furniture, and cooking pots. It had been, she said, like a dream, a terrible dream.

What was happening to Olivia was also like a dream. Although no one could have been more matter-of-fact than the women attending her: two homely, middle-aged midwives doing the job they had been commissioned for. The maidservant who had brought her had also been quite matter-of-fact. She had dressed Olivia in a burka and made her follow her on foot through the lanes of Khatm. No one took any notice of them—they were just two women in burkas, the usual walking tents. The street of the midwives was reached by descending some slippery steps (here Olivia, unused to her burka, had to be particularly careful). The midwives' house was in a tumbledown condition—very likely it would go in the next monsoon; the stairs looked especially dangerous. They were so dark that her escort had to take Olivia's hand—for a moment Olivia shrank from this physical contact but only for a moment, knowing that soon she would be touched in a far more intimate manner and in more intimate places.

PSALM

Alina Stefanescu

For the crochet hook and
    the knitting needle,
makers of homes and warm bodies.

For the slender wooden dowel
    that broke inside a
woman no one dared help.

For the raspberry leaf and
    the stinging nettle,
boiled across centuries.

For the pliable metal
    coat hangers that
we hid in household closets.

For all who have died
    female bodies
the merciless felled.

ON THE DEATH AND HACKING INTO A HUNDRED PIECES OF NINETEEN-YEAR-OLD BARBARA LOFRUMENTO BY AN ILLEGAL ABORTIONIST, 1962

Pat Falk

A botched abortion and the whole world bleeds.
Or so it seemed to the doctor
who didn't want to do it in the first place.
He had panicked when she died on the table.
So much blood he could not tell
the fetus from the woman,
so he kept on cutting, delivering
decisive strikes to the chest, finding that
the buzz saw carried from the shed worked best.
How hard was her skull?
How quickly did he gather, bag, and drag
the parts to the kitchen sink?
How does one stuff chunks of flesh
and lengths of bone down a long steel drain
where thin-edged blades,
spinning like the law
that brought him to this madness,
grind the matter down to soft pink pulp?
The earth, he prays, will heal this wound in silence.
He turns on the tap, washes the woman away.

FROM *SELF-RITUAL FOR INVOKING RELEASE OF SPIRIT LIFE IN THE WOMB*

Deborah Maia

During ritual today, I sat naked in the midst of a circle of red silk, red wool, garnet, and red coral. I drummed and chanted to Mother Earth . . . to Mother Spirit . . . to Spirit Life within my Womb. A chant came forth while in trance:

> Great One who lives within my Womb
> I accept with Love

> Great One who lives within my Womb
> I release with Love

> Great One who lives within my Womb
> I accept with Love

> Great One who lives within my Womb
> I release with Love

In a south window of my house stands a circle of iridescent red glass. I create a ritual with this circle of redness as my focus . . . as my altar. It is midday, the Sun shines brightly through the red circle.

The connection with the South, and the gifts of fire, passion, and sparks of life, became most apparent. The vision of fire grows before me and within me.

> This fire within me is releasing
> the Spirit Life within my Womb.

I sense the embrace of Mother Earth as She guides me to the South:
the gateway to passion . . . to love . . . to One who lives within my
Womb.

I walk outside. The icy air is very still and large snowflakes are falling.
I stand for several minutes, in deep appreciation of winter's beauty,
when quite suddenly I feel a warm moist ooze coming from my vagina.
When I look inside my pants, my eyes meet with a loose formed clot of
bright red.

I feel uplifted to a peak of elation.

I offer gratitude
    to my Body for strength.
I offer gratitude
    to my Intuition for guidance.
I offer gratitude
    to my Heart for love.
I offer gratitude
    to my Mind for knowledge.
I offer gratitude
    to my blessed Spirit for balance.

As the day moves on, the slight cramping, the heaviness, the spotting
decrease. By evening all has stopped.

AND THERE IS THIS EDGE

Lauren R. Korn

> *I don't believe in God, but I do have some pretty*
> *interesting thoughts concerning ghosts.*
>
> —Ada Limón

the relief of itching
                around
something that itches
        the containment
                of [something harmful]
                held by winter's still
in my body a foreign object
in my body, a foreign object

        I cannot identify the tree outside my kitchen window, and so
approved street trees for the city of Missoula, Montana
                                there is snow on the ground, browned
and melted on concrete
stained by street salt, the [*Acer saccharum, Acer glabrum*]
                                has stopped its bleeding,
        [there is another word for this] and I am no longer looking out
my kitchen window but at *wikiHow, WebMD,* and *Homeland Security*

        and there is this edge, this something missing
        after one month, I am still bleeding
        I am ever conscious of the sun
                of its drop and of its rise
[of my circadian rhythms]
        in darkness, I see only the tree's silhouette
and not the tree itself
        but of its life I am certain

      but of its life I am certain am I of its leaves, once stuck to summer
sap

      but of its life I am certain am I of its leaves, once stuck to the
windshields of cars its life I am
below my kitchen window

      but of its life I am not a god buried, but a god strewn

              I do not believe in God

                    what do I believe in

        in a dead garden, a sapped maple

        in seeing a thing clearly [and knowing absence]

TUGGING

SeSe Geddes

It's the final moment—the tugging—
that's the worst. A sucking deep within the pelvis,
where the body contracts as if
to cling to that tiny growth. Everything
seems to fight for life, the way a moth
with wings bent and tattered by the cat
still stretches its proboscis to an offered cap of water.
The uterus does not easily let go.
My body's instinct is deeply woven, dense
as the bird's nest the house painter found
beneath the eaves. He gasped at the eggs
in their bowl of twigs, cupped it
in his sunburned, paint-speckled hands, placed it
back before dusk, but the birds never returned.

FROM *HAPPENING*

Annie Ernaux

I was seized with a violent urge to shit. I rushed across the corridor into the bathroom and squatted by the porcelain bowl, facing the door. I could see the tiles between my thighs. I pushed with all my strength. It burst forth like a grenade, in a spray of water that splashed the door. I saw a baby doll dangling from my loins at the end of a reddish cord. I couldn't imagine ever having had that inside me. I had to walk with it to my room. I took it in one hand—it was strangely heavy—and proceeded along the corridor, squeezing it between my thighs. I was a wild beast.

O's door was ajar, with a beam of light. I called out her name softly, "It's here."

The two of us are back in my room. I am sitting on the bed with the fetus between my legs. Neither of us knows what to do. I tell O we must cut the cord. She gets a pair of scissors; we don't know where to cut it but she goes ahead and does it. We look at the tiny body with its huge head, the eyes two blue dashes beneath translucent lids. It looks like an Indian doll. We look at the sexual organs. We seem to detect the early stages of a penis. To think I was capable of producing that. O sits down on a stool. She is crying. We are both crying in silence. It's an indescribable scene, life and death in the same breath. A sacrificial scene.

We don't know what to do with the fetus. O goes to her room to fetch an empty melba toast wrapper and I slip it inside. I walk to the bathroom with the bag. It feels like a stone inside. I turn the bag upside down above the bowl. I pull the chain.

In Japan aborted embryos are called *mizuko*—water babies.

The motions we went through that night came to us naturally. They seemed the only thing to do at the time.

Nothing about her bourgeois ideals or her beliefs had prepared O to sever the umbilical cord of a three-month-old fetus. Today she may have dismissed this episode as a temporary aberration, an inexplicable moment of chaos in her life. She may also hold anti-abortion views. But it was she, and she alone, who stood by my side that night, her small face crumpled with tears, acting as an improvised midwife in room seventeen of the girls' dormitory.

Translated from the French by Tanya Leslie

SARASWATI PRAISES YOUR NAME
EVEN WHEN YOU HAVE NO CHOICE

Purvi Shah

*Patel, a thirty-three-year-old woman who lives in Indiana, was
accused of feticide—specifically, illegally inducing her own
abortion—and accused of having a baby whom she allowed
to die. The facts supporting each count are murky, but a jury
convicted Patel and she was sentenced to twenty years in prison.*

—Emily Bazelon, "Purvi Patel Could Be Just the
Beginning," *New York Times Magazine*, April 1, 2015

You had a name no one
could hold between their

       teeth. So they pronounced
    a sentence. Had you the choice,

you would pilgrim
to the Vermilion. It is no

Ganges, but you could dream for tiger's
      blood, for eight tributaries to open

into palms bearing girls unfettered. Before your baby

was a baby,   could it float? Could
a stillness of breath   be the air asking

for alchemy   as you cast your life as a spell? These days
the world is looking   for witches. You had been

searching for a day   beyond labor, option

of pleasure, a choice unscripted
by parents, borders unscripted

by choices, a passing
salvation. You had not

expected this state—punishment
for a wrung womb. These days

you mourn: when you are free, you won't
be able to bear   the children you

wanted. In silence, you pronounce   your name as if it came
from the crucible of river, from the first   throat broken
                     into a cobra of desiccated streams.

"RECRUITING NEW COUNSELORS" FROM
JANE: ABORTION AND THE UNDERGROUND

Paula Kamen

CHARACTERS:

JUDITH ARCANA (married name of Pildes): (1943–) Late twenties. Very intense. Mostly takes over lead role in play after JODY. Her manner is very sensual, as if she is always aware of her body and sexuality. Her clothes, always very loose and sometimes revealing, convey this attitude. Unusually articulate, she speaks with a blend of intelligence and inner passion. Her views are so strong that when she speaks, she states her opinions as if they were proven facts. Jewish.

MICKI: (1940s–) In early twenties. She is very much into excitement and extremes of counterculture and the revolutionary "scene" of the period, but is always acting in the background. She is one of the few members of The Service who is black and/or working class. From the South Side of Chicago, and a pre-law student at Loyola University. Not knowing if she'll survive these turbulent years, she lives in the moment, allowing the use of her apartment for the abortions. Grew up Catholic.

(JUDITH passes the clipboard to MICKI, who fills out her contact info by the end of the scene. MICKI and JUDITH stand to face audience. Lights shift.)

MICKI: I'd been involved in the Chicago Conspiracy Trial, of "The Chicago Seven," they were called . . . I was on the legal defense team. I helped them do research. . . . [In news footage,] I'm the black female sitting next to Bobby Seal, holding his hand when he's being gagged and stuff. And I'm holding the notebooks so he can write notes. . . . So, you know, I've demonstrated against the war in Vietnam and, you know, all that kind of stuff. And then . . . I was somewhere on the North Side a couple years after the trial was over and somebody handed me a leaflet, and I might have read about the Chicago Women's Liberation Union. (An aside) . . . My opinion about Heather and the people that she associated with was that they were a bunch of liberals, even though they thought of themselves as radicals or revolutionaries . . . I didn't think highly of them at the time. So, I didn't associate with them, and that's kind of how you did it in those days . . . [But] I went up the office [of the Women's Union] and kind of looked around, and the first thing that attracted me was the posters because the Graphics Collective was active then. And I was like really intrigued by the art, [the iconic, bold, colorful pictures of women from all races] (We see projected images of art in background), which really spoke to me. And, you know, I had years of Catholic education on holy cards that they give you . . . usually it was of a mother and child and, I mean, you know, it was totally unfeminist, you know, even if it was a picture of the Virgin Mary . . . And then there was this stuff, (looking to images) which was just like really revolutionary for me. . . . I mean, it was just like, it was more of a 'yeah!' kind of thing for me where I just . . . I wanted to be connected to this . . . .

JUDITH: I was in my teaching job trying to figure out what was wrong, why everybody hated high school, why my students were so unhappy. And so I asked them. And they told me. And I learned what the public education system really was, and all of those things . . . and my life was coming apart very dramatically, and I was having this affair, and I wouldn't eat, and I thought, 'Ugh! I'm pregnant.' I called a friend who was a medical student, and he called me back and said, 'Everyone here [in his medical school] says call this number and ask for Jane.' So, I called the number, and a woman called me back, and we talked for a very long time. I can't remember the specifics, but it was a very political conversation, you know. She asked me a lot of stuff about my life, and I was in a mood to tell her, because I was changing in every possible way. . . .

MICKI: How did I know you were going to ask that question? . . . For a long time, I was the only [black woman] in the Women's Union [and the only working-class woman]. I think there were a couple of other black volunteers in Jane . . . I got my sense of injustice from just being black in this society, and I got my sense of politics from my dad. . . . He was very involved in his union, and he worked at the steel mills at a time when blacks had the more undesirable jobs. And so he was always, you know, he was always in both the union's face and management's face about that, and gained a great deal of respect from black and white steelworkers alike. He worked in the wire mill at Republic Steel for thirty-five years. [When organizing,] I always looked to see what kind of white people they were. Were they white people with class consciousness because they came out of a white working-class background? Or were they people who were faking it, people with long hair and dirty clothes who talked about how they were down with the people? Excuse me, but I take a bath every day. Don't insult me like that. So I guess from that point on I looked at people based on their practice and their background. . . . Yeah, it was pretty lonely but you know, I ignored that stuff because of the bigger picture, the bigger social issues that needed to be addressed. And as long as there was one black voice in there, then I felt like I was making a contribution. . . . I'm sure when I opened the door for people who were coming in, and several of them were black, they were like 'OK, good. I'm all right. I've had [enough of] this all-white thing.'

JUDITH: And then I found out I wasn't pregnant, just very, very, very, very late. And so I didn't need an abortion, which was lucky, and this woman and I, who I called Jane, I guess we agreed that we might talk again at some future time. I was looking for the women's movement. . . . And if I had met somebody who was doing employment work about women or daycare work about women, maybe I would have gone that way. I don't know. But I didn't. I met these people, and so I went to the meeting and I became a counselor.

MICKI: People were so desperate for abortions. And again, the issues of whether I was the only black woman or the only whatever, there were women who were dying, there were black women who were dying because of back alley abortions. So I didn't care what organization was doing it or what color they were. They were somebody who was doing something about the problem, and I wanted to be a person who did something about the problem.

FROM "BOX SET"

Sue D. Burton

For my Great-Aunt Antoinette (Nettie) Bope (1880–1902)

I.

Is it true Nettie wasn't pregnant? But she *thought* she was—did she try one of those mail-order concoctions? The parsley seed cure? Did it screw up her hormones? *Everybody* took them. Ads in church bulletins: *for blocked menses.* But she was seen by doctors. Hoskinson and Cookes. Did they even know how to do a pelvic exam? They *inserted implements.* Bent spoons. Penholders, *wire attached.*

    but   *can't—*

repeat?   1968. Baltimore. X waiting in a bar. While I go to the doctor's. To get a "rabbit test." To get a phone number so somebody could drive me someplace in Pennsylvania. Blindfolded. X had had a few beers by the time I got back to the bar. The doctor's waiting room was standing-room-only. Thick with smoke.

II.

Standing-room-only. Thick. I was twenty-four. Nettie was almost twenty-two. I found her. Loved her. Made her into myself. For years, I had only one newspaper clipping: *It is said the girl was taken to the place of a Mrs. Beatty on South Pearl Alley some time ago, and it was claimed she was in a delicate condition at the time.* Beatty, no first name. *Licensed midwife,* whatever that meant in 1902. But in 1902, university-trained doctors (*regular* doctors) were on a crusade to license themselves. To squeeze out the competition—the *irregulars,* like Mrs. Beatty. Who *diluted the profession.* Like me in 1976, apprentice-trained at a women's health center. For years, I had only one clipping and thought Mrs. Beatty was the abortionist. Nothing in the paper about doctors. *You don't do abortions, do you, Sue*, Moo asked me once.

III.

No one should do abortions, said the regular doctors. Except themselves. Hospital boards. *Yes. No.* Checks, boxes. *Regulars* will *regulate*. Begottens. Though *concerns re preserving the stock.* Who is this Antoinette Bope? Frenchified. Farmer's daughter. Grocery clerk. *Convalescing* for weeks. Who is *the author of her ruin*? Cy Stewart? Regular docs? *Sudie, don't brood.* A student at Ohio State, Cy Stewart *claimed to know a great deal which he could tell about the girl if the press would promise not to use his name, but as he intimated it was reflections on the girl's character rather than facts in connection with the case at hand, he was informed his story was not wanted.* My white dress Emily Dickinson Nettie. Who was *hardworking and held in high esteem.* Doctors and their boxes. They should've let the midwives keep the work.

BIRTH

Wendy Chin-Tanner

bone-scraping
    labor is
        nothing like

the pangs that
    wracked me for
        after

    the vacuum
        emptied my
            womb and what

    spilled from me
        was bleak and
            nacreous

        for years I
            was tethered
                to terror

        led by the
            nose a beast
                pierced through its

        septum I
            had cast veils
                over it

        defiance

            denial
              and though it

            had left my
             sight smoke

still

              issued from

             my mouth as
           if I had
           swallowed fire

            as if its
          violence had
        smoldered and

           sunken down
         into ash
       live embers

           still glowing
        now in these
      volcanic

        surges in
      the burning
    ring as she

      crowns she leaves
    my dwindling
  starless night

    as sacrum
  and pelvis
and inward

        spiral let
     go I yield
I open

                                                     my body
                                                    turns itself
                                                   inside out

THE SCARLET A

Soniah Kamal

The following reenactments are based on separate and extensive interviews with students from one high school class in Pakistan. These women agreed to share their experiences under the condition of using pseudonyms.

Aminah, 1995

Hours after arriving home in Lahore for summer break from college in America, I told my mother I had to go to the store to buy sanitary napkins, my decoy. I drove to a pharmacy in another neighborhood and purchased two pregnancy tests with cash scrounged up from the insides of old handbags. My boyfriend, Mike, and I had used a condom from a dispensary in the girls' dorm bathrooms.

I was pregnant.

Sarai, my best friend, came over immediately.

Can you and Mike get married? she asked.

Sarai was married; the ultimate goal for good girls. I certainly did not want to get married just because I was pregnant. In the Bollywood films I'd grown up on, an unwed pregnant girl *always* commits suicide to save her family's honor, but life is not a movie.

Pre-Mike, I was a virgin in a committed relationship of five years with my Pakistani paramour, Q. One weekend, Q had paid me a visit from his college. Perhaps because five years seemed testimony of everlasting love and because we planned to marry, we had sex. Also what happens in America stays in America and so good Pakistani girls learn the art of subterfuge in order to survive what, in other cultures, are simply rites of puberty: dating, kissing, sex.

Soon after, I discovered Q was cheating on me. Although Islam forbids premarital sex for both genders, Sarai consoled me that 'boys will be boys' and that I was Q's one true love. This double standard upset me, so I cast off the shackles of purity, honor, and reputation and broke up with him.

A few months later I'd started dating Mike because if boys could be boys, then why couldn't girls be girls?

I had two options: abortion or adoption.

"I can't abort," I told Fatima. "I don't want to."

I was roughly two and a half months gone. My due date was in December, which meant back in college and winter break. I would secretly carry the baby to term while at college, not return to Pakistan during winter break, and, instead, deliver the baby and give it up for adoption. Under this plan, I would not get to keep my child, but I was determined to someday have a relationship.

I slept soundly for the first time in a long while only to awake the next morning to pandemonium. My sister's in-laws-to-be had set the wedding date: December. In some cultures, "out of wedlock" and "illegitimate" are archaic terms, but in honor-purity cultures they remain relevant. If I returned to Pakistan in December, unwed and pregnant, the scandal would destroy and taint everyone—friends, extended family, parents; my sister's wedding could be cancelled.

But there was *no* excuse valid enough to miss a sibling's wedding.

I had to get an abortion. In Pakistan, premarital sex, let alone being unwed and pregnant, is a crime. Abortion is legal only in order, save the mother's life and in cases of "necessary treatment," whatever that means. In Islam, an abortion is legal until the fetus's organs have formed and "life is breathed into it," which, according to most Islamic scholars, is around 120 days. I was already nearing ninety days.

At home, I was dying of guilt. My mother is a doctor. She believes girls who abort are hell bound, doctors who perform/aid abortions are devils, and she will not work with a colleague if she finds out they are "soft" on abortion.

Sarai and I knew we had to find a doctor who did not know my mother. After two frantic weeks, Sarai managed to find a friend whose cleaner had used the services of a cheap doctor who asked no questions. The doctor's place was situated by a well-known bridge.

Sarai drove me. An elderly woman in a floral shalwar kurta—the doctor—opened the door to a small side room. We huddled in plastic chairs in front of a wooden desk with a prop-up calendar. The doctor stared at us. I was frightened she would recognize me as my mother's daughter.

"Who is getting it done?" she said.

"Me," I squawked.

"Married?"

I lifted a hand temporarily wearing Sarai's wedding ring. The doctor barely glanced at it.

"Why isn't your mother with you?"

"Dead." Blood rushed to my face for figuratively murdering my mother.

"Husband?" The doctor asked, stone-faced. "Mother-in-law? Sister-in-law?"

Sarai jumped in. "She is newly married and does not want a child so soon."

"*You* are?"

"Friend."

I feared the doctor would guess this was all a farce and kick us out, in which case the miracle I'd asked from Allah would be delivered and the baby would not be aborted, but then I'd be back to step one.

I wanted to know what she would do with the remains but I was terrified of the answer. I wanted to ask if the procedure was safe. But what right did I have to care about my safety? I did inquire at which hospital the abortion would take place, my fingers crossed that it would not be one where my mother practiced.

"There's your hospital." She pointed to a run-down gurney against one wall. I stared at the rickety bed, the gray wrinkled sheet, a huge black-and-white clock on the wall.

"Return in three days. No eating after midnight. Cost—two thousand rupees, cash only."

Whenever I wanted to buy anything—music, makeup, shoes—I asked my parents for money and was expected to show what I'd spent it on. There was no way I could ask for two thousand rupees and not be held accountable.

To borrow from girlfriends, I made up a story about losing jewelry I needed to replace, but no one had any money. Desperate, I approached a male family friend with a liberal outlook. To my relief, he handed me the full amount, assuring me there was no need to return it. However, his expression conveyed disappointment and disgust that comes with trusting a girl enough to allow her to study abroad only to have her betray her morals and Muslim upbringing.

Three days later, I pay the doctor first, and then I undress from the waist down. My feet are placed in stirrups. Sarai sits on a stool next to the gurney. She does not flinch at my bone-crushing grip. At the foot of the gurney there is a steel trolley with surgical tools waiting to invade me. Sarai keeps whispering it'll be okay.

The doctor gives me an aspirin.

"How long will it take?" I stammer.

"Five minutes."

She tells me she is going to scrape the lining of my uterus and that I will feel some pressure. She bows between my legs and I hear a muffled roar like a vacuum cleaner. An excruciating spasm begins in my lower abdomen. I once stepped on an anthill and was bitten so badly I'd felt my foot was on fire. This was worse. This was boiling acid blistering, devouring, disintegrating my insides.

I scream. The doctor slaps my inner thigh. "Shut up." I whimper. She slaps me again. "Shut up or I will stop." She says that her husband is just beyond the door leading from the side room clinic into the house.

"What," she demands, "is he going to think is happening in here if he hears you?"

I bite my tongue. I try to think happy thoughts. I scream again. The doctor stops the machine.

"One more sound. . ." she says, half punching my exposed tummy, "and I will send you home with the deed half done."

I concentrate on the black-and-white clock hanging above me. The long hand and the short hand and the second hand are all moving. Five minutes are long up.

I can hear my baby being sucked out. I had wanted to deliver this baby and give it up for adoption but all I have to offer is death. I would like to see the remains but I'm scared I'll be denied this request and I do not want to give the doctor further control.

For the first time I fully fathom the gulf between the crimes of a man and the crimes of a woman. As I lie there, the clock ticking, my uterus being cleansed, I realize I hate this culture which has forced me to kill my baby. But my culture will say I only have myself to blame: *I had premarital sex and it is fitting that I suffer.*

After it is done, the doctor informs me to take over-the-counter painkillers for cramps and heavy bleeding.

"How heavy?" I ask, weak from pain. "For how long?"

"Heavy," she says. "One week. One month. It varies."

I did not know then that, having aborted the way I had, I risked uncontrolled bleeding, uterine damage, infections, a punctured uterus, septic shock, punctured bowels, possible chronic pain syndrome, and infertility. I would not know this until, years later, I looked up on the Internet the risks of an illegal unhygienic backstreet abortion. When I returned to college, I told Mike about the abortion and relief flooded his face. I broke up with him days later.

I'd dream one night of a chubby baby boy who said, "It's okay, I forgive you, forgive yourself, we'll meet again." Perhaps it was my subconscious assuaging my emotions so I could live with myself, but I'd like to believe it *was* my baby, because, since I'd always wanted only daughters, I had no reason to dream up a son.

The doctor tells me to get rest and dismisses us. Sarai helps me hobble towards the car where her husband has been waiting. I get in. I shut my eyes. I return her wedding ring.

Hajra, 1997

What leads a studious girl like me who barely looked at boys, not that they looked at me, to start dating one? I agreed to chaperone a friend from high school, Khadijah, on her clandestine date just to see what all the fuss was about. When we arrived at the ice cream parlor, her boyfriend, Omar, had brought along his younger brother, Osman. Osman was courteous and cute. He kept smiling at me, making small talk, politely, respectfully, and I was flattered.

On our fifth chaperoning, Osman asked me for my phone number. Soon we were speaking regularly. Each time, I begged Allah to forgive me for deceiving my unsuspecting parents. Anyway, all we talked about were studies and future plans and I would shyly brag about my grades and dreams of a career of my own. Osman was studying engineering in college.

A few months later, Osman paid me a surprise-midnight-birthday visit at my house. I smuggled him in and, after accepting his gift bag and quick kiss on my cheek, smuggled him out. My parents did not wake up and I took that as a sign from Allah that our relationship was not tawdry. However, gossipy Khadijah had told our clique about Osman, and, though I wish she hadn't, their excitement at bookish me scoring a boyfriend made me bold.

On Osman's birthday, I surprised him at his house while his parents were at work. After cutting the cake, Omar and Khadijah disappeared and Osman and I were alone in his bedroom. Osman locked the door and whispered that I was driving him crazy: Was it all right if he kissed me? For my parent's sake alone I should have said "no." Instead, basking in my ability to drive a boy crazy, I nodded even as I beseeched Allah to forgive me the sin of kissing. Next thing I knew, we were making out and he was saying "I love you."

I had never felt happier. Or guiltier.

After that, I frequented his house even if Khadijah couldn't go, and justified it because we were in love and would eventually get married.

One day Osman had a condom and we went all the way.

Afterwards I was shocked at what a big thing I'd done, but also at how little time it had taken doing this *sacrosanct* act which should have happened on our wedding night. I wept. I kept saying how I was no longer deserving of respect and Osman kept assuring me that he respected me all the more because we had *made love* and that even Allah recognized the sanctity of love.

The second time we "made love," Osman didn't have a condom. I *truly* believed pregnancy was a matter of consistent timing and effort and that no one got pregnant easily.

But I did.

I had watched too many Bollywood films to be naïve about my nausea or my missed period: Could this be Allah's way of telling me to get married to Osman?

The thought of having to get married because of pregnancy and forfeit my studies in order to look after a child jolted me into realizing that

a) I was in no way equipped to be a mother and b) I wanted a career more than anything else in the world.

Osman was shaken at the news. "Are you sure?" He kept asking. "Are you absolutely sure?"

Osman and I did not know that home pregnancy tests were available over the counter at pharmacies. We believed only clinics with laboratory facilities could conduct pregnancy tests. And that is why I found myself peeing into a glass bottle, skulking to the edge of the garden at midnight, and handing the bottle to Osman.

The lab results were positive.

I was on the phone with Osman when he told me a second test was positive too.

"My parents are going to kill me," he said.

My knees buckled. Osman's tone had hammered in the fact that we were teenagers with uncertain futures and no independent incomes.

"If my father finds out," Osman was saying, "he's going to beat the crap out of me. My parents will never let me get married at this stage of my life."

"My parents," I said, my voice breaking, "aren't exactly going to be thrilled over this situation either."

"What do you want me to do?" Osman said. "Marry you?"

His curt tone injured my pride. I informed him that I didn't want to marry him. We were silent for a moment before I brought up the "A" word. My family cook had terminated an unwanted pregnancy—she already had seven little children—by ramming twigs up herself and drinking herbal concoctions—and I could ask her for help.

Osman said he'd heard there was a nurse in the Old City who performed abortions, charged ten thousand rupees, and was reputed to be safe. I flinched as he uttered the "A" word with such obvious relief. I began to cry. This situation was my fault: I was a wicked person who had deceived her parents, and Allah was punishing me.

I heard my mother hollering for me. I hung up on Osman, dried my eyes as best as I could, and went to my mother's room.

My mother was clutching the second cordless phone. In a deathly still voice, she asked, "Are you pregnant?"

I nodded slowly. I was faint with relief at my mother having found out even if she was looking at me as if a snake had bitten her. I wished she'd hit me or scream at me; anything other than that stricken stare. I wished she'd hug me like always and tell me Allah would solve every problem and that all I had to do was pray.

Finally, she managed to say, "Your father will die if he finds out."

My mother began to cry as she told me I was an impure woman, one that even Allah would forsake given the fact that I'd had relations outside of wedlock.

"You are worse than a prostitute," she said.

A deep disgust for myself took root in me. I had defiled myself with my eyes wide open, and yet, had I not gotten pregnant I would still be with Osman. My mind reeled with contradictory thoughts.

"You were going to tell the cook, a servant, about your situation." My mother cringed. "We would have become the talk of the town. Do your friends know?"

I shook my head. Scared of their reactions, I'd not told them about my situation.

"Is the boy from a good family? How old is he? Is he financially stable enough to marry you?"

When I made it clear that marriage was not an option, fresh tears engulfed my mother. I tried to kiss her, beg her forgiveness, but she pushed me away as if I was impure.

I *was* impure. And dirty. And disgusting.

"You were going to let that *boy* take you to an unhygienic abortionist in the Old City. She could have stuck hangers up you! Given you poisonous herbs! You could have died, do you understand, you could have died and I wouldn't have even known." She began to wring her hands. "Who will marry you now? Who will marry you? And even if someone does, once he discovers you're not a virgin, he will divorce you."

What had I done to myself? How had I allowed myself to ruin my life?

"You have broken my heart," my mother said. "You have broken my heart forever."

That evening, after my father returned from work, my mother said she was ill and took to her bed. Alone with my father, I kept looking at his unsuspecting face as he regaled me with tidbits from his day, and, when he kissed me good night and told me I was a good daughter, my heart broke.

I spent the night on the prayer mat begging Allah to forgive me and to put me back on the *siratul-mustakeem*, the straight and righteous path from which I had obviously allowed the devil to lead me astray. I begged Allah to help my mother overcome this shock and I promised that, in return, I would do everything my parents ever asked of me.

Osman kept calling. I kept hanging up. My mother's stunned face coupled with my father's trusting one broke any spell Osman had over me.

The next day, my mother made discreet inquiries at her workplace on the pretext that a servant needed help. A colleague who'd aborted her pregnancy because of financial struggles informed my mother of a cheap and efficient doctor who lived by a well-known bridge. We were going to check this doctor out, my mother informed me. In order to look married, I was to wear a heavily embroidered outfit, gold earrings and bangles, and my diamond pendant that spelled out *Allah* in Arabic, and to apply kohl, a bright lipstick, and rouge.

We drove to the bridge in silence and found the doctor's house. A girl who looked around my age was squatting in front of the main door and vomiting into a potted plant. For the first time I realized that my mother's presence could not keep me safe from harm. For the first time it struck me that while Osman was probably sitting in his room watching a movie, I was about to undergo something potentially fatal.

My mother told the doctor I was newly married and had recently discovered my husband was a heroin addict, and therefore we wanted to terminate this pregnancy and perhaps even the marriage.

The doctor smiled. "Our menfolk are useless," she said, "but it is the mother's duty to make sure daughters do not get married unless they are able to stand on their own two feet."

At that moment I promised myself that, come what may, I would study and become independent. My mother asked the doctor if the procedure was safe. The doctor replied that while the procedure was safe, death and mishaps were in Allah's hands, but that my mother was to feel free to call her at any time with any questions. My mother handed three thousand rupees to the doctor's helper while I climbed on a gurney underneath a wall with a massive black-and-white clock.

My mother recited Qur'anic verses from across the room and blew them over me to keep me safe. I wanted her to hold my hand, but when the doctor injected a narcotic into my leg, my mother turned away as if she could not bear to see me in this state.

I turned my face toward the wall. It didn't hurt that much physically and by this time I was so exhausted by the past few days that I was numb to the emotional pain; I just closed my eyes and repeated surahs from the Qur'an and prayed to Allah to protect the soul of the unborn child.

When I returned home, I phoned Osman one last time to tell him that my mother had found out and that we'd taken care of it. Before he could respond, I hung up.

I thought life would return to normal after the abortion. But a new nightmare began as my mother constantly feared that, upon marriage, my husband would discover I was not a virgin and divorce me. For the first time in my life my grades dropped over the anxiety of being married and divorced on the same day. I found solace in reading the Qur'an and praying for hours on end—my mother thought I was turning into a religious nut, "going from one extreme to another," she called it—but I was praying to Allah that, were I lucky enough to get married, my husband should not find out that I was not a virgin.

Finally, I told my mother to agree to the very next proposal I received. I wanted to get my wedding night over with. She found someone for me, and I met him once before we married. He was a billion times better looking than Osman and intelligent too.

All my high school friends, including a girl named Sarai, attended my wedding. Sarai had dropped out of school to get married, and though we'd envied her love marriage, I recalled my bewilderment, at the time, over her decision. But now, as I sat on the dais in my wedding finery, I wondered about what might have caused Sarai to leave school for marriage.

On my wedding night, terrified out of my mind, I received proof of Allah. There on the white bridal-suite sheets were spots of blood. I thought all my fears were over, but Khadijah ended up married to Omar, who told her about my abortion. Given Khadijah's propensity for gossip, I became increasingly paranoid my husband would find out and, despite the child we now had, divorce me. In order to avoid this catastrophe, I urged my husband to find a job overseas, far away from Pakistan. And he did.

I still live abroad. A home and a husband and children: many would say these are all the requirements for a happy life. And I am happy. As happy as I deserve to be. In loving my husband, I realized I never loved Osman. He was a crush, one that would have died a natural death had it not been for my pregnancy accelerating events.

I will say that as grateful as I am to my mother for being there for me, I wish she hadn't made me feel that my virginity was everything. I also often wonder if, had we known about hymen reconstruction, how different my life might have turned out. I still harbor hope that, *inshallah*, God willing, one day I will return to studies and have a career. Osman completed his studies in a timely fashion and is an engineer.

Sarai, 1999

I fell in love with L because he was sweet and sexy. But I married him because I wanted to escape the oppressive atmosphere in my home. My father and stepmother fought constantly, and too often my stepmother turned her anger on me. Minor transgressions such as leaving my shoes in the wrong place could ignite massive fights. She would always end by saying she couldn't wait for me to go to my *real house*, for in Pakistan a girl's home is not considered the one into which she is born but the one into which she marries.

After a particularly bad fight, I decided to expedite matters. L was always telling me that we should elope—he thought eloping romantic, a marker of true love—so we did.

"You are so lucky to be getting married," my school friends said, despite the fact that L was finishing up high school and I had dropped out. My stepmother was pleased I'd be gone, but my father and biological mother called us rash. L's parents declared wily me had ensnared their innocent son and ruined his life. L's mother had had grand plans for L, which included his going to college abroad and then getting married to a girl of her choice, a girl who was not, like me, from a "broken home."

I decided to prove to my mother-in-law that I was her dream daughter-in-law. I began to cook, even though I'd never stepped foot inside a kitchen, and help in running the household. But the nicer I was, the worse my mother-in-law treated me. Although L would apologize on his mother's behalf, he never defended me to her.

Because our elopement coincided with L's final high school exams, he underperformed and was unable to gain admission to a good college in Pakistan, let alone one abroad. Instead, he settled for a mediocre job at a bank. L never blamed me for his situation, but his mother constantly found occasion to let me know I was the root of his failure.

My father-in-law was no better. "Yes," he would say, concurring with my mother-in-law, "Sarai oversalts the food. Sarai makes terrible tea. Sarai is arrogant because she speaks English rather than Punjabi. L was the perfect son before Sarai got her claws into him."

I was a prisoner in that house, without dignity, without money, day in and day out losing any sense of self. I complained to my father and biological mother, but because I hadn't bothered asking their advice before eloping, they said I had only myself to blame.

Around this time, a classmate of mine, Hajra, had an arranged marriage. I recall thinking how lucky she was because her in-laws obviously approved of her. I also recalled feeling like a fraud at the wedding, with all my classmates envying my love marriage.

I became pregnant seven months into my marriage. I was overjoyed and believed a baby would mend all relations. But my mother-in-law was livid. After demanding to know why L hadn't used the prophylactics she'd given him, she threatened to poison me. I spent my entire pregnancy too frightened to eat. After nine terrifying months, I had a blessedly easy labor and delivery and gave birth to a beautiful baby.

My in-laws helped with the baby only when L was around, and when the baby became colicky and demanding, even L lost interest. He increasingly envied his college-going friends their ability to do whatever they wanted without the interference of a wailing newborn, a warring mother and wife, and an underpaid bank job. Through exaggerated sighs, L complained that the baby made him feel "stuck and suffocated" and that he hadn't wanted to be a father so soon. The baby made me feel stuck and suffocated too, but I battled these feelings and concentrated on being a good mother.

I still thought L a decent man. When my best friend, Aminah, returned from college needing an abortion, L insisted on driving us to Aminah's appointment. "Shit happens," he said. I really loved him for his nonjudgmental attitude, and I encouraged him to re-sit for his high school exams. This time L received scores high enough to get into a college abroad.

I was ecstatic at the thought of leaving Pakistan and getting far away from my abusive in-laws. When I finally realized that L was going abroad *by himself*, I was heartbroken and angry. L assured me he was doing this for our future, and that it would be much easier for him to navigate studies abroad without a wife and a child tagging along.

After L's departure, my in-laws withheld all affection for their grandchild and begrudged me every bite and every breath. How I survived those two years, God only knows. I spent each day fantasizing about leaving my in-laws behind to join L abroad.

But when L kept stalling about procuring visas for me and our child, I realized that he would never send for us. I reached my breaking point the day my mother-in-law sat my toddler in her lap and told stories of children who fell out of windows, or came under a car, or died in their sleep. That night my child had nightmares.

The following morning, I bundled my child into L's car and, swallowing my pride, drove to my father's house. L telephoned me and, as usual, refused to hear anything negative about his parents. When I hung up, I finally realized, here or abroad, I did not want to be with someone who valued his parents over his wife and child.

After I began divorce proceedings, I heard that my soon-to-be ex-mother-in-law had already lined up girls from unbroken homes willing to marry her foreign-educated son.

At my return, my stepmother became increasingly quarrelsome and I knew that my child and I needed a place of our own. Through my father's connections, I landed a job with enough salary to rent an annex, hire a maid, and put my child in preschool. My child began to thrive, and with my newfound financial independence, I began to regain confidence and security.

A year after my divorce, I met K. Though I was not looking for a relationship, K pursued me until I changed my mind. We'd kept bumping into one another on the party circuit. He was always attentive of my needs—refilling my wine glass, lighting my cigarettes—without my asking. He had a gentle touch and a soothing voice. He was always telling me I was a pure and strong woman and a remarkable mother.

Five months after I began dating K, I ran into J, an ex-classmate of L's. He'd heard about the divorce and he was sorry—he smiled—but not too sorry. I agreed to go for coffee with him and we ended up talking the whole night.

J was working overseas but visited Pakistan every month. Soon, each time he visited we would go out for dinner, which would stretch into breakfast. He made me laugh. He also made me aware that L was poorer for having lost me, and it certainly didn't hurt that J was very cute.

I wanted to tell K and J about each other, but I was scared one or the other would ask that I choose between them. I suppose I was greedy—I had been without affection and intimacy for so long that I wanted them both.

When I became pregnant six months later, I didn't know who the father was. I had to tell them both. J rushed back from abroad and K happened to follow me to the hotel where J was staying. That's how my two-timing got caught. While K and J agreed that I was a horrible woman, they each offered to support me as long as I chose one of them. But I feared that, were I to marry either J or K, sooner or later, he might feel "stuck and suffocated" by the baby and I would be back to square one: financially and physically on my own and responsible for yet another child.

I told J and K that I chose neither one of them and was getting an abortion. J left in a huff. K told me to do what I thought was best for me. I thought it best to abort.

I refused to go to that *butcher* by the well-known bridge. I remember the butcher giving Aminah a paltry aspirin instead of proper anesthetic. Her brusque slaps and Aminah's cries were the stuff of *my* nightmares. Since Aminah's abortion, I'd grown older and wiser. Abortion might be illegal, but in the Islamic Republic of Pakistan everything is available for the right price.

My OB-GYN looked at me for a long second before telling me to come to *** hospital the day after tomorrow during a time slot the operating theatre was idle. I was not to go to the reception. Instead her head nurse would be on the lookout for me. I was to pay the nurse fifteen thousand rupees. She would then guide me from there. And yes, the OB-GYN assured me, there would most definitely be anesthesia.

I wished Aminah was here, but she'd married and chosen to leave Pakistan. K drove me to the hospital. He offered to pay for the abortion. But I could afford to pay myself. Even though we didn't utter a single word on the way, he held my hand the entire time.

I didn't know it then, but in a few years K, like J, would be gone from my life.

At the hospital, the head nurse was waiting for me. I handed her the fifteen thousand rupees thanks to my having a good job, even as I recalled Aminah's struggles to collect two thousand rupees. The nurse led me to an operating theatre where two junior nurses were put on guard outside the door so no one would intrude on this illegal procedure. Soon after the OB-GYN and anesthesiologist arrived, a drip was attached to my toe. Soon I was numb, and even sooner it was over.

K drove me home. He wanted to stay with me but I sent him away. Once he left, I cried—with relief and with regret over depriving my child of a sibling. Finally, I forbade myself from crying. I could not allow myself the luxury of remorse or guilt, the luxury of self-pity, the luxury of falling apart—after all, I had a child to feed and clothe, and I had rent to pay. I promised myself to get on with the future and not dwell on the past, and that is what I did.

Aminah, 2001

In Pakistan, married women routinely have abortions. These abortions are often performed for financial reasons, or to space out children, or as birth control. My married cousin, Hawwa, was admitted into the hospital this morning for an abortion though officially it will be recorded as an appendectomy. She sits propped up against pillows from home on a comfortable hospital bed in her private room. She looks fresh, as if she's just come back from a spa. I think what a difference anesthesia and painkillers can make. My mother and Hawwa's are opening plastic food containers and the room is flooded with the comforting smell of soup.

I thought my mother was against abortion for any reason. Perhaps she has softened her stance; perhaps now I can come clean, tell my mother about my ordeal.

"Ami," I say, "do you know about this doctor by *** Bridge who used to, maybe still does, perform abortions?"

My mother makes an ugly face. "That woman performs illegal abortions. She is a disgrace. She should be put away."

I sputter that Hawwa's abortion should also be a disgrace since her pregnancy did not endanger her life. Hawwa and her mother are used to my harboring *hatke*, or far-from-the-norm opinions, and ignore my statement.

My mother asks how I know about that woman by the bridge. *Because I went there*, I want to scream. *I went there in order to save our family from disgrace.* I want to tell my mother everything. But I don't. I don't want to witness the censure in her eyes for that unwed me even as she spoons love into my married cousin's mouth. Though now that I'm married, my mother, I am sure, will be more than pleased to hold my hand and feed me soup should I too have a pregnancy I want to abort.

Postscript

Aminah cried as she related her abortion. "If I could reverse time, I would go back and have my baby. Not a day goes by when I do not think of that 'choice' with rage and regret."

Hajra told me she lives in daily terror that her husband will yet find out that she wasn't pure and a virgin at marriage and so divorce her. She added that in telling her tale and knowing that it would be written down, she'd found a sense of closure she hadn't even realized she'd been seeking. "I rarely think of my abortion and I have zero regret."

Sarai related her story to me in an even tone. Afterward she said that since she was two-timing guys, she didn't expect sympathy from this society, or anyone. "Past is past. I don't have time to dwell, and, really, what's the use of regret?"

Author's Note: Aminah, Hajra, and Sarai were three who shared their stories in that high school class of twenty-one. Premarital sex in Pakistan remains a crime punishable by a five-year prison term.

SORRY I'M LATE

Kristen R. Ghodsee

She strode into the restaurant about forty minutes late. Bulgarians don't always share the same concept of time with Americans, so I had ordered a Shopska salad and decided to wait. Svetozara worked for a local nongovernmental organization dealing with domestic violence, and I needed to interview her about a piece of legislation working its way through parliament.

"Sorry I'm late," she said to me in the perfect English of a young professional who had earned a master's degree in the UK. "I had an abortion this morning and had to run some errands, and then my tram didn't show up and I had to take a taxi. The traffic was awful."

I looked up, stunned. In America we have this acronym TMI, which means "too much information." But I wasn't so much thinking TMI as I was thinking, "Wow, how can she be so nonchalant about something like that?"

Svetozara studied my half-eaten pile of cucumbers, tomatoes, and onions covered with shredded white sheep's-milk cheese and said, "Have you ordered anything else?"

I shook my head. "No, just some wine."

"Oh great," she said, picking up the menu. "I know you must be busy, so you can go ahead and ask me your questions. I'll try my best to answer you."

I opened up my notebook and glanced down at my queries, but I was still reeling from the abortion comment. In the abstract, I knew that Bulgarian women, and indeed, most women in the former communist countries, relied on abortion as their primary form of birth control. Most of my Bulgarian friends and colleagues had already had at least two, if not three or four, abortions. Like menstruation and menopause, abortion was just part of a woman's life cycle in this part of the world.

Still, it was hard for me to wrap my head around. I'd spent almost all of my adult life on hormonal birth control to avoid getting pregnant because I was terrified of both having an unwanted child and of having an abortion. In my mind abortion meant trauma, regret, and emotional *sturm und drang*. In the US, abortion was a big deal. People killed over it. Could it really be that in Bulgaria it was just something you did on the way to the post office?

"So, I understand that the legislation is being drafted in committee right now," I said. "How much influence do lobbyists have over the proposed text?"

Svetozara leaned back in her chair and began to explain the draft language that her organization had submitted for consideration. If she felt any remorse at all for her lost baby-that-might-have-been, it didn't show. With the exception of Albania and Romania, most Eastern Bloc women not only enjoyed full reproductive rights but lived in societies where abortion carried little stigma. Everyone's mother (and sometimes grandmother) had had at least one.

The waiter came and brought us a carafe of Bulgarian rosé. We each ordered grilled kebabs made of mixed ground pork and beef infused with Balkan spices and roasted spicy peppers. These were called "nervous meatballs."

It was the Russian revolutionary Alexandra Kollontai who had legalized abortion in the Soviet Union back in 1920, making the young workers' state the first country in the world to guarantee women's reproductive rights. Although Stalin reversed the decree from 1936 to 1955, abortion had been accessible to all women in the USSR since 1956. Abortion had been legal in Bulgaria to varying degrees also since 1956, which meant that Svetozara was born into a country where women had enjoyed their reproductive freedoms for more than fifty years.

"If you want to interview one of our allies in parliament," Svetozara said, "I can give you the contact information of Minister Peeva. She could give you the inside perspective."

"That would be wonderful," I said, pouring Svetozara wine. I wanted to ask her how she was feeling and if she might like to go home and rest, because I worried that she was silently suffering and doing her best to carry on with her day after a difficult morning. But I didn't say anything. I poured myself some wine and thought about my own morning: What's the first thing I do every day? Take the pill. I'd been doing that almost every day for over sixteen years. Because I was sensitive to medication, I'd been on various different versions. Some made me gain weight. Some gave me mood swings. Some induced headaches. When I thought about the hassle, and expense, and side effects, I actually hated the pill.

As Svetozara explained that not all of the women in parliament supported the domestic violence legislation because they feared it would make women seem like victims, I wondered what my reproductive life would have been like if I'd been raised in a country where a women's right to control her own body hadn't been seriously challenged in decades. Where going to an abortion clinic didn't mean risking your life to get inside. Maybe having multiple abortions is actually better than pumping yourself full of hormones for decades. I didn't know, but that day I realized that for women born in most Eastern European countries, the medical removal of a fertilized egg was no more traumatic or shameful than the pharmaceutical prevention of the egg's fertilization in the first place.

"*Nazdrave*," Svetozara said, holding up her glass, and smiling. "To women's rights."

I clinked my glass against hers. "Yes, *Nazdrave*. To women's rights."

PELICAN

Mahogany L. Browne

She quit every job she owned on a Friday
Left the shabby chairs and floor to squeal farewell
She's never been the kind to exit in a sentimental way
A poet, an exposed bone, a girl too fragile, a shaken empty well
To be a forgotten song in the throat of a corpse
To be a washed-up basin on the edge of an ocean's mouth
She crawls towards the sea, towards the sun for a morsel
She lives off the sandcastles blown away, a flimsy house
She wants riches of mangoes and dumplings pinched by brown hands
She wants what her hands can't carry, she wants what she should not
know exists
Sweet bread from her mother's kitchen and green crops from good land
The pelican, intersection death, beak w i d e with its flushed pink
stomach persists
Don't ask her what she does not know, don't ask her about marriage or
honor
Ask her of the children buried, after a sweet medicine wrecked her
insides into order

NAMES OF EXOTIC GODS AND CHILDREN

Valley Haggard

In the parking lot, there were protesters everywhere. I hated them. How dare they make something so hard so much harder? I'd never really felt the need to wear armor, but I wanted it then. To be shielded, invisible, invincible. To have the privacy of my own pain. There were a lot of forms to fill out and papers to sign. Big Will and I split the price fifty-fifty from our tips from the ranch, a big chunk of the money we'd planned to travel with when we were free. I scanned a list of horribles as I signed my name: bleeding, cramping, fatigue, and then, the worst of all, continued pregnancy. I thought that possible outcome worse than the possibility beneath: death.

I hyperventilated on the table with the doctor's hands and heavy metal tools crammed into my body. "Keep looking at my beautiful face," the nurse said again and again, squeezing my hand as I tried to breathe, pain and fear and blinding lights tight and clamping down on the black hole between my legs. Finally, it was over, and somehow, they sat me up and put me back together as best they could. When Big Will pulled out of the parking lot, I mouthed "fuck you" to the protesters shouting in our wake, but the truth was, I didn't know who I hated more: me or him or them.

We returned to the ranch up Coffee Pot Road, leaving government land behind, zigzagging up the bumpy, impossibly deep grooves in the earth. I returned to the kitchen and the wringer-washer washing machine and the dishes and laundry as best I could. But I didn't feel like singing along to the country songs on our little FM radio anymore. On my afternoon break, instead of exploring or hiking or writing, I wrapped myself in quilts and curled up like a baby.

It was one week later that I got a call from my mother. The singular phone on the ranch was in a little alcove next to the kitchen and worked rarely. Phone calls were uncommon, though not unheard of. My mother's voice came through the crackling static on the other end of the phone, reached through the line, and homesickness ached through my bones. "Valley!" my mom shouted. "The clinic's been trying to reach you. They couldn't get through." I'd given my mom's number as my emergency contact. I'd gotten into the habit of living places one could not call.

"Oh?" I yelled back. The wranglers were starting to mill about, gathering for dinner. I tried to pretend I was alone in the room. "The procedure didn't work," I heard my mother's voice say. The news bounced off and then thunked into my belly like a heavy stone. There was still a baby alive inside of me. "Mom," I said. "I want to come home."

She sent me a plane ticket and by the next week I had packed up my canvas army-navy bag and was gone. It was too much to say goodbye to those mountains, to that valley, to the cabins and the lodge and Hooker and the horses and the flowers and my fiancé and all of the other wranglers I'd grown not to like but to love. I said this lie, "see you soon," and returned to the clinic before getting on the plane so they could redo the job that had failed before. I cried the whole plane ride home, suspended in the sky above our country, freed from the cluster of molecules, the magical cells, the holy organism in my body that had refused to die.

My mother picked me up from the airport and moved me into her queen-sized bed back home. I was bleeding and cramping and full of rage and sorrow and grief. Pain took hold of my guts and squeezed hard like those cold metal clamps were still there, as if they always would be.

The hydrocodone and valium did not take away the pain but wrapped it in a flimsy layer of gauze. I lay in the fetal position, twisted up in blankets on my mother's bed for a week as she nursed me back to health with broth and tea and love. Sometimes I still turn over names for the child that could have been, but I never come up with one that is good.

DATE OF LAST PERIOD

Amy Alvarez

The first time I had my period, we had burnt
Jamaican beef patties and broccoli for dinner.
Blood came as a surprise—and not. All the other
girls in my grade had already bled. The cheery red
on my white cotton underwear would readmit me
to their ranks.

Over dinner, Mom explained pregnancy: endgame
of this bleeding between my legs. Terrified of tearing
as she'd described, I kept my legs closed for the next
seven years—no glimpses, not a finger. Even tampons
threatened the flower. It took a team of three girls
outside a stall door barking instructions—*tilt back, put
one foot on the edge of the seat*—before anything could enter.

The first night I didn't get my period, I don't remember
what I ate. He and I talked about whether this was what
we wanted under a dim pendant lamp over the kitchen
table. I decided on pills. I remember feeling my body
readjust—like swaying at boat's bottom, that gentle
watery nausea. I remember mucus, and finally, the joy
blood brought: bright red with clots the color of crushed
violets.

REMEMBERING HOW MY NATIVE AMERICAN GRANDFATHER TOLD ME A PREGNANT WOMAN HAD SWALLOWED WATERMELON SEEDS

Jennifer Reeser

> *You might as well cut a five-year-old child's head*
> *off!... A woman will... take the risk of dying with*
> *her baby, rather than to live without a child.*

—Cherokee Shaman Wili-Westi, on learning of the white
man's abortion procedures, in "Cherokee Belief and Practice
with Regard to Childbirth," Olbrechts, *Anthropos*

The shamans can't contain what they don't know.
Showing such astonishment, they curse.
They call it "murder medicine." *Wado.**

They shame, ". . . for Womanhood would rather go
And die than live without a child to nurse."
The shamans can't contain what they don't know.

While she receives a bowl, but he, a bow;
While warriors shake scalps, avowed in verse,
They call it "murder medicine." *Wado.*

Into the osi menses shack, all flow.
The midwives murmur, "Swallow Shepherd's Purse. . ."
The shamans can't contain what they don't know.

---

* "Thank you" in Cherokee

Since Suicide Root* will keep an embryo
From coming—till the purchase of her hearse—
They call it "murder medicine." *Wado.*

The watermelon seeds inside her grow
Till she becomes taboo—and what is worse?
The shamans can't contain what they don't know.
They call it "murder medicine." *Wado.*

---

* Cicuta maculata was reputed among the Cherokee to be an oral contraceptive, though it was discouraged with a social stigma of immorality attached to the woman taking it, and prescribed with a warning that the woman's resulting infertility would be permanent.

FROM "MAKE YOUR OWN WAY HOME"

Leila Aboulela

FRIDAY AFTERNOON

It is strange to visit Tracy in a nursing home. Somehow Nadia associates the words with the old and the infirm, and Tracy has not yet said goodbye to her teens. But that is what the elegant gold letters say, and when Nadia rings the bell she asks herself, *but what else do you expect them to write on the front door?*

Cosy, unobtrusive, the house is like any other in this quiet north London street. A quaint gate, a small front garden, and when she goes inside Nadia can see the back garden with a clothesline, a green lawnmower propped against the wooden fence of next door. There are four women in the room. Tracy, three others, and two empty beds. It's not one of our busy days, the nurse later says. The curtains separating the beds are open and Oprah beams down from the TV, which protrudes from the wall high above.

Bullying is the topic of the show. Childhood victims of bullying are telling their stories to a sympathetic audience.

Tracy in a pink nightgown, lank hair, a little pale. No, it doesn't hurt much now; it did at first. We all had it done, one after the other. I was first, then they brought me back here in a wheelchair. She tells Nadia about the other women in the room. The old-looking woman is Irish, Mandy or Maggie; Tracy isn't sure. Her husband is sitting with her on the bed, they are laughing at the television show. The skinny woman with the permed hair, Kay. And the blonde with the great tan, she's come all the way from South Africa. She was far ahead of us, Tracy whispers; you can still see now how big her stomach is. And believe me, Nadia, she soaked her bed with blood.

The South African girl has a visitor, a similar-looking friend who arrives with flowers. Kay's boyfriend appears shortly after Nadia. Fat and reluctant, he edges his way into the room, empty-handed. I should have brought flowers, thinks Nadia. But then she consoles herself with the thought that if she hadn't come, Tracy would have been the only one without a visitor.

Do you have change for the phone?

Tracy takes twenty pence and gets up slowly from the bed, shuffling her feet around in search of her slippers. When she walks to the door, she holds her lower stomach with one hand and Nadia sees dark stains on her friend's nightgown.

Nadia lied to her parents to be here. Of course. What could she have told them? Long ago Lateefa unwittingly bestowed glamor on Tracy, making her friendship even more desirable. Lateefa said, That girl Tracy is no good. Don't be her friend anymore. Perhaps she saw warning signs in the streak of color on Tracy's lips, the awareness in her eyes. When Tracy wore a short skirt, she no longer crossed her bare legs carelessly like a child but did it deliberately with all the calm knowledge of an adult. She'll have a bad end, Lateefa said, and Nadia knew that her mother's mind held images of the fallen women of the Egyptian cinema screen. The wrathful uncle from the south of Egypt stalking his niece with a loaded gun. Only blood could wash his family's dishonor. And off the screen, in urban Cairo, where there were no guns, there would be shame. Lateefa could imagine the shame. Mothers get divorced for this kind of thing. Sisters remain unwed. Grandmothers go to their graves before their time, crushed by sorrow. A girl's honor is like a matchstick: break it, and it can never be fixed.

Tracy has no gun-wielding uncle from the south. Her father will not divorce her mother because he already did so years ago. He went to Australia, and Tracy's dream is that she will visit him there one day. She watches *Neighbours* with obsessive love, she has three stuffed koala bears in her bedroom.

Tracy threw a tantrum when the perfect blue circle showed up on the stick she dipped in her morning urine. She could not believe it; such a thing could not happen to her. And today is a kind of relief; it is over at last. Time to get back to normal, to start pretending that nothing has happened.

Her mother paid up the two hundred and fifty pounds without a fuss. Then she packed and drove with Tracy's stepfather and the twins to a house-swap holiday with a family in the Black Forest. The travel plans were made ages ago, house-swapping takes a long time to arrange, and there was absolutely *no way* they could cancel. And as Stepdad said, was it fair that the family's holiday be disrupted because of Tracy's carelessness?

So yesterday Tracy was counseled, as the law prescribed, today she is to spend the night at the nursing home, and next day she will go back to her everyday life. End of story.

They called me white trash. Oprah's guest says this and bursts into tears. Compassion gurgles around the studio audience. Only Oprah reigns plump and polished—the softest baby cheeks—coiffured, and coated with a yellow designer suit.

Now the show reaches new heights: former bullies appear to confront those people whose childhood they ruined. Boos and hisses from the audience. Irish laughter from the bed in the corner. Nadia can see that Maggie and her husband are holding hands. I never get to see this show, she is saying to him. It's the time when the children are always watching their programs on the other channel.

But Nadia cannot laugh like them, her own childhood is still too close to her. She is moved by the pain unfolding before her on the screen. Was she bullied? Did she ever bully anyone? Uneasy thoughts. And why is it that, so many years later, it is so easy to distinguish the bullies from their prey? Adult bodies surrounding the children of long ago. The years have changed nothing.

He wasn't there. Tracy gives the coins back to Nadia. Let's go upstairs. We're not allowed to smoke in here.

Upstairs is a bright room overlooking the front of the house. Oriel windows with seats all around, a high ceiling, sandwiches on a tray. Coffee, tea, a kettle. Magazines and pamphlets on the low coffee table, posters on the walls. "Have You Considered Sterilization?" . . . "The Morning-After Pill—Ask your GP about it."

Nadia chews a cheese sandwich, makes tea, leafs through the pamphlets. So what are you going to use now, Tracy, progesterone injections, the low-dose mini-pill, the IUD? She reads them out as if she is choosing lunch from a menu.

Shut up, Nadia.

Tracy lights her second cigarette, and for an instant the flame gives her features a delicate glow as if she is painted, not real. She snaps the match in her hand into two before she throws it in the ashtray.

They sucked it out. The vacuum roared and sucked and gobbled. It's a very loud noise, I told the nurse. Not really, she said, you must be imagining it. All the painkillers that you took. She held my hand and chatted to me to distract me. I lay down and it was like an initiation rite in those weird ceremonies they have in horror films. The contents of your womb, she called it. This is what they call it here. So many words for such a tiny thing.

AN AVOCADO IS GOING TO
HAVE AN ABORTION

Vi Khi Nao

An avocado is going to have an abortion. What is the grapefruit going to do about it? It hasn't gotten it pregnant. Certainly not. It
rolls its thick yellow rind back and forth when it pleases. Being a rocking
chair isn't going to help the helpless, pseudo-alligator pear whose flesh has
turned vegan, whose blood has coagulated green. Six plump equidistant
apples sit on the windowsill watching the landscape become an enclosed
wardrobe. Tomorrow the six queenly apples will rot; today their bruised
flesh will watch the horizon fold its polychromatic shirts into a void. The
cucumber wilted in a clear plastic bin sighs, turning its round shoulders
inward. Tomorrow its insides are going to slowly drip on its own crispy
precipice before desiccating. The avocado can't sympathize, but thinks:
how can I carry a child that is larger than the rest of me, who looks nothing like me, until, of course, I rot? Is it possible that color dictates herit-
age? And nothing more? The avocado arches its back, twisting from side
to side. The avocado won't rotate any more after this. It is not a pervert
in that way. No, no, no. Never that way. The avocado arches its back so
that its round child can slip easily out of its blackish orifice. Having no
hips and no pelvic bones doesn't make it any easier to convert a life into
stillbirth. It lives near indecent neighbors like the carrots. The firm long
orange legs of the carrots have gotten very soft. So soft, like latex. That
kind of tenderness is never good in the kitchen. The knife won't know
how to assert its whetted vocal cord. The pear is willing to compare itself
to the avocado. It tells the soft, non-pearly neighbors: sometimes my flesh
is so crispy that I can't even pee out a seed. However, I am willing to force
myself to pee out an eye or two—so that I can see what I am made of. So
that I can gaze at my own image. Others, having gazed at me, tell me that
I have hips like an avocado. I have enormous potential to birth a child.
But I have a seed like an eye, a crack in the door, that won't and can't gaze

back at me. The avocado replies, I don't feel for you. I am only capable of an abortion. It won't be long before I have to endure this annihilation that has blown into a planet.

yolk (v.)

Emily Carr

he's gonna havta reach inside you.

he's gonna do it. you asked him to. he's gonna tell you how old it is.
he's gonna decide when old is too.

then you're gonna wait.

you're gonna stand against the wall in your paper gown.

you're gonna wait in line. wait for him to vacuum inside you.

you're gonna listen. the other girls, like a sorority, they don't consider
this any more than the Piggly Wiggly line. for all they know, they
could be buying lipstick.

you're thinking this is gonna hurt. he's gonna havta reach inside, again.

what're you gonna do then?

you gonna scream? you gonna clench your teeth?

you gonna say to yourself, you gotta do this?

he's waiting, too. there's a window, a TC, two face-to-face rows of
stained upholstery. by now,

it'd be Regis & Kathy Lee. he wouldn't watch it; he'd be out smoking.
he doesn't smoke inside anymore, not since May.

you're gonna do this, for him, who doesn't smoke inside anymore,
who's out there, wrapping his lips around the filter. his saliva wetting
the paper, his fingers absorbing the sweet raw tobacco smell. he,
who doesn't know anything about this: how it's like an assembly
line, except it's not assembling, it's taking apart, tossing out, special
receptacles.

you're gonna do this, right?

you havta. you are not, you are not gonna chicken out now, not now. the corridor pans out, thins, readjusts.

you are just not gonna do this. the fluorescents fracture into halos. time spools.

you gotta remember what is now, what is here. the light disco-balls, in/out, light/dark. you can't feel your toes, can't feel your fingertips. the line of girls shimmies, sways.

you gotta dance if you're gonna keep perspective.

gotta put one foot in front of the other & dance. you gotta find somebody's hand, you gotta find their hand & hold on.

you gotta find somebody who's gonna help you do this, who isn't chickenshit, whose knees aren't buckling as she kneels, who isn't letting the room go black, who isn't skipping ahead, to a rust-stained recliner, a handful of saltines, sour OJ in a Dixie cup, & a wastepaper basket. you lean over now, if you feel sick, the nurse says. her voice is centuries away, filed away behind a metal desk.

you better come back later, she says, you can't speak because you're leaning over the wastebasket, because the room smells like talcum powder & citrus fruit, because your womb feels like an argument, because you are,

you're chickenshit. you wipe your mouth, exhale.

I gotta do this, you say. we drove three hours for this. I already paid. I gotta do this now. I can't send you in like this.

you gotta pull yourself together. the words are like a steel-trap, snapping. you gotta explicate yourself. the room bulges, contracts. you bowl over, you

hold your stomach & you forget. she's standing over you now. her fingertips cool on your forehead, cheek. this your first time, honey? her words syrup, slush.

you gotta close your eyes to make sense.

you gotta lean over the wastepaper basket, you gotta wipe your mouth, you gotta swallow.

you haven't got to answer. you gotta do it, that's all.

THIS DOCTOR SPEAKS:
ABORTION IS HEALTH CARE

Sylvia Ramos Cruz

Abortion.
Nobody likes the word.
Why not? asks the doctor.
"Abortion is health care," she says, looking down to check the overnight
tweets of trolls who call her killer, promise death.

Later, at the hospital, she navigates the maze of laws conceived by scores
of part-time legislators who know little about the science, ritual, real-life
consequences of practicing medicine—legislators who wage a stealth
campaign against women, waving clubs of medically unsound mandates
for—
    intrusive ultrasounds
    three-day waits
    scripted counseling
    parental consent,
    twelve-week bans
    painkillers for twenty-week-old fetuses
    and more . . .

And when that's done, the doctor turns to what she enjoys—
    talks birth control with teens
    counsels women about mammograms
    examines patients with high-risk pregnancies
    delivers babies
    screens for cancer
    cuts out tumors
    makes treatment plans for patients

who can't afford even basic
generic drugs . . .

And once a month she joins a handful of providers, travels to the only two
clinics left in this vast
wind-sculpted state, brings abortion services to almost a million women
and girls sixteen and over.
She does this because she knows
                        abortion is health care.

IN WHICH I AM A VOLCANO,
FROM *TERMINATIONS: ONE*

Lynne DeSilva-Johnson

In volcanic eruptions, I read, magma rises through cracks or weaknesses in the Earth's crust. When the pressure is released, e.g., as a result of plate movement, magma explodes to the surface, causing a volcanic eruption. The lava from the eruption cools to form new crust. The rock builds up, and a volcano forms.

It's hard to locate the origin of shame in my body. No, that's not exactly true—it's more that it's hard to locate the entry point in the story. I have vague, dreamlike memories of not feeling ashamed, embarrassed, or uncomfortable in my body, but it is so early that I can't identify the precise shift, but I know that by eight years old, it was going strong.

When do we start telling the human children we call "girls" that they can't sit with their legs spread, that their shirts can't hang down below their nipples when they turn upside down on the monkey bars? When do those children learn that their value is inextricably linked to their ability to be attractive to the opposite sex—to their *body's* ability to do so?

For those of us with nothing in our pockets, fighting against abuse, or eking out survival, this lesson has an additional set of teeth—the ability to attract and manipulate sexual attention becomes a capital negotiation, a cost-benefit analysis.

I grew up in a household that looked from the outside like a "liberal" one, but where conservative, sex-negative body-shaming was the norm. As a preteen I was dragged out of sex-ed classes ("human education," they called it) where my school was using *Our Bodies, Ourselves*, and told by my mother that my school was being irresponsible, as she went on a vocal campaign to recommend the adoption of an abstinence-only text, that no other parents (bravo!) went along with. So, only I was removed from these classes.

My friends were jealous, they said it was a drag, and I got to work on homework in a study hall, which was generally considered the better deal. But I was mortified—both because my experience in school was already that of imposter, other, different, and all I wanted was to seamlessly fit into normal experience.

I wanted desperately to be liked and accepted, and from first or second grade, conversations with other little "girls" (I use quotes because there was no option to be other than your cisgendered origin) were already concerned with which boys we liked, and with stories of teenage romance, boyfriends, and the role of the body and clothes in this.

I also wanted to understand and feel legitimized in my instincts that body exploration was not evil and degenerate and that my quickly growing body was not something to hide. In fifth grade, I was the tallest person in my class, and the first bra I ever bought was a C cup. As my breasts grew, my mother shifted all my clothes into tent-like sizes and insisted my bras be matronly, taupe, and white devices with the intent of taming and obscuring my breasts. Any desire for color or pattern or pretty was a place for shame: *Why was I thinking about who was going to see my bra? SLUT!* Touching myself was verboten. Wanting contact or sex was verboten. Early experimentation, written down in a secret diary read without my permission, resulted in repeat visits to a priest for repentance and retraining in classic Catholic shame, fire, and brimstone. Not only was I dirty, low, broken, I was a sinner, and I would be punished not only in this world but beyond.

There is no boundary where shame "about body" or about self ends and shame "about abortion" begins. For me, it is inextricably entwined. Its roots come in a deep-seated fear of my own true self—my desires—being something to be repressed and hidden, and the learned belief, repeated to me so many times by my mother, that left to my own devices, I would be a disaster.

My inescapable abortion, like a toxic waste spill on the timeline of my life, was a beacon of this inner programming for nearly twenty years. *It was true*, the inner voice said. *Left to your own devices, you fuck everything up. You become a statistic.*

The thoughts woven tightly with these aligned with my mother's perspective; the gaslighting that was so constant came to live in my head, a voice I misunderstood as my own inner voice, rather than a programmed recording I hadn't been able to dub over. Any time I couldn't get a job, struggled with a class, was unsure of my next steps, the abortion appeared like a warning flare—reminding me of my weakness, my lack.

For nearly twenty years, the abortion loomed, as illness and broken relationships and labor precarity and a string of traumas each as damaging as the next made childbearing a seem a diminishing possibility. With each misstep, I thought to myself, *you killed the only child you will ever conceive.* When my reproductive system remained riddled with pain and cysts and in need of surgery and then medication, for many years the words in my head weren't *was there a medical problem with the abortion or could there be a metaphysical, psychological root of this illness,* but only, ever, *you fuckup, you ruined your chances at children.* My shame remained rooted in my feelings of weakness and inadequacy, and of self-blame. I was told again and again, in doctor's offices where the "termination" was discussed, that I was a ticking clock. My womb was broken, and my promiscuity was often inferred as the probable cause. Endometriosis being rarely identified, the going theory was, usually, unchecked STIs. *Judging your-fault faces, judging your-fault official diagnosis.*

And: no one talked about it. I didn't know a single woman who'd come forward about an abortion until I was much older. No doctors understood—few doctors do—the manifestation of trauma in the body as chronic illness. It took until the magma collecting under my surface erupted and I ended up in countless hospitals and emergency rooms, nearly twenty years later, for me to understand.

It was only as I worked my way out of trauma that I realized the source of my programming and started to reclaim my story, and to see that my shame was learned—it was not mine. There is no shame in these stories. If we can find a safe, supportive container for their release (and if we create these soft landings for each other) we can begin to truly heal. And when we begin to release the chokehold of other people's shame, the shift begins. I barely recognize myself stripped of this burden I too long called by my name.

I am building my body anew, and these stories are the foundation. The lava hardens, and becomes the landscape. Even on that burnt landscape, new growth appears.

COLD CUTS AND CONCEPTIONS

Julia Conrad

Few daughters know how many abortions their mothers have had. Few daughters even know their mothers have had an abortion. When my friend Ella found out, at sixteen, about her mother's, she was so shocked she didn't speak to her for a week—and her mother had only had one.

"You're the sole survivor!" my mom said jokingly after she told me she had had five. "It's because I'm hyper-fertile," she added. "You might be, too. When I was getting my fifth, the doctor said he was really impressed by how fertile I am."

She told me that after the first abortion, my grandparents took her out for lunch at the Carnegie Deli in New York. She got a corned beef sandwich. My grandfather got two hot dogs. After all, it was the seventies, a time when, if you lived in Greenwich Village, as my mother and her family did, such events were framed by more urgent concerns: The Weathermen detonating their townhouse headquarters by accident, Diane Arbus committing suicide upstairs, the Stonewall riots three blocks away.

Her first one was by far the worst—only a year after Roe v. Wade legalized abortion. The whole process was nothing like it is today. She waited for hours in her Wrangler jeans at that first clinic in Greenwich Village, listening to women scream from inside the operation rooms. The procedure was less refined, and the doctors seemed to be trying to teach a moral lesson with their curettes. None of the others hurt, she said. She never heard cries again like that, and her last one was as painless as a pelvic exam. She jokes about how she owes the world a seminal memoir (pun intended) entitled *Abortion Throughout the Ages*, showing how as politics changed, technology improved, and ubiquity increased, an abortion became less of an ordeal.

Certainly, an abortion can be an emotionally or morally difficult procedure. But it's strangely rare to hear about the instances when it isn't. Even though almost everyone I know is staunchly pro-choice, people look at me with horror for divulging the great secret of my mother's five abortions. They do not understand that, although she's definitely not proud of the number, she talks about it openly, whether at a party, in a crowded subway car, or to me for many years.

"I'm the only one who didn't get one!" cried my mom's childhood friend Emily at a gathering at our home one afternoon. "But that was because I wasn't getting laid." Everyone in the room laughed.

"I had three," her friend Sheila added. "Two with pennyroyal. It was too expensive otherwise. That was horrible though. I wouldn't do it on my own again, but the clinic one was fine."

"If there's one thing that never changes," they all told me sagely the week before I got my IUD, "it's that you can't always trust men to use condoms."

My IUD insertion appointment was at 9 a.m. later that week. I tried to convince my mom that she didn't need to come, but she didn't listen. She said she needed to bring the insurance card. She sat in the waiting room for the fifteen minutes it took, and when I emerged, upon seeing that I wasn't keeled over in abject pain, she asked me if I was hungry. It was barely 10:30 a.m., but we went to Katz's Deli, and both got pastrami sandwiches.

MY EXCUSE: I HAD AN ABORTION. WHAT'S YOURS?

Laura Wetherington

after Paul Verlaine

One can't begin to assume how much room there is in a room.
The joy which overtook you,
my friend, had roots in my abdomen.
The desire, I thought,

the desire-brimming dream broke down
when I tried to draw it out.
None of my best enemies
had even the appetite
for vocal violence—their horror
at the living lacerations
and the local nightmare!
Little limbs overrode the afterbath.
My robes felt able-bodied.
I matured.

I could grow back the legs I never knew I'd lost.
My palms felt softer and the training
overcame all ways to water.
But disquiet is a problem of dialect,
and sex is an unusual number.
In my torso: the open mouths of all kinds of
dead informants. I'll pardon your
please, roll back your torment, torch
all the long confessional letters, only,
stop leaving me messages.

THE JEWEL OF TEHRAN

Sholeh Wolpé

She was still bleeding, three days later, still in pain. We returned to the clinic on the other side of town. Her feet were put back into the stirrups, her legs pulled apart. There were pieces still clinging to her womb like strands of red algae. The procedure had to be repeated.

No, no, she sobbed. *I can't do it again.*

* * *

He sits in the clinic's spotless waiting room. She lies on a cold, hard bed, legs sprawled. She scrunches her face, bites her lower lip, lifts her shoulders and neck, arms tensing with pain, and squeezes my hand so hard I want to scream. I reach over with my other hand and brush away strands of brown hair from her eyes, this girl who was once the jewel of Tehran.

Between her thighs, the doctor is playing a war game with her body's desire to hold on to what has been imposed . . . by nature, God, angels, chance. Does it matter now?

They were once in love. Or lust. He has two kids and a conservative wife. She is divorced and has a child. He is ambitious. She is from a religious family. Perspectives make any story into play dough. You can shape and tell it a hundred ways.

Silence. Then a plop followed by a clink of metal against metal. The doctor walks over to the counter, puts the bowl in the sink, then leaves; his leather shoes suction the linoleum floor. I get up (shouldn't have) and casually wander towards the sink. What's inside that metal bowl melts my marrow—not because it's gruesome, violent, or vile, but because it's nothing but slimy pink spit; because this is how we all begin and live lives of various lengths, between happiness and misery, love and lust, belief and unbelief; between many, few, or no sunrises and sunsets. In the end, bones are buried, burned or crushed, and time bends and bounces, always true to its own form and direction.

She moans, *it hurts,* and I don't know if she means her heart or her womb. I look away from the sink, and something catches fire between my eyebrows, a scalding ache like the sting of a scorpion. I pull a blanket over my friend. She closes her eyes. Her face is swollen. Lines around her eyes and mouth spread like runaway roads to nowhere.

Making true love must be skin to skin, he had insisted, refusing to wear a condom. Pills nauseated her. She imagined she was too old to sprout his seed. He bought her dresses, a diamond necklace; delivered promises fragrant as tuberoses he brought her every week wrapped in golden cellophane.

In the bathroom, I throw up my breakfast. Yogurt and peaches that look like a whirling universe of pink starfish. The doctor comes back, asks my friend how she is feeling. She cries. I go to the waiting room, watch her Persian lover, doused with Paco Rabanne aftershave, pay the bill in cash. The nurse says I look pale and offers me a glass of water. His wallet is black. He counts the bills one by one.

How is she? he asks. I shrug. He drops his head, shakes it east to west, west to east. *I do love her,* he says. I rub the pain between my eyebrows. He looks at me. His eyes are the color of burnt toast. I tell him he should go home. *She doesn't want to see you,* I say. He nods, turns to leave but then stops, says, *Please, tell her I'm sorry. For this. For everything.*

I want to say, tell her yourself, jellyfish. But my tongue is suddenly stone. I go back to the room. My friend has dressed and is ready to go. Walking is difficult. Living is difficult. Especially today. Shame is indelible. If you let it, it will stain your forehead like a tattoo.

The doctor puts his hand on her shoulder, pats it gently. I think to myself, he is like that steel bowl; he holds within himself what he yanks out. This is his sacrifice.

He looks at me, straight at me, and I know he's read my thoughts, or maybe every friend who comes to hold hands has the same thought, this same grateful look; maybe he registers us all in his eyes and stows us away in the vaults of his consciousness for the days that he battles fear, doubt, or fatigue. *Come see me again in two weeks*, he says, jotting down notes. *The nurse will give you instructions.*

At my friend's apartment, I tuck her in, make her chicken soup. She wants a cigarette. I give her two. She smokes five. Drinks tea. Refuses soup. I pick up her daughter from school, buy her glitter lip gloss. The girl is happy. Life is that simple when you are nine. At Johnny Rockets, she mixes ketchup and mayonnaise, spreads it on her burger. Pink, I think. Pink.

HEART

THE MOTHER

Gwendolyn Brooks

Abortions will not let you forget.
You remember the children you got that you did not get,
The damp small pulps with a little or with no hair,
The singers and workers that never handled the air.
You will never neglect or beat
Them, or silence or buy with a sweet.
You will never wind up the sucking-thumb
Or scuttle off ghosts that come.
You will never leave them, controlling your luscious sigh,
Return for a snack of them, with gobbling mother-eye.

I have heard in the voices of the wind the voices of my dim killed
    children.
I have contracted. I have eased
My dim dears at the breasts they could never suck.
I have said, Sweets, if I sinned, if I seized
Your luck
And your lives from your unfinished reach,
If I stole your births and your names,
Your straight baby tears and your games,
Your stilted or lovely loves, your tumults, your marriages, aches, and
your deaths,
If I poisoned the beginnings of your breaths,
Believe that even in my deliberateness I was not deliberate.
Though why should I whine,
Whine that the crime was other than mine?—
Since anyhow you are dead.
Or rather, or instead,
You were never made.

But that too, I am afraid,
Is faulty: oh, what shall I say, how is the truth to be said?
You were born, you had body, you died.
It is just that you never giggled or planned or cried.

Believe me, I loved you all.
Believe me, I knew you, though faintly, and I loved, I loved you
All.

PLACES

Mariana Enriquez

This is what it's like to grow up in a country where abortion is illegal. Teenage girls in a provincial town, scared because the pill is expensive and they can't pay, because they don't know how to use a condom—this isn't taught in schools and their parents don't know they're already having sex—and pregnancy tests are bought, together with antacids and aspirin in the drugstore. Silent crying in the bathroom when the test shows positive and then trying to find help. Drink rue tea. Throw yourself downstairs. Put some parsley in your vagina. Nothing works, the blood doesn't appear, and it's time to visit the "places," because that's what we call them. "A place" where a "señora" sees to you.

Places don't have names or, rather, they can't be named. They are ghost houses, anonymous houses, with facades that are so inoffensive they look suspicious. One of the "places" is an apartment. The stairs are very steep, narrow, and in almost total darkness. The door of the apartment is white. The woman who answers the doorbell keeps her face in the shadows, wants to know who told you about the "place," and asks "how far gone" (referring to months of pregnancy). "Tell the truth because after three I don't do it." She then says the price and gives a date for the procedure.

That's it. No advice, no medical history, no preparation, no who will do it, no what to do afterwards. The amount is high. Then the money's stolen, usually from parents. Or the computer is sold. Or marijuana is sold. If your boyfriend agrees about the abortion, he might contribute. But usually boyfriends don't know what's happening because boys tend to like the idea of being fathers and then they become one more obstacle.

In one of the "places" on the outskirts of town, the clinic where the abortions were done coexisted with a small puppy mill. Rumor had it that the doctor was no such thing, but a vet who knew how to deal with human patients.

A girl from my school, Bernie, had her first abortion there. She told us about it as she smoked a cigarette in the schoolyard. She said it wasn't a dirty place, despite the animals. And if she got pregnant again, she'd go back to see them because they were cheap.

Bernie was strangely pretty: she had a squinty eye and she had attitude. I was fascinated by it. At school, they said she was a tart, but insult tends to come with admiration and, with Bernie, the admiration was evident. The gray skirt of her uniform, which she wore very short, pulled up and folded over her belt, was the envy of everyone. Her long legs and laddered tights. The multicolored barrettes she wore in her hair and the adolescent rage in her blue eyes. The way she leaned against the wall, her white shirt, the cutest boy in the school kissing her in front of a female guard.

They expelled her. I don't know why, maybe for smoking or for all sorts of misbehavior or some stupid thing. After she stopped coming to school, we still saw her in the street, in bars, at concerts. She was a famous girl, which is what bold, pretty girls tend to be.

We didn't see her for some weeks and soon the word got around. Bernie had died in the street. She'd bled to death. Well, not exactly. She died in hospital, but she was close to death when she was found on the sidewalk. Someone who lived nearby called an ambulance when he saw her lying on the curb in a pool of blood, with a perforated uterus. I imagine her long white legs, covered in blood. Her hands full of blood as she tried to staunch the hemorrhage.

She was near the famous clinic with the dogs but not too near. About five hundred meters away. Did she walk there alone, mad with pain? Did the people who did the abortion dump her in this place? After how long? Had they put her in a car so they could leave her far away? Had someone been capable of holding her hand, lying to her, telling her not to be afraid, that she was going to be fine? I can't stop wondering why they didn't take her to a hospital. Why they punished her like that.

WOMEN'S LIBERATION

Judith Arcana

Every week we went to a meeting,
but not like now. No one stood up
and said, My name is Jane and I'm
an abortionist. No. Because we didn't
want to stop, we weren't trying not to do it.
We sat in apartments, passing the cards.
One card is Sandy from West Lafayette,
eighteen years old, coming in on the bus.
She's got about sixty-three dollars, she thinks
she's nine weeks pregnant. The next card is
Terrelle, who's thirty-two and angry. Her
doctor gave her an IUD that didn't work;
he says there's nothing he can do.
Here's Mona, fifty-four years old, has one
hundred dollars, wants to keep this secret
from her family. And Carlie, a long term—
twenty weeks pregnant, may have ten dollars,
twelve years old like Mona's youngest—she
got herpes from her brother when he did it.
Every week some of the cards were passed
around for hours; none of us wanted
to counsel those women, take one
into her life. The longest of long terms,
they lived far away, had no one but us,
no one to tell, no one to help, no money.
They needed everything. Cards went around
the room while we talked: dilation, syringes,
xylocaine, the Saturday list. At the end
of the meeting, all the cards were taken.

CARDBOARD POPE

Galina Yudovich

Stranger on the sidewalk says,
don't kill your baby. he's holding a sign and running after women
and careful not to step in the parking lot where
guardians in orange watch for violations.
Across the street is a shop selling
PARROTS PARROTS PARROTS
of glorious yellows and greens and blues unbothered by abortions.
Nun on the sidewalk says,
they kill babies in there. she stands with a line of
churchgoers, church pray-ers, hallowed be thy name,
and all the rest of it, again and again, but more
around Easter, when the sin is worse.
Angry Old White Man on the sidewalk says,
you're no better than Muslims
who go around killing people. he spends his days
with his sidewalk family. Sanctimony is thicker than blood.
Cardboard Pope on the sidewalk says,
give me your baby. there's a man named Frank who
tells brown people in Spanish that his name is Francis, like the Papa.
he wants your baby too. i want to ask who does he offer his prayers to.
are his vigils for dead women—
dead from bleach, dead from poison, dead from knitting needles in
their vaginas?
where is his burning candle for sepsis, for bleeding tissue, for suicide?
But i have signed a pledge of non-engagement.

silence is political.
inside, the women reach home base, safe, Ollie ollie oxen free.
they battle cardboard popes to be here. They want to explain to me

why not now:
money, school, work, no man, bad man, too many kids to love.
they cry or they don't. they say *sorrysorrysorry* for:
crying, not crying, asking questions, needing to check when someone
can drive them.
they say *sorrysorrysorry* for using my tissues, for
being pregnant, for not understanding why before, for needing
another one, for their kids running around the office.
i think, do they apologize to the Cardboard Pope, ask for:
absolution, forgiveness, mercy, understanding, unconditional godly love.
inside there is propofol and cookies for when you wake up and
doulas to hold your hand or ignore. Inside there is sisterhood telling you:
don't cry, oh my kids are teenagers too, i can give you a ride.
outside there is Papa Frank, and there is no baby to give him.
he wants nothing from you now.

FROM *GRANICA (BOUNDARY)*

Zofia Nałkowska

That night had been a bad one for Justyna, full of dreams and sudden awakenings, damp and sticky from sweat. "What's the matter with me?" she thought and sank back into sleep. She had to get inside somewhere, reach some sort of people, some kind of dwelling place. She was walking down an unpleasant black corridor, with her head bowed, and a feeling of suffocation in her throat. It was a passageway leading to Jasia's basement, the very same yet worse and more terrifying than it actually was. She was walking along this corridor, on and on, until she stumbled upon a wooden door made only of bare planks. She groped with her fingers over the surface for a lock with an iron latch, and a key jutting out of a lock. She turned the key, because it had been locked from the outside, and opened the door. No one was inside, no one responded. She entered the dark interior and felt with her hand for the bed. There were no covers, only boards. On the bare boards, directly on the wood itself, lay Karolina Bogutowa just as she had after she had died, fully clothed in her black dress, swollen, holding a little crucifix in her hands. It was as if she had been lying there for a long time, as if they had forgotten to bury her. And that, too, was worse than the truth that her mother had died.

She woke up and again imagined something was the matter with her. The next dream was beautiful. She was sailing across the sea. But what a strange craft it was—no people, no deck or chimney. There was no sky above it. Only through what seemed like huge gates was the sea visible and its boom and swell tangible. But the gates were made entirely of rock and the whole ship was of stone. And thus, it rumbled over the sea without a single human on board, only her.

Only at daybreak did she dream about the child. Tiny, completely naked, healthy, and robust. It was alive, but as though hewn out of white stone, not flesh. Pretty and sunny. Then it became soft, flopped in her arms. Its little head hung on its neck and rolled onto her shoulder. It grew sad like little Jadwisia. And then, when it died, it actually was Jadwisia.

She awoke from her dream weeping. In the room it was still dark and cold. She remained in bed and, as she lay there, continued to weep silently, for a long time. It may have seemed that she dreamed of Jadwisia, but it was not for her that she wept. Jadwisia had lived in the world and seen the sky and earth before she went blind, played with the cat, exchanged hugs with her mother. But that child of hers, which was to be and was no more, was poorer by far. She had gone to the midwife of her own accord, allowed the thing to be done to her that women do, and so she was the one who had squandered its life. Most of all she remembered—and it kept coming back to her—how when she was lying on the bed at night after those pains, keeping quiet so as not to wake anyone, she was suddenly in motion. And then it had slipped out of her, like a little mouse. The whole world hadn't wanted it, its own natural father hadn't wanted it—only inside her had it had a safe hiding place. She alone in the whole wide world could have helped it wrest itself into life. Only in her did it have refuge and shelter. And she too, its own mother, had risen against it. So where was that tiny infant to turn for rescue when she herself, she too, had done this to it?

She lay in bed until midday and thought round and round in circles about the same thing. On the far side of the yard, the sun was shining on the pales of the fence. Outside the window a single small tree was writhing in the wind and scraping its branches against the pales. The snow was melting. The March sky was a clear blue from the wind, and dotted with dark azure cloudlets. Yet Justyna had no desire to get up, or eat, or go out. She felt happy only when lying down like that, weeping and thinking of the one thing. She had no idea whether it would have been a boy or a girl, could not imagine how it might have grown up. She thought only of the small, blind, almost nonexistent little nobody, still ignorant of the created world around it, which had hidden inside her and only inside her found protection.

In the afternoon someone knocked at the door. She rose from her bed, wrapped herself in a shawl, and turned the key in the protruding iron lock, just like the one she had dreamed about.

"Again, you're lying in bed all day," said Niestrzepowa as she entered. "Aren't you ashamed of yourself? Who's going to light the stove for you? Who are you waiting for? You want to cook something? Tidy up."

Justyna got up in silence, washed in the water in the wash basin, rummaged around with a piece of wood in the ashes in the grate. While Niestrzepowa stood over her, she lit a fire in the stove, picked up first one and then another object in her hand, poured water from a bottle into a pan, looked into a drawer and then into various bags to see if she still had some kasha.

"You can't go on like this. You'll die of starvation!"

Niestrzepowa went out, brought Justyna a little of her homemade soup, and urged her to take her coat, go to the shops, and buy at least a piece of sausage from the butcher.

Justyna made her bed and swept the floor, then she sat and watched the flames as they burned and flickered, running along each log until it eventually caught fire. She would get up, add fresh logs, close the stove door, and then sit down on the edge of the bed.

Again, she recalled how she went to that midwife on Mostowa Street, a few doors from the end of Swietojanska Street, near the train station. She lived in a red brick house. There was a kitchenette and one reception room. First was the kitchen, where the woman slept with her husband and three boys, while the main room was for patients. But when Justyna was lying there, there were no other patients. The woman's mother cooked for them and swept the room. She told Justyna that the last patient before her had been a wealthy young lady, unmarried, not even sixteen years old. In the greatest of secrecy her uncle, who had a wife and children, had driven her there from the country, where she had been living with them.

As soon as Justyna arrived, the midwife ordered her to get onto the large table and lie down at the very edge while she brought in from the kitchen some sort of wires and tongs on a shallow dish and waited a moment for them to cool down. They were very poor people but took great care that everything was clean. In the evening the woman's husband came home, a railwayman who drank heavily, and then there was a row in the kitchen. The kitchen door opened in the dark, and the old woman crept in silently on tiptoe. Evidently, she was hiding from her son-in-law;

perhaps she stood in his way and it was on her account that he bullied his wife. These were the worst days of Justyna's life since her mother's death.

After what the woman had done to her on the table, Justyna lay during the night unaware of what was happening to her, until she was seized by sharp pains. She screamed, but the woman immediately came in and told her to stop or she would be the ruin of them both. She stopped screaming and lay quietly for a few hours until everything ceased. And then, toward dawn, when she was all in motion, she felt—without any pain, without anything like that—the tiny thing come out of her. She lay there for another two weeks but what was wrong with her, she could scarcely remember. A doctor came. She had a high fever. They did various things to her. When she left there, she was still not entirely cured, but she gradually recovered and by the autumn was able to work at Torucinski's. But the thought of that child was to remain with her forever.

Translated from the Polish by Ursula Phillips

INTERRED

Pratibha Kelapure

*For Purvi Patel and countless other women in India and anywhere else in
the world*

How do you speak of an event that didn't happen?
Time goes by and you don't trust your memory,
Veiled for so long it is impossible to bare the truth.
You remember it well, but no one else does,
Because no one else knew about the weekend
You spent holed up in an old hovel of a clinic
While blood, hope, and the whisper of a life flowed away.
Now no one would believe it. It doesn't fit
The frame of the flawless family picture. It's easier
To forget, pretend, and propagate the family lore.
You hate to disturb other people's dreams, always
Altering your own narrative to fit theirs, to bury
Your hurts and deny your suffering, and simply
Carry the elephant of guilt on your shoulder until
Your heart is buried too deep to pulse with life.

SHE DID NOT TELL HER MOTHER
(A FOUND POEM)*

Kenyan Teenagers and Annie Finch

"Are there young girls who have died during abortion?"

"Yes."

"What happened?"

"She took the medicine, but she did not tell her mother. She started crying at night. Her mother gave her painkillers, and she died."

"A woman used a stick to perforate the amniotic fluid. . . . She inserted the stick and rotated it like this . . . the placenta came [out], but the girl died."

"She did not tell her mother. She started crying at night. Her mother gave her painkillers."

"There is a lady who was trying to help her daughter abort, so she took three different types of trees, mixed them and mashed them, and then mixed [it] with water, and gave it to her daughter . . . and the girl died."

"She started crying at night. Her mother gave her painkillers."

"My roommate, last year in January, left school. It was an old woman in the village who advised her on the method she used. After she used it, she bled and bled until she died."

"We don't have anywhere to go for help."

"She did not tell her mother. She started crying at night."

---

* "She Did Not Tell Her Mother (A Found Poem)" is based on quotes gathered from Mitchell, Ellen H.H. et al., "Social Scripts and Stark Realities: Kenyan Adolescents' Abortion Discourse," *Culture, Health, and Sexuality*, Volume 8, 2006, pp. 518–528.

THE LADY WITH THE LAMP

Dorothy Parker

Well, Mona! Well, you poor sick thing, you! Ah, you look so little and white and *little*, you do, lying there in that great big bed. That's what you do—go and look so childlike and pitiful nobody'd have the heart to scold you. And I ought to scold you, Mona. Oh, yes, I should so, too. Never letting me know you were ill. Never a word to your oldest friend. Darling, you might have known I'd understand, no matter what you did. What do I mean? Well, what do you *mean* what do I mean, Mona? Of course, if you'd rather not talk about—Not even to your oldest friend. All I wanted to say was you might have known that I'm always for you, no matter what happens. I do admit, sometimes it's a little hard for me to understand how on earth you ever got into such—well. Goodness knows I don't want to nag you now, when you're so sick.

All right, Mona, then you're *not* sick. If that's what you want to say, even to me, why, all right, my dear. People who aren't sick have to stay in bed for nearly two weeks, I suppose; I suppose people who aren't sick look the way you do. Just your nerves? You were simply all tired out? I see. It's just your nerves. You were simply tired. Yes. Oh, Mona, Mona, why don't you feel you can trust me?

Well—if that's the way you want to be to me, that's the way you want to be. I won't say anything more about it. Only I do think you might have let me know that you had—well, that you were so *tired*, if that's what you want me to say. Why, I'd never have known a word about it if I hadn't run bang into Alice Patterson and she told me she'd called you up and that maid of yours said you had been sick in bed for ten days. Of course, I'd thought it rather funny I hadn't heard from you, but you know how you are—you simply let people go, and weeks can go by like, well, like *weeks*, and never a sign from you. Why, I could have been dead over and over again, for all you'd know. Twenty times over. Now, I'm not going to scold you when you're sick, but frankly and honestly, Mona, I said to myself this time, "Well, she'll have a good wait before I call her up. I've given in often enough, goodness knows. Now she can just call me first." Frankly and honestly, that's what I said!

And then I saw Alice, and I did feel mean, I really did. And now to see you lying there—well, I feel like a complete *dog*. That's what you do to people even when you're in the wrong the way you always are, you wicked little thing, you! Ah, the poor dear! Feels just so awful, doesn't it?

Oh, don't keep trying to be brave, child. Not with me. Just give in—it helps so much. Just tell me all about it. You know I'll never say a word. Or at least you ought to know. When Alice told me that maid of yours said you were all tired out and your nerves had gone bad, I naturally never said anything, but I thought to myself, "Well, maybe that's the only thing Mona could say was the matter. That's probably about the best excuse she could think of." And, of course, *I'll* never deny it—but perhaps it might have been better to have said you had influenza or ptomaine poisoning. After all, people don't stay in bed for ten whole days just because they're nervous. All right, Mona, then they *do*. Then they do. Yes, dear.

Ah, to think of you going through all this and crawling off here all alone like a little wounded animal or something. And with only that colored Edie to take care of you. Darling, oughtn't you have a trained nurse, I mean really oughtn't you? There must be so many things that have to be done for you. Why, Mona! Mona, please! Dear, you don't have to get so excited. Very well, my dear, it's just as you say—there isn't a single thing to be done. I was mistaken, that's all. I simply thought that after—Oh, now, you don't have to do that. You never have to say you're sorry, to *me*. I understand. As a matter of fact, I was glad to hear you lose your temper. It's a good sign when sick people are cross. It means they're on the way to getting better. Oh, I know! You go right ahead and be cross all you want to.

Look, where shall I sit? I want to sit some place where you won't have to turn around, so you can talk to me. You stay right the way you're lying, and I'll—Because you shouldn't move around, I'm sure. It must be terribly bad for you. All right, dear, you can move around all you want to. All right, I must be crazy. I'm crazy, then. We'll leave it like that. Only please, please don't excite yourself that way.

I'll just get this chair and put it over—oops, I'm sorry I joggled the bed—put it over here, where you can see me. There. But first I want to fix your pillows before I get settled. Well, they certainly are *not* all right, Mona. After the way you've been twisting them and pulling them, these last few minutes. Now look, honey, I'll help you raise yourself ve-ry, ve-ry slo-o-ow-ly. Oh. Of course, you can sit up by yourself, dear. Of course, you can. Nobody ever said you couldn't. Nobody ever thought of such a thing. There now, your pillows are all smooth and lovely, and you lie right down again, before you hurt yourself. Now, isn't that better? Well, I should think it was!

Just a minute, till I get my sewing. Oh, yes, I brought it along, so we'd be all cozy. Do you honestly, frankly and honestly, think it's pretty? I'm so glad. It's nothing but a tray-cloth, you know. But you simply can't have too many. They're a lot of fun to make, too, doing this edge—it goes so quickly. Oh, Mona dear, so often I think if you just had a home of your own, and could be all busy, making pretty little things like this for it, it would do so *much* for you. I worry so about you, living in a little furnished apartment, with nothing that belongs to you, no roots, no nothing. It's not right for a woman. It's all wrong for a woman like you. Oh, I wish you'd get over that Garry McVicker! If you could just meet some nice, sweet, considerate man, and get married to him, and have your own lovely place—and with your *taste*, Mona!—and maybe have a couple of children. You're so simply adorable with children. Why, Mona Morrison, are you crying? Oh, you've got a cold? You've got a cold, *too*? I thought you were crying, there for a second. Don't you want my handkerchief, lamb? Oh, you have yours. Wouldn't you have a pink chiffon handkerchief, you nut! Why on earth don't you use cleansing tissues, just lying there in bed with no one to see you? You little idiot, you! Extravagant little fool!

No, but really, I'm serious. I've said to Fred so often, "Oh, if we could just get Mona married!" Honestly, you don't know the feeling it gives you, just to be all secure and safe with your own sweet home and your own blessed children, and your own nice husband coming back to you every night. That's a woman's *life*, Mona. What you've been doing is really horrible. Just drifting along, that's all. What's going to happen to you, dear, whatever is going to become of you? But no—you don't even think of it. You go, and go falling in love with that Garry. Well, my dear, you've got to give me credit—I said from the very first, "He'll never marry her." You know that. What? There was never any thought of marriage, with you and Garry? Oh, Mona, now listen! Every woman on earth thinks of marriage as soon as she's in love with a man. Every woman, I don't care who she is.

Oh, if you were only married! It would be all the difference in the world. I think a child would do everything for you, Mona. Goodness knows, I just can't speak *decently* to that Garry, after the way he's treated you—well, you know perfectly well, *none* of your friends can—but I can frankly and honestly say, if he married you, I'd absolutely let bygones be bygones, and I'd be just as happy as happy, for you. If he's what you want. And I will say, what with your lovely looks and what with good-looking as he is, you ought to have simply *gorgeous* children. Mona, baby, you really have got a rotten cold, haven't you? Don't you want me to get you another handkerchief? Really?

I'm simply sick that I didn't bring you any flowers. But I thought the place would be full of them. Well, I'll stop on the way home and send you some. It looks too dreary here, without a flower in the room. Didn't Garry send you any? Oh, he didn't know you were sick. Well, doesn't he send you flowers anyway? Listen, hasn't he called up, all this time, and found out whether you were sick or not? Not in ten days? Well, then haven't you called him and told him? Ah, now, Mona, there is this thing as being too much of a heroine. Let him worry a little, dear. It would be a very good thing for him. Maybe that's the trouble—you've always taken all the worry for both of you. Hasn't sent any flowers! Hasn't even telephoned! Well, I'd just like to talk to that young man for a few minutes. After all, this is all *his* responsibility.

He's away? He's *what*? Oh, he went to Chicago two weeks ago. Well, seems to me I'd always heard that there were telephone wires running between here and Chicago, but of course—And you'd think since he's been back, the least he could do would be to do something. He's not back yet? He's not *back* yet? Mona, what are you trying to tell me? Why, just night before last—Said he'd let you know the minute he got home? Of all the rotten, low things I ever heard in my life, this is really the—Mona, dear, please lie down. Please. Why, I didn't mean anything. I don't know what I was going to say, honestly I don't, it couldn't have been anything. For goodness' sake, let's talk about something else.

Let's see. Oh, you really ought to see Julia Post's living room, the way she's done it now. She has brown walls—not beige, you know, or tan or anything, but brown—and these cream-colored taffeta curtains and—Mona, I tell you I absolutely don't know what I was going to say before. It's gone completely out of my head. So you see how unimportant it must have been. Dear, please just lie quiet and try to relax. Please forget about that man for a few minutes, anyway. No man's worth getting that worked up about. Catch me doing it! You know you can't expect to get well quickly, if you get yourself so excited. You know that.

What doctor did you have, darling? Or don't you want to say? Your own? Your own Doctor Britton? You don't mean it! Well, I certainly never thought he'd do a thing like—Yes, dear, of course he's a nerve specialist. Yes, dear. Yes, dear. Yes, dear, of course you have perfect confidence in him. I only wish you would in me, once in a while, after we went to school together and everything. You might know I absolutely sympathize with you. I don't see how you could possibly have done anything else. I know you've always talked about how you'd give anything to have a baby, but it would have been so terribly unfair to the child to bring it into the world without being married. You'd have had to go live abroad and never see anybody and—And even then, somebody would have been sure to have told it sometime. They always do. You did the only possible thing, *I* think. Mona, for heaven's sake! Don't scream like that. I'm not deaf, you know. All right, dear, all right, all right, all right. All right, of course I believe you. Naturally I take your word for anything. Anything you say. Only please do try to be quiet. Just lie back and rest, and have a nice talk.

Ah, now don't keep harping on that. I've told you a hundred times, if I've told you once, I wasn't going to say anything at all. I tell you I don't remember *what* I was going to say. "Night before last"? When did I mention "night before last"? I never said any such—Well. Maybe it's better this way, Mona. The more I think of it, the more I think it's much better for you to hear it from me. Because somebody's bound to tell you. These things always come out. And I know you'd rather hear it from your oldest friend, wouldn't you? And the good Lord knows, anything I could do to make you see what that man really is! Only do relax, darling. Just for me. Dear, Garry isn't in Chicago. Fred and I saw him night before last at the Comet Club, dancing. And Alice saw him Tuesday night at El Rhumba. And I don't know how many people have said they've seen him around at the theatre and night clubs and things. Why, he couldn't have stayed in Chicago more than a day or so—if he went at all.

Well, he was with *her* when we saw him, honey. Apparently, he's with her all the time; nobody ever sees him with anyone else. You really must make up your mind to it, dear; it's the only thing to do. I hear all over that he's just simply *pleading* with her to marry him, but I don't know how true that is. I'm sure I can't see why he'd want to, but then you never can tell what a man like that will do. It would be just good enough *for* him if he got her, that's what *I* say. Then he'd see. She'd never stand for any of his nonsense. She'd make him toe the mark. She's a smart woman.

But, oh, so *ordinary*. I thought, when we saw them the other night, "Well, she just looks cheap, that's all she looks." That must be what he likes, I suppose. I must admit he looked very well. I never saw him look better. Of course, you know what I think of him, but I always had to say he's one of the handsomest men I ever saw in my life. I can understand how any woman would be attracted to him—at first. Until they found out what he's really like. Oh, if you could have seen him with that awful, common creature, never once taking his eyes off her, and hanging on every word she said, as if it was pearls! It made me just—

Mona, angel, are you *crying*? Now, darling, that's just plain silly. That man's not worth another thought. You've thought about him entirely too much, that's the trouble. Three years! Three of the best years of your life you've given him, and all the time he's been deceiving you with that woman. Just think back over what you've been through—all the times and times and times he promised you he'd give her up; and you, you poor little idiot, you'd believe him, and then he'd go right back to her again. And *everybody* knew about it. Think of that, and then try telling me that man's worth crying over! Really, Mona! I'd have more pride.

You know, I'm just glad this thing happened. I'm just glad you found out. This is a little too much, this time. In Chicago, indeed! Let you know the minute he came home! The kindest thing a person could possibly have done was to tell you, and bring you to your senses at last. I'm not sorry I did it, for a second. When I think of him out having the time of his life and you lying here deathly sick all on account of him, I could just—Yes, it is on account of him. Even if you didn't have an—well, even if I was mistaken about what I naturally thought was the matter with you when you made such a secret of your illness, he's driven you into a nervous breakdown, and that's plenty bad enough. All for that man! The skunk! You just put him right out of your head.

Why, of course you can, Mona. All you need to do is to pull yourself together, child. Simply say to yourself, "Well, I've wasted three years of my life, and that's that." Never worry about *him* anymore. The Lord knows, darling, he's not worrying about you.

It's just because you're weak and sick that you're worked up like this, dear. I know. But you're going to be all right. You can make something of your life. You've got to, Mona, you know. Because after all—well, of course, you never looked sweeter, I don't mean that; but you're—well, you're not getting any younger. And here you've been throwing away your time, never seeing your friends, never going out, never meeting anybody new, just sitting here waiting for Garry to telephone, or Garry to come in—if he didn't have anything better to do. For three years, you've never had a thought in your head but that man. Now you just forget him.

Ah, baby, it isn't good for you to cry like that. Please don't. He's not even worth talking about. Look at the woman he's in love with, and you'll see what kind he is. You were much too good for him. You were much too sweet to him. You gave in too easily. The minute he had you, he didn't want you anymore. That's what he's like. Why, he no more loved you than—

Mona, don't! Mona, stop it! Please, Mona! You mustn't talk like that, you mustn't say such things. You've got to stop crying, you'll be terribly sick. Stop, oh, stop it, oh, please stop! Oh, what am I going to do with her? Mona, dear—Mona! Oh, where in heaven's name is that fool maid?

Edie, Oh, Edie! Edie, I think you'd better get Dr. Britton on the telephone, and tell him to come down and give Miss Morrison something to quiet her. I'm afraid she's got herself a little bit upset.

FROM *RUBYFRUIT JUNGLE*

Rita Mae Brown

"Are you sure you're pregnant?"

"Yes, I am goddamn fucking sure. Enough to make you vomit, isn't it?"

"Where can we get an abortion?"

"I know a guy in med school who will do it. But I have to give him $500. Can you believe $500 to scrape a tiny bit of gook from my insides?"

"Do you think he's safe?"

"Who knows?"

"Well, when are we doing it?"

"Tomorrow night. You're driving me there, Cookie."

"Okay. Did you tell Cathy you were going tomorrow?"

"No. At least I had sense enough not to spill that. I don't even know why I told her in the first place. It was on my mind and it popped out. Stupid."

The next evening we left the dorm at nine and drove out west of the town. We pulled in the driveway of the med student's trailer and Faye climbed out.

"I'm coming with you."

"No, you're not. You stay here and wait."

It seemed hours and I was so nervous I threw up. The whole thing was creepy and the Spanish moss in the night looked like ragged fingers of death coming to get me. All I could think of was Faye in there on some kitchen table with him doing God knows what. I thought maybe I should go in there, but then suppose I barge in at the critical moment and he pushes a hole in her or something. Eventually Faye wobbled out. I ran out of the car to help her.

"Faysie, are you all right?"

"Yeah, I'm all right. A little weak."

As we neared the dorm I turned out the lights and pulled into the macadam parking lot. We walked slowly back to the basement window that was permanently unlocked at the price of ten dollars per week to the guard. I lifted Faye through because it was high up. As I dropped to the other side I noticed blood oozing down her leg. "Faye, you're bleeding. Maybe we should go to a real doctor."

"No. He told me I might bleed a little. It's okay. Shut up about it or you'll make me think about it." We started up the four flights of stairs to our room and Faye was going painfully slow. "I'm so goddamned weak this is gonna take a fucking hour."

"Put your arms around my neck and I'll carry you up."

"Molly, you crack me up. I weigh one thirty-five and you must weigh about a hundred."

"I'm very strong. Come on, this is no time to pull a Weight Watchers. Put your arms around my neck."

She leaned on me and I picked her up. "My hero." She laughed.

I cut classes the next two days to hang around the room in case Faye needed me. She recovered in record time and by Saturday was ready for another liquor-sodden weekend.

"I'm going over to Jacksonville to raise hell."

"Don't be an asswipe, Faye. Take it easy this weekend."

"If you're so worried you can come along and play nurse. We can stay at my house and come back Sunday night. Come on."

"Okay, but promise me you won't pick up some stud and bust open your stitches or whatever you've got up there."

"You crack me up."

We started out at a bar near Jacksonville University, black walls, Day-Glo paint on them and a huge sea-turtle shell here and there. An enormous basketball player bought us drinks and insisted on asking me to dance. My nose hit his navel and I got cramps in my arches from dancing so long on my toes. We left there and headed toward the inner city. "I'm gonna take you to a wild bar, Molly, so gear yourself."

The bar was Rosetta's, named after the owner, who walked around with a black lasagna hairdo teased up nearly a foot with chopsticks stuck in it at various angles. Rosetta smiled at us as we came in and demanded our IDs. They were fake, of course, but we passed Checkpoint Charlie and went over to a table in the corner. As we sat down, I glanced in the direction of the dance floor and noticed that the men were dancing with each other and the women were dancing with other women. I had a sudden urge to clap my hands in frenzied applause, but I suppressed it because I knew no one would understand.

"Faye, how'd you find this place?"

"I get around, Toots."

"Are you gay?"

"No, but I like gay bars. They're more fun than straight ones, plus there's no jocks to paw at you. I thought I'd bring you here for a little treat."

"Thought you'd shock me, right?"

"I don't know. I just thought it would be fun."

"Let's have fun then. Come on, smartass, how'd you like to dance?"

"Bolt, you crack me up. Who the hell is going to lead?"

"You are because you're taller than I am."

"Wonderful, I can be butchess."

Once on the terrazzo dance floor, we had a hard time keeping our balance because Faye was laughing uproariously. Every two steps she mangled my sandaled foot. Then in a burst of concentration, she gave me a Fred Astaire twirl and made use of her cotillion training. As the final strains of Ruby and the Romantics died down, we started for our table to be intercepted by two young women on the other side of the dance floor.

"Excuse me. Don't you all go to Florida and live in Broward?"

Faye volunteered the information. Then the short one asked us if we'd come to their table for a drink. We agreed to that and trotted back to our corner table to retrieve our drinks.

"Molly, if that little one tries to pick me up, you tell her we're going together. Okay?"

"Instant marriage, is it? In that case, I'll do anything for my wife."

"Thanks dearie. I'll do the same for you. Remember we're the hottest couple since Adam and Eve. Wrong metaphor—since Sappho and whoever. Come on."

FROM *LA BÂTARDE*

Violette Leduc

My period did not come. I did not want to keep the child. Sometimes I told Gabriel about my visits to the so-called midwives, sometimes not. A curious man: he still continued to keep himself in check, yet he still wanted the child. As for my mother, she treated her married daughter as though she were an innocent maiden who'd been seduced. But despite this confusion I must admit her appraisal of my situation was astute enough. I was torn in two directions at once. When I fell on a staircase I imagined I was saved. I was mistaken. The months passed and the five months' ripened fruit in my belly gave me the strength of a lion. If it moved, what would I decide? It didn't move, I wasn't forced to say to myself that there was a heart beating in my insides. It was while we were eating in a restaurant that specialized in the dishes of the Auvergne that Gabriel told me how he was going to rent a sunny apartment in a modern block, how we were going to bring up the child together. The rosé wine was sending me to sleep, Gabriel's voice was like a cradle rocking me. Since his mother's death and his sister's marriage, he'd been living on the top floor of a new building just around the corner from our musty room. I came to my senses, I went to live with my mother. I was full of mistrust. My mother has no idea of the love I showed her or the sacrifice I made for her then.

A Sunday afternoon in winter without a fire. Michel was taking a course in sheep farming at a school in the country. He had to leave again that evening. I knew how passionate they both were about the cinema and persuaded them to go to one. My mother was unaware of what a serious condition I was in after my final attempts at an abortion the day before. The door banged behind them, the lift came up. I was warm as I lay in my mother's bed writing a story for the magazine. Writing: it meant entering the struggle; it meant earning my livelihood as religious people earn their right to enter heaven. I blew on my fingers, I massaged my hip, the infection was beginning, I went on writing, and every now and then I glanced through the glass front of the dresser in their dining room. Inside, I could see the drawer in which I had put away ten thousand francs, a fortune acquired in one fell swoop, thanks to an advertising story I had written for the firm of Lissac: in it I had demonstrated how a shortsighted girl who wore glasses was more attractive than her twin sister who had arrogantly refused to adopt a long view of things. They came back from the cinema at six that evening and I told them I was in no pain. I *was* in pain. Unforgettable afternoon with my paper to be filled and my single woman's determination to stand by herself and not to fall.

I have described the sequel to that afternoon in *Ravages*: the following evening I was dying in a clinic. I didn't want my mother to spend the night in an armchair by my bed. I begged her to go home and rest in her own bed. But the one spark of life left in me kept flickering the same message over and over: she will stay, you'll see, she'll stay. She left. She told me later that she went to the cinema, otherwise she couldn't have got through the evening. I understand her and I don't understand her. The next morning, she didn't dare telephone the clinic. She thought they would tell her I was dead. I suffer from her sufferings as well as my own.

A terrible winter without coal. I had been discharged from the clinic and spent several months in bed at my mother's. She got up at six in the morning, she broke the ice in the kitchen, then she put the pieces of ice in the rubber bag I had to keep in my belly all day long. I listened: the pieces of ice fell on to the tiled floor, and because her hands were cold, when she had finished picking them up she'd let them all slip on to the floor again. I accused myself of being sick, of lying in a warm bed, of making her wait on me. I upbraided my immobile legs.

A yellowing light coming through the window. The sky had snow in store for us. I panicked. Night was coming, I couldn't switch on the light. My mother had gone out to bring medical supplies from a chemist's near Gare Saint-Lazare and she should have been back by now. I called to her with all the strength of my lungs. Someone rang the doorbell. I sensed that it was Gabriel. Nailed to the bed, I loved him without desire and without regret. I heard him going away, I called to my mother again in the darkness. What had happened to her, what would happen to me, alone in her big bed? The door was double locked. Gently, in the silence, I began to weep. Crying rhythmically like that kept me going in the darkness behind my closed eyelids.

My mother came back and flew into a temper. She'd been held up by the queue in the chemist's, the crowd in the Métro, the crowds everywhere she went. I asked her the time. She'd been away six hours, I said piteously between sobs. I would have liked her to take me in her arms. She was getting ready the permanganate, the boiled water, the douche. . . . She began giving me my treatment. The doorbell rang. She thrust the douche into my hands and went to the door. She came back into the room and went on attending to me. Wearing his long cape and his beret, leaden faced, he had followed her into the room. He looked at me and he looked at the pink rubber tube, the crimson blood. He left without a word.

Translated from the French by Derek Coltman

I AM USED TO KEEPING SECRETS ABOUT MY BODY

Josette Akresh-Gonzales

A bottom drawer of just-in-case ovules—
treasure of *Candida*—
ointment *if you do not feel some relief.*

* * *

Bathroom door locked, rashes I've treated in the mirror.

The doctor I had for ten years—never not awkward
and when I revealed the pink pustules exploding,
oystershell yellow and white, my breast,
the underside of the breast,

he only glanced, said he suspected poison ivy—
shy (or maybe horny) doctor referred me to derm.

* * *

In camp, I remember, a girl whose boobs had come
overnight like she had hidden a bicycle pump under her bed—
I stared at her and me, me and her—funny mirrors.
Behind the hook-and-eye latched door,

one of those girls taught me how to shove a tampon in.
When I failed over and over, my knee high over the toilet,
my bare toes balanced brown with mud on the sole, my face
reddening more with each attempt,
there was relief in flopping down on the bed with a pile of *Seventeen*—

tips on how to break up with a boy: *It's not you, it's me.*

* * *

I try to hike up in the Green Mountains,
focus on not peeing as I step a foot-high boulder
down, way behind my husband and boys,
our friends and their dog so far ahead, their voices damp
at the summit. I watch the horizon, a done deal:
I quit I quit I quit.

* * *

About ten years ago, a woman I worked with
took me for a walk by the river, opened up like a storm:
that guy she'd hooked up with—who she thought she might marry,
who'd profiled on IndianCupid as square-jawed but smart and steady
almost too good to be true—
and saw again at a friend's party—

Well, now I'm pregnant. Pale, nauseated
morning, noon, and night—
she wondered if I had a doctor I liked who could do an abortion.
Her eyes had never strayed up from the pebbled map
of river path under our boots.
So how far along are you, I asked—
splash—a false contraction overcoming me.
I was pregnant too, and the body quickening,
a kick in the guts.
I don't know, she said, *it could be two months.*
I don't know.

I gave her the number of my doctor
and promised that he would be for her a thing with feathers—
this was Massachusetts in 2008—

and a few weeks later, upstairs, quiet,
she told me that it was done—
of course, it was never purely one thing—
no, she had bled too much,
she had to return to the surgeon,
had to keep her secret from even her closest sister.
She told me, *Look, I can never tell my mom,*
my father would disown me, I could never get married.
Working in her cubicle next to mine, she took pills for the pain—
she would not be an exile.

In time her sisters would paint her in henna
and she would wear a pink sari and many gold bracelets.
She would enjoy the sweet smile of her child, like mine—
the border of before motherhood/after motherhood
like a wall which is a grassy hill on one side,
stones stacked up on the other.

WEATHER

Lisa Coffman

When I sit teaching among my red-lipped girls sugaring to ripeness
among the flushed necks prideful as mine has been
and feel in myself only the new wish
to lie down in the earliest dark and turn my face

or when I go among pleasured women filling with first child, oh
when I want to go over what is gone and done
then I come to my high room that faces the river
and the wide light the river moves ceaselessly under.

OF THE MISSING FIFTY MILLION

Shikha Malaviya

*According to statistics from the United Nations, there are fifty million more
boys than girls under the age of twenty in India. Sex-selective abortions,
despite being illegal in India, are often performed, as boys are considered
more desirable.*

In the celestial realm
of abandoned girls
you will find all parts
tiny fingers and toes
thumbnail-sized hearts
silver anklets barely an inch wide
kohl to ward off the evil eye
and tiny ovaries dotting the skies
Rupees five thousand for a simple operation
saves you a dowry of fifty thousand
for daughters are a father's burden
legs closed, mouths open
decked in red
when they are wed
we welcome the bride
as Lakshmi, goddess of wealth
uttering blessings, of them one
putravati bhava
be the mother of a son

MY SISTER GROWS BIG AND SMALL

Linda Ashok

Okay, listen, you need
to calm down. It was just a dream,
you know that. If you promise me
and calm down, I will get you
the joker-box in which his laughter
spills into candies.
But Ma, could that be his tongue?
Could those candies be his tongue?

No! Now you are annoying me.
Listen there is no bad dream
like an empty stomach
and now I must go,
gather firewood
and cook
a warm and loving meal for you.

But Ma, you know that dream is not unreal.
I see a girl by the pond every day;
she wears my school dress
and tells me that she misses you.
She has your mole and her lips, Ma,
are as red as yours. Hers,
not snaggletooth but as perfect as yours.

No, that is not real! Come with me
to the woods. We'll burn the spell
of this bad dream.

Ma, she is real. She follows me home
till I wake up and she grows big and small
and I cannot catch her. She says
she will take me away with her.
She knows you and grandpa
and brother all by their names.

She gets me toffees. But I cannot take them;
there is something between us;
she tells me it is you.

See, when you gather the wood,
check them if they are soggy, as the wet ones
take longer to burn, might be a waste of all your time.

Ma, could I be a soggy branch?

You are too little to know how she fell off
me. You are not responsible. She dropped
off me.

Next time, if you meet her, tell her
that Ma wanted her as much.
She'll understand.

TWEETS IN EXILE FROM NORTHERN IRELAND

Jennifer Hanratty

Dedicated to our son Linus, born Liverpool, September 2018

At our twelve-week scan, we were told that they suspected our baby had anencephaly. At fourteen weeks the diagnosis was confirmed. The termination itself we coped with; we knew it was the right choice for us, and the NHS staff were incredibly kind and understanding. But the weeks before our son was delivered were horrific. It took two more weeks to find a provider abroad, get an appointment, make childcare arrangements, and book travel. The journey was torture. I will never not feel the pain of being exiled and tortured by my country during the worst moments of my life.

I documented our journey on Twitter (**RatherBeHome @HomeRather https://twitter.com/HomeRather**) so that people could understand the real impact of the law: not in an abstract way, but its real visceral human impact. I began from home, outside of Belfast, covered the trip to Liverpool and the procedure there, and ended with our return to Belfast, where we should have been all along.

October, 18, 2018 [Thursday at home]
9:58 a.m. Anencephaly is a neural tube defect. Anencephaly literally means "without a brain". It is fatal. Incompatible with life,

Basic biology lesson: When an egg and sperm fuse you get a zygote. That cell splits in two, they split into four and 8, 16, 32 and on and on till you get a ball of cells.

Part of the ball of cells will become the placenta and amniotic sac, the other part becomes the fetus. The group of fetal cells starts off in a disk shape, that disk folds up to form a tube.

The "top" bit of the tube seals up and becomes the skull and brain. The bottom bit seals up and becomes the spine. Any problems in this sealing process lead to a "neural tube defect."

It happens between the 23rd and 26th day of pregnancy. Most women won't have missed a period yet so won't even realize they are #pregnant. That's why, if you are thinking of getting pregnant, you'd be wise to take #folicacid NOW @SHINEUKCharity.

There are different types of neural tube defects, depending on where in the "tube" things went wrong. For our little one, the problem was at the top. This meant that the skull and brain would never form. No brain. #Brainless. Headless? Not quite but nearly #nearlyheadlessnick

We were told that our baby had anencephaly at the twelve-week scan. It is fatal. No chance of survival. The #midwife said we were "lucky" because sometimes these defects can't be seen until twenty weeks.

Maybe it's lucky to know the devastating news before you've really allowed yourself to believe that the #pregnancy was real. Maybe it's lucky to have time to consider your options. Except if you live in Northern Ireland. #nowforNI @DianaJohnsonMP.

If you live in Northern Ireland your choices are: 1. Stay #pregnant and endure the long slow torture of feeling your baby grow while you wait for them to die or 2. Become some other country's problem. @Alliance4Choice

Follow our journey for #healthcare tomorrow. Flight leaves at 6:30 a.m. #belfast @NowForNI

October 19, 2018 [Friday 5:30 a.m. Belfast City Airport]
5:30 a.m. We just left a sobbing two-year-old. Her little face, tears streaming, staring out of her seat in the back of her Granny's car nearly broke me before this torturous journey even started.

This morning her sleepy begging was too much. . . "but I want to go, too, Mummy." Big tears rolled down her tiny perfect little face. I told her I wished I could stay with her. I cried big stupid tears of my own and snuggled her close so she wouldn't see #motherhood #ToddlerLife

She's still in her pajamas because it's so early. We had to wake her up to come to the airport with us before going to her Granny's for the weekend @BELFASTCITY_AIR

5:52 a.m. We haven't told toddler what's happening. How do you explain to a two-year-old that the tiny baby swimming in mummy's tummy is dying? #BabyLossAwarenessWeek @TFMRIRE

How do you explain that our country would rather torture us and force us to leave her than allow our doctors to care for us as they want to, without fear of prosecution? @duponline I don't know. @RCObsGyn @MidwivesRCM

I do know that none of the people responsible for maintaining NI's barbaric laws were there this morning to dry her tears. And none of them care about us. #nowforNI

Boarding @flybe #HealthcareNotAirfare #RepealThe8th @NowForNI

7:42 a.m. I'm so fucking tired.

My stomach hurts from holding it in. I want to hide because I'm afraid someone will notice and ask the usual questions. . . When are you due? Is it your first? Do you know what you're having? I can't handle that.

9:05 a.m. The next salesperson who tries to strike up one of those faux friendly conversations "what brings you here today" "business or pleasure" is getting an honest fucking answer. I'm too tired to save other people's feelings with plain lies about visiting friends.

I leave himself to deal with the sales pitch at the car hire desk and go to the loo. The little hope that I'll see blood in my knickers reminds me again why we're here. As if I could forget. My baby has a fatal abnormality. A condition that is "incompatible with life." #nowforNI

If there was blood it would mean we could just go home now. If the baby's heart stopped beating on its own we would be welcome at home. We'd be cared for as grief-stricken parents.

9:54 a.m. We've arrived at the hospital. I don't want to get out of the car. Getting out means that it's real. That this is happening to me. To us. It's not someone else's story, it's ours. It's not just something that happened to @MrsEtoB years ago it's happening now.

10:18 a.m. We got lost looking for the clinic. Here now waiting. There are six other women here, one has a partner, one is with her mother, the rest are alone. There are a range of ages.

10:22 a.m. I was worried that I'd feel angry or upset seeing women with presumably healthy pregnancies here. But I don't. I feel sorry for them. I feel sorry for me. None of us want to be in this situation. We're here because we need to be.

I don't know the circumstances of their lives. They don't know mine. #trustwomen

10:27 a.m. The nurse calls women one by one to take BP, height, weight. She struggles when she calls an Irish name. The young woman, here on her own, corrects the nurse and pronounces her name for her. It's not a difficult one.

Imagine being here, away from home, all alone, where people can't even say your name. Thank fuck for #repeal #trustwomen @simon (health minister) @alliance4choice @nowforNI @tfmr

10:31 a.m. One woman comes back to the waiting room really upset. She's on her own. I want to comfort her but I hesitate. Everyone else pretends not to notice her, so eventually I feel compelled to do something. I get up and sit beside her. I offer her a hug. We chat a bit.

She tells me she's already got two young kids. She doesn't look more than twenty years old. She tells me that she'd used hormonal contraception but it failed. She felt she had to justify herself, to a total stranger, in an abortion clinic. #noneofmybusiness #trustwomen

I mention that I will have to stay for the weekend and she's surprised to learn that abortion is illegal in Northern Ireland. I don't tell her that it's even illegal when the baby has no chance of surviving. I don't want her to feel even worse about her own situation.

10:45 a.m. I get called in to get my bloods taken. The nurse steps out to get something and suddenly I am bawling. I have spent so much time doing the admin to get us here that I haven't allowed myself to be upset about losing my baby.

11:03 a.m. We get called in to see the midwife I've already spoken to her on the phone and she gives us both a hug. She's sorry. She understands how awful it is for us to be stuck here all weekend.

Himself looks pale when she mentions that there is a risk of uterine rupture and hysterectomy. The risk is really, really small, but he looks terrified and it's the first time I realize how much he has to lose, too, and how scared he is for me, for our family and for the future.

11:48 a.m. The bereavement specialist midwife comes to see us. She talks through our options for the remains. The product of pregnancy. Our child.

We could have brought "everything" home if we'd come by ferry but it was so expensive and would have meant leaving the toddler for longer. There was also the small horror of bringing our baby home in a plastic bag.

I've heard stories of people having to buy bags of frozen peas on the way home so that their beloved child doesn't decompose on the ferry. #horrorstory #gruesome

We could arrange a cremation locally through funeral directors or the hospital but that would mean coming back here again to collect the ashes. #nevergoingback

Or we could choose a "communal cremation" where our baby would be cremated with others and the ashes scattered in a remembrance garden and all the babies' names would be read out during the service.

We chose the latter. It felt right for us that our little person would be remembered with others. Or maybe we just couldn't face any more admin, or having to make this journey again, before we allowed ourselves to grieve. #babylossawarenessweek @lullybytrust @shine

13:03 p.m. Finally, all the necessary boxes have been ticked, bloods checked, and forms signed. I am given a pill. I have to swallow it in front of the midwife. I feel like grabbing it and running to the airport but I can't.

We have to hang about for thrity minutes and if nothing happens, we can go. Not go home of course, just go and wait. For forty-eight hours.

While we are waiting we get some food in the hospital canteen. Next to us is a couple holding fertility brochures. Everyone has their struggles. #trustwomen

14:08 p.m. We check in to the hotel. Thankfully we don't have to wait for the room to be ready. I realize I'm holding in my stomach again, and I'm sweating in my big coat but I don't want to take it off in case someone notices. This is bullshit. #RatherBeHome

14:20 p.m. The hotel looks grand from the outside but it's actually pretty shit. In fact, it's so bad it's actually funny. Himself and I joke about the fake marble. I'm thankful that we can still be ourselves in the midst of this shit. Even for a few minutes.

14:35 p.m. Our plan, to spend the forty-eight-hour wait cocooned in the hotel, is out the window. It's too depressing, the "free Wi–Fi" is free for twenty minutes and the TV doesn't work. We're starving, but there's no room service, so we have to go out for food.

We have to wander about this strange city, pretending everything is normal #RatherBeHome #nowforNI

17:13 p.m. I could have a drink with dinner. I certainly feel like having a skinful. But it tastes awful because I'm still #pregnant. I can't finish my pizza because I feel sick if I eat too much. Still pregnant. I'm not expecting a baby though.

19:58 p.m. We decide to go to the cinema #blackklansman. We haven't been out together like this since toddler was born. We hate leaving her. The film is excellent @spikelee. Suddenly and for no reason, a wave of despair and rage and grief hits me and I want out.

I want to run away and hide so I can wail and sob and let all of this rip out of me. But I'm stuck here three hundred miles from my safe place. At least the cinema is dark so I can weep quietly.

October 20, 2018 [Saturday morning]

If we were #home this morning I'd be making pancakes and supervising toddler cracking the eggs. Instead I'm in a strange city, getting breakfast. It's pretty nice tbf. The breakfast I mean. Being tortured by your own country is fucking horrendous. #nowforNI @duponline @BelfastLive

HELP ME https://nowforni.uk/take-action/

We were told that our baby had anencephaly at the twelve-week scan. No chance of survival. Himself said the news was like being hit with a sledgehammer. We decided immediately that ending the pregnancy was the least awful choice. #nowforNI

But @duponline have created fear in the medical profession. They are threatened with murder charges and prison. So, even though our medical team wanted to help us, they couldn't. Or wouldn't #tfmr @RCObsGyn @bpas1968

If you live in Northern Ireland your only "choice" is staying #pregnant and waiting for your baby to die. Dreading feeling kicks. Hiding from the world. Hiding from your own body, to protect yourself from the incomprehensible reality that your child will not survive. Or, become some other country's problem. At least we don't have to pay for treatment anymore. Just #travel @Alliance4Choice

October 20, 2018 [Saturday evening]
18:45 p.m. We've spent the day wandering around killing time. We took an open-top bus tour as if we're here on purpose.

Dinner was nice, Peruvian. We're doing a good job of pretending we're on a romantic weekend away. Until himself goes to the loo and I'm alone at the table. Suddenly I'm gasping and fighting to keep from sobbing and screaming.

I stare at a mural on the wall and try to calm down. When toddler was born I used #hypnobirthing. I find myself using the relaxation techniques to get my emotions under control. I should be at home. I shouldn't have to suffer so publicly. It's inhumane. #nowforNI

Toddler had lovely day today with her cousins. Back at Granny's now. At bedtime she had a screaming meltdown. The novelty of Granny's has worn off. She wants her Mummy and Daddy. She wants to go home. Same as us really.

October 21, 2018 [Sunday]
Today our baby will be born. We have to be at the hospital at 9 a.m. Thankfully we will have a private room off the main gyne ward. Breakfast is a banana and some watery instant porridge we bought yesterday (shitty hotel has no fridge). Bag packed in case I have to stay overnight.

9:05 a.m. At the hospital now. Waiting. Really upset. I just want to be at home. With familiar faces and accents and skyline out the window.

The nurse that showed us in said she'd get bedpans for the bathroom. That makes me really sad.

Granny sent a video of toddler this morning. Her sweet voice says "hello, Mummy, hello Daddy." Then she picks her nose, shows Granny and says "there's another snot" and wipes it on her chair. She's hilarious. I miss her snotty face.

10:40 a.m. Still waiting.

11:02 a.m. The doctor has just come in to place a canula, a thing that pokes into your vein and sits there just in case you need fluids (or presumably blood) urgently. He's not the gentlest and it hurts.

He says "Ireland really is so green. Must be why you people all like wearing green so much." WTF? Is that some casual racism or just social awkwardness? Bit of #hibernophobia at the bedside, all part of the service. Lovely.

11:16 a.m. The nurse comes in to "administer tablets." This is code for place them up your doot. Vaginal "administration" reduces side effects apparently.

The Wi–Fi in the hospital is much better than the shitty hotel so we decide to watch a movie on @netflix @MelissaMcCarthy and @IMKristenBell are hilarious. Bet they never thought their movie would help a woman cope with the shittiest day of her life. #thankyou

12:30 p.m. We don't have anything for baby. We've been too focused on just getting through this awful journey that we didn't think. Should we have brought a blanket to wrap baby in and then bring home with us? The blanket. We won't be bringing baby #home

12:32 p.m. A hat. A hat to shield us from the defect that's taken our baby away from us.

12:48 p.m. Feeling a bit crampy now so take paracetamol and a good whack of codeine. Normally I avoid taking painkillers. Especially while

#breastfeeding and #pregnant. But toddler is three hundred miles away and baby doesn't have a brain so won't be affected by the codeine #brutaltruth

13:35 p.m. Mucus plug and waters just came out in a big rush of blood and fluid into the green bedpan in the toilet. Feeling light cramps but nothing too bad.

I'm aware that I know what's happening. I know what a mucus plug is and what that whooshy feeling of water escaping from a burst balloon is. Only because I've birthed a baby before. Not because I was actually told what to expect from this process in any detail.

14:03 p.m. our baby was born.

The nurses talked about "passing the pregnancy." That's just what it was. It passed. No pain, just gently emerged. This tiny perfect body followed by the placenta and some blood and clots. Gently slid away into a green bed pan.

When the baby emerged, I looked. Still attached by the cord with tiny arms and legs. I looked away. Himself came in. I didn't move because I didn't think he'd want to see and asked him to call the nurses. Then I sat, held his hand as he stood beside me, and waited for the placenta to emerge.

The nurses came in, all ready for action, but I could feel that the placenta hadn't come out yet. They saw that we were ok so gave us some privacy till we were ready. Slowly and softly we parted ways.

The nurses take the bedpan away. They are gone for what seems like forever. Eventually they come back with a tiny blue knitted crib and we get to meet our baby. Our son.

He is so small. Barely identifiable as a "he." His skin is translucent, so we can see every vein and vessel. He is red. His fingers and toes are tiny and perfect. His mouth looks like his Daddy's. He looks almost like he's smiling. #Childofmine

I'm fascinated by him. How he is perfect aside from one fatal defect. It is so extreme. His eyes bulge, he has no forehead, his skull stops just above his ears and then there is nothing. We name him. We hold him. We take pictures.

I go to clean myself up and come back to find himself holding our boy and sobbing. I haven't seen him cry like this since this nightmare began. I'm not even sure he did cry till just now. He had to be strong to get us through this journey that we shouldn't have had to make.

Eventually we feel ready to say goodbye. I rip a piece of my nightdress. I squeeze out some colostrum #liquid-gold, dot it on the cloth, and tuck it into his little crib. My only gift, a part of me to keep him company.

The bereavement team have left a memory box for us. It has a little certificate to acknowledge his birth. A copy of "guess how much I love you" and a card with our baby's tiny hand and footprints in ink.

They tell us that we can go "home" when the bleeding settles and I feel well enough to go. But we aren't going home are we?

Back at the shitty hotel. Himself goes out to get us food and I message @BfN_UK #breastfeeding #medication to find out how much codeine I can take and safely feed the toddler tomorrow evening #ratherbehome #nowforNI

October 22, 2018 [Monday]

4:19 a.m. On Monday morning I'm ruining everyone's day with our news. Trying to remember who knew we were expecting and who didn't know. If the long or short version of this shitty story is needed. Thank goodness for WhatsApp because I can't handle the conversations right now.

I should be at home in the privacy of my own home. Instead I'm trying to discretely bleed in a shitty hotel knowing that some low-paid worker, probably a woman, is going to have to empty a bin full of bloody sanitary pads. There's no dignity here. There's no privacy.

8:27 a.m. The drive back to the airport is a relief. I'm so glad we could afford a hire car instead of public transport. At least one small part of this journey is private.

We navigate the airport without delays and board quickly, #thanks @ flybe

The flight home. I feel myself crumbling as we board. When the doors close I can't hold it together any more. Relief to be going home, loss, grief, exhaustion. I shake and sob. Himself holds my hand and the engines down me out.

My overwhelming thought is that we have left him. We left him alone. I know that we made the right choice, but my body is desperate to hold him, to have him with me. If we were treated at #home he'd be with us.

Home. Landed in Belfast. Toddler is at the gate to meet us. She does a little excited dance and I scoop her up. She clings to me. Was she this strong when we left? I am so relieved to be home to hold my precious girl in my arms.

1:45 p.m. Home. Home. Toddler has a nasty cold. She demands milk as soon as I get my coat off. We sit on the sofa, she snuggles up, latches and I can feel her body relax. She's exhausted and falls asleep in minutes. I'm relieved to be home with her, #breastfeeding is a comfort to us both.

We're so relieved to be home—that this journey is over—so our grief can finally begin. But other women are only beginning their stories of exile. Other families don't know our story might be theirs one day. Unless we change it https://bit.ly/2CYudeF @All4Choice @bpas1968

THE VIRGINITY THIEF (A LETTER TO MY MAN)

Thylias Moss

Dear H,
      I'm sixty-five, retired, mixed-race with one term-pregnancy—my son, who is thirty-seven, the best son anyone could ever want—and I'm an award-winning poet, Professor Emerita at a major research university where I was Full Professor of English and Full Professor of Art and Design, and finally in Love with the finest man on the face of the earth, you, a poet also, a life made possible because I had an abortion following my loss of virginity: rape at age fifteen that resulted in pregnancy fathered by Charles Jones, twenty-five-year-old deacon in my mother's church, and director of the choir I was in.

I can't tell you why I didn't fight, instead giving in to paralysis. Each rough ripping of a button breaking in that harshness, mother-of-pearl molar and canine destruction like being bit into with rotting teeth, green at the gumline like Patrina's, seemed more a misapplication of makeup than deliberate placement of gum disease finding its rot path. No way did I want anything like that to touch me!

D-Con assuring himself that no pregnancy could happen if I sat up, still draped in smelly blanket so semen could run down my legs in a carnivalesque application of cheap lotion. Smelly blanket over me like cloth privacy shield in case he was stopped and could easily explain just taking soloist home from Assembly Baptist Church, just alphabet: ABC.

To get home, I had to run, as he didn't drive me. Made me get out of the car, I was glad to escape, ten baths weren't enough; I didn't stand up straight, found scoliosis out there also, specious muscle relaxant, repackaged snake oil oleo. Blue choir robe stained with a narrow stream of semen twisted as a poisonous snake, the full length, my virginity snaking away, subdividing into tributaries, snakelettes, seeking hem, him too for hellfire; I had very long natural fingernails, at least I could've scratched his face, but I didn't want contaminated fingernails. I didn't want to touch him anywhere. I wouldn't get to give it to someone I chose (and I didn't choose till you). Contaminated robe. That too I burned. Backyard ritual of fire (although I was terrified of matches), always plenty around because my father smoked Pall Malls, my hair having been caught in stove's flames when I was eight, my signature braids burnt. Crispy.

But no period. Two weeks passed and no blood. I tried to tell D-Con that I was pregnant. What else could it be? Trying also to be back in school. Trying to talk with the only possible man, but he or his wife hung up the phone every time. I persisted. I wanted him to know what he'd done. My body was thickening with his baby, despite what he wanted to think. My large breasts swelled even larger. I kept calling and eventually he agreed to take me to his wife's OB-GYN, all the bumpy ride hiding me under the ragged, stinky blanket, as if never washed. D-Con said he would call me with results of the test, but he never spoke to me again.

Abortions were legal then (1969) in only one state, New York, and mine performed by a Greek doctor at St. Luke's Medical Center, Dr. Panayotopoulos. Fifth month of pregnancy—many premature babies just that age survive. Nineteen-seventy—I was sixteen when the abortion was performed, assigned to the maternity floor. I could hear the newborns.

I could've been another young woman having a live birth. But I wasn't. There may have been a heartbeat. I didn't want to hear it. Rhythmic. That baby's solo for the D-Con Choir. My father was with me. Not sure where my mother was. She liked me the least she ever had so was done with me.

A large syringe withdrew amniotic fluid. Lethal saline solution—salt— replaced it, burned baby. An essential nutrient; no salt in the body and no life. Baby barbecue. Infant flambé. A horrible death, but death penalty seemed right. Labor all night. The next day I delivered the stillborn vaginally and got admonishment from Dr. P: "Don't do this again, young lady!"—as if I would want to repeat this! I never checked for fetal movement. The baby must have sensed it wasn't wanted. I did nothing to celebrate it, nothing to memorialize that striped blanket, its stank odor, that D-Conning deacon.

My most fertile days of this cycle for rape, but I didn't scream. Maybe I could've. I don't know because I didn't try. I opened my mouth, drained of sound, only mouthing words of an ineffective heavenly song. Nor did I bite him, staining my teeth, rendering them useless for eating anything. I would surely need prosthetics. Voice and virginity gone. And a pregnancy that would follow me to this day. Having to say to every OB-GYN that I have had, not one, but two pregnancies and only one son.

You might think that this would be the end, but two more things: my mother said, "Be sure to tell no one about this. They will never understand. No man will want you. It will always hold you back." And her prediction seemed to happen, because the person she insisted I marry the very next year, John Moss, who attended that church, said to me, "Charles Jones is laughing at me for having his used goods."

ABORTION HALLUCINATION

Larissa Shmailo

In the corner of the basement where my father used to lie I
watch, interested, as the snake
grows larger and more menacing I am
taken slightly aback but remember him remember that I like
handling snakes and smile
and as always he softens grows smaller
becomes a hippopotamus I have won again I have stared him down
made him warm
and the Nile gives up its life to me
animals carnivorous and calm come home to me
two by two

I watch for the longest time
until the largest fills the window with his face
black as light
Agnus Dei

BRASS FURNACE GOING OUT: SONG, AFTER AN ABORTION

Diane di Prima

I
to say I failed, that is walked out
and into the arctic
  How shd I know where I was?
A man chants in the courtyard,
  the window is open
someone else drops a pecan pie
  into the yard
two dogs down there play trumpet
  there is something disturbed
about the melody.

and what of the three-year-old girl who poisoned her mother?
that happens, it isn't just us, as you can see—
what you took with you when you left
remains to be seen.

II
I want you in a bottle to send to your father
with a long bitter note. I want him to know
I'll not forgive you, or him, for not being born
for drying up, quitting
  at the first harsh treatment
as if the whole thing were a rent party
& somebody stepped in your feet

III
send me your address, a picture, I want to
keep in touch. I want to know how you
are, to send you cookies.
do you have enough sweaters? is the winter bad?
do you know what I've done, what I'm doing?
do you care?
write in detail of your day, what time you get up,
what you are studying, when you expect
to finish & what you will do.
is it chilly?

IV
your face dissolving in water, like wet clay
washed away, like a rotten water lily
rats on the riverbank barking at the sight
do they swim?
the trees here walk right down to the edge
conversing
your body sank, a good way back
I hear the otters will bring it to the surface

and the wailing mosquitoes even stop to examine
the last melting details of eyelid & cheekbone
the stagnant blood
who taught you not to tangle your hair in the seaweed
to disappear with finesse

the lion pads
  along the difficult path
in the heart of the jungle
and comes to the riverbank
he paws your face
I wish he would drink it up
in that strong gut it would come
to life.

but he waits till he floats
a distance
  drinks clean water
dances a little
  starts the long walk
again

  the silent giraffe lets loose
a mourning cry
  fish surface
  your mouth and the end of your nose
disappear.

the water was cold the day you slipped into the river
wind ruffled the surface, I carried you on my back
a good distance, then you slipped in
red ants started up my leg & changed their minds
I fed my eyeballs to a carnivorous snake
& chained myself to a tree to await your end.
your face no sooner dissolved than I thought I saw
a kneecap sticking up where the current is strongest
a turtle
  older than stars
walked on your bones

V
who forged this night, what steel
clamps down?
like gray pajamas on an invalid
if I knew the name of flowers, the habits
of quadrupeds, the thirteen points of the compass. . .
an aged mapmaker who lived on this street
just succumbed to rheumatism
I have cut the shroud to measure
  bought the stone
a plot in the cemetery set aside

   to bury your shadow
take your head & go!
& may the woman that you find know better
than talk to me about it

VI
your goddamned belly, rotten, a home for flies.
blown out & stinking, the maggots curling your hair
your useless never used cock, the pitiful skull
the pitiful shell of a skull, dumped in the toilet
the violet, translucent folds
   of beginning life

VII
what is it that I cannot bear to say?
that if you had turned out mad, a murderer
a junkie pimp hanged & burning in lime
   alone & filled w/the rotting dark
   if you'd been frail and a little given to weirdness
   or starved, or been shot, or tortured in hunger camps
   it wd have been frolic & triumph compared to this—

   I can't even cry for you, I can't hang on
   that long

VIII
forgive, forgive
that the cosmic waters do not turn from me
that I should not die of thirst

IX
oranges & jade at the shrine
my footprints
wet on the stone
the bells in that clear air
wind from the sea

your shadow
flat on the flat rocks
the priestess (sybil)
spelling your name
crying out, behind copper doors
giving birth
atone
    silence, the air
moving outside
the door to the temple blowing on its hinges
that was the spirit she said
it passed above you

the branch I carry home is mistletoe
& walk backwards, with my eyes on the sea

X
here in my room I sit at drawing table
as I have sat all day, or walked
from drawing table to bed,
or stopped at window
considering the things to be done
weighing them in the hand and putting them down
hung up as the young Rilke.
here in my room all day on my couch a stranger
who does not take his eyes
off me as I walk & walk from table to bed.

and I cannot stop thinking I would be three months pregnant
we would be well out of here & in the sun
Even our telephone would be polite
we would laugh a lot, in the morning.

XI
your ivory teeth in the half light
your arms

flailing about, that is, you
age nine months,
  sitting up & trying to stand
  cutting teeth.
  your diaper trailing, a formality

elegant as a loincloth, the sweet stench
of baby-shit in the house; the oil
rubbed into your hair.
blue off the moon your ghostshape
  mistaken as broken tooth

your flesh rejected
  never to grow—your hands

that should have closed around my finger
what moonlight
  will play in your hair?

I mean to say
  dear fish, I hope you swim

in another river.
I hope that wasn't
rebuttal, but a transfer, an attempt
that failed, but to be followed

quickly by another

suck your thumb somewhere
dear silly thing, explode
make someone's colors.

the senses (five)
  a gift

to hear, see, touch, choke on & love
this life
the rotten globe
to walk in shoes
what apple doesn't get
   at least this much?

a caramel candy sticking in your teeth
you, age three
bugged

      bearing down on a sliding pond.

your pulled tooth in my hand
  (age six)
your hair with clay in it,
   your goddamn grin

XII
sun on the green plants, your prattle
among the vines.
that this possibility is closed to us.
my house is small, my windows look out on grey courtyard
there is no view of the sea.
will you come here again? I will entertain you
as well as I can—I will make you comfortable
in spite of new york.

will
you
come here
again

my breasts prepare
to feed you: they do what they can

WHAT WAS, STILL IS

Alida Rol

Although the how matters
little, she blamed herself
as women do. She told only

those she had to and nursed
her shame alone. There was
never a question. There were no

what-ifs. She knew there must be
no baby. It was legal and yet
so difficult to lie on a strange

man's table, trust his hands
inside. It was hard to feel the
delving, hear the motor, taste

the pain. It was as right
as it was unbearable. She held
these thoughts side by side

and carried them into her future
where she treats the women
who've come to lie, often afraid,

on her table. Now there are
pills to take and probes
instead of fingers, but there is

no proxy, still, for the plain

words and kind touch
    of someone who was there.

FROM "ABORTION"

Anne Finger

Amber and I ate a p.m. breakfast at a diner near her house. A man in a stained white apron came over to the booth to take our order, carrying a pencil but no pad. He pointed the pencil eraser end outwards (as if pointing with the sharpened end were rude) first at Amber, repeating, "Bagel, scrambled, grapefruit, coffee," and then at me, "Poached, bacon, whole wheat, coffee."

"Amber, when you had your abortion, did you . . . "

"Jesus," Amber said. "Jump right in."

"I'm sorry." I took a cigarette from her pack but didn't light it. "I think I feel guilty. About having had one."

"You?" Amber asked. "Guilty?"

"What do you mean, *me*, guilty. I'm guilt-*ridden*. It's my sap, my second blood."

"It's just that you always seem so in control. Like the heroine of a nineteenth-century novel. Tempering her passion with ideals."

"Hmmm," I said, more puzzled than flattered.

"I don't mind too much talking about it," she said. "I feel like I'm a relic from the past, living history. You know, some of the kids—listen to me, *kids*—I taught at Binghamton don't really believe that abortion used to be illegal. They know it, but they say things like, 'You couldn't even get a private doctor to do it for you?' I told them it even used to be impossible for girls to get birth control, and they looked at me, gaga, and said, '*You* don't remember that.' I feel called upon to tell my tale." Amber laid a melodramatic hand on her breast.

"God, I was so dumb," she said. "The thought of me, at fifteen, pregnant, seemed so ridiculous, so impossible. I thought it just wouldn't happen. Couldn't. So I never did anything. But I knew I was pregnant, even before I missed my first period."

"I remember that," I said. "It wasn't just that I was so tired. I just *knew*."

"I was scared to tell Hank," she said. "When I finally did, he was a real sweetheart. We sat in his bedroom—his mother was at work—and he cried and I cried. . . . I walked around the Pembroke campus, stopping each woman walking alone. 'I'm pregnant. Do you know anyone who can help me?' Finally, one woman gave me a phone number, she knew it by heart, a doctor in West Virginia.

"I called him from a phone booth, I was afraid to have the long-distance call show up on my parents' bill. The woman had told me, don't say *pregnant*, don't say *abortion*. He sounded so gentle. I told him I was fifteen years old, that I understood he might be able to help me. He kept saying 'Uh-huh, uh-huh,' and then I blurted it out, I said the word, *pregnant*, and the phone clicked dead. I called right back, and it rang and rang and rang."

SONG OF THE EMMENAGOGUES

Lesley Wheeler

> *Vincent drank a potion Mother had concocted*
> *and walked and walked and walked.*
>
> —Norma Millay, quoted in *Savage Beauty*

> *I tell everybody how my mother feeds me on nettles*
> *and thistles, the heartless old thing.*
>
> —from *Letters of Edna St. Vincent Millay*

She was caught, fallen, over her time,
a blossomy month on the road.
Think and think twelve miles a day,
up and down hills near Shillingstone.

    Mugwort, nasturtium, rue,
    primrose, angelica, parsley.

The sun's clock ticked into summer
and down. Bigger than her sorrow.
Unmothering flower crouched in grass.
Scour the paths tomorrow.

    Henbane, gentian, all-heal,
    hyssop, thyme, bitter apple.

Some herbs provoke a woman's courses.
Says the book: decoct in wine.
The blue-petaled one, darling of Venus,
draws forth the undreamed-of child.

Tea of the raspberry leaf. Ginger,
cohosh, tansy, pennyroyal.

Refusal grew of her weeks in Dorset,
blooming from red-rooted alkanet.
Rhymes with secret, the pretty weeds whisper.
Thatch hushes the cottages yet.

FROM *THE HUNDRED SECRET SENSES*

Amy Tan

"Simon, you don't have to explain." I stood up on shaky legs. "Let's just forget it, okay?"

"Olivia, sit down. Please. I have to tell you. I want you to understand. This is important."

"Let go of me. Forget it, okay? Oh, shit! Just pretend it never happened!"

"Wait. Come back. Sit down, please sit down. Olivia, I have to tell you this."

"What the hell for?"

"Because I think I love you too."

I caught my breath. Of course, I would have preferred if he hadn't qualified his declaration with "I think" and "too," as if I could be part of an emotional harem. But infatuated as I was, "love" was enough to act as both balm and bait. I sat down.

"If you hear what happened," he said, "maybe you'll understand why it's taken me so long to tell you how I feel about you."

My heart was still pounding wildly with a strange mixture of anger and hope. We sat in nervous silence for a few minutes. When I was ready, I said in a cool voice, "Go ahead."

Simon cleared his throat. "This fight Elza and I had, it was in December, during the quarter break. I was back in Utah. We had planned to go cross-country skiing in Little Cottonwood Canyon. The week before, we'd been praying for new snow, and then it finally came in truckloads, three feet of fresh powder."

"She didn't want to go," I guessed, trying to hurry up the story.

"No, we went. So we were driving up the canyon, and I remember we were talking about the SLA and whether giving food to the poor made extortion and bank robbery less reprehensible. Out of the blue, Elza asked me, 'What do you feel about abortion?' And I thought I heard wrong. 'Extortion?' I said. And she said, 'No, abortion.' So I said, 'You know, like what we said before, about Roe v. Wade, that the decision didn't go far enough.' She cut me off and said, 'But what do you *really* feel about abortion?'"

"What did she mean, really feel?"

"That's what I asked. And she said slowly, enunciating every syllable: 'I mean emotionally, what do you feel?' And I said, 'Emotionally, I think it's fine.' Then she blew up: 'You didn't even think about the question! I'm not asking you about the weather. I'm asking you about the lives of human beings! I'm talking about the real life of a woman versus the potential life in her womb!'"

"She was hysterical." I was eager to emphasize Elza's volatile and unreasonable nature.

He nodded. "At the trailhead, she jumped out of the car, really pissed, threw on her skis. Just before she took off, she screamed, 'I'm pregnant, you idiot. And there's no way I'm having this baby and ruining my life. But it tears me up to abort it and you're just sitting there, smiling, saying it's fine.'"

"Omigod. Simon. How were you supposed to know?" So that was it, I thought: Elza had wanted to get married, and confronted with the prospect, Simon had refused. Good for him.

"I was stunned," Simon continued. "I had no idea. We were always careful about birth control."

"You think she slipped up on purpose?"

He frowned. "She's not that kind of person." He seemed defensive.

"What did you do?"

"I put on my skis, followed her tracks. I kept shouting for her to wait, but she went over a crest and I couldn't see her anymore. God, I remember how beautiful it was that day, sunny, peaceful. You know, you never think terrible things can happen when the weather's nice." He laughed bitterly.

I thought he was through—since that day, he and Elza hadn't seen each other, end of story, time for the sequel, me. "Well," I said, trying to sound sympathetic, "the least she could have done was given you a chance to discuss the situation before jumping all over you."

Simon leaned forward and buried his face in his hands. "Oh, God!" he said in an anguished voice.

"Simon, I understand, but it wasn't your fault, and now it's over."

"No, wait," he said hoarsely. "Let me finish." He stared at his knees, took a few deep breaths. "I got to this steep fire road, and there was an out-of-bounds sign. Just beyond that, she was sitting at the top of a ledge, hugging herself, crying. I called to her and she looked up, really pissed. She pushed off and headed down this steep wide-open bowl. I can still see it: The snow, it was incredible, pristine and bottomless. And she was gliding down, taking the fall line. But about halfway down, she hit some heavier snow, her skis sank, and she sagged to a stop."

I looked at Simon's eyes. They were fixed on something faraway and lost, and I became scared.

"I yelled her name as loud as I could. She was mashing her poles against the snow, trying to kick up the tips of her skis. I yelled again—'Goddamnit, Elza!'—and I heard the sound, like a muffled gunshot, and then it was perfectly quiet again. She turned around. She was squinting—she must have been blinded by the sun. I don't think she saw it—the slope, two hundred yards above her. It was slowly tearing, no sound, like a giant zipper opening up. The seam became a crack, an icy blue shadow. And then it was snaking fast, straight across. The crack slipped down a little, and it was huge, glassy as an ice rink. Then everything began to rumble, the ground, my feet, my chest, my head. And Elza—I could tell she knew. She was struggling to get out of her skis."

Like Elza, I knew what was coming. "Simon, I don't think I want to hear any more of this—"

"She threw off her skis and her backpack. She was jumping through the snow, sinking to her hips. I started yelling, 'Go to the side!' And then the mountain collapsed and all I could hear was this train roar, trees snapping, whole stands of them, popping like toothpicks."

NOTHING BUT THE WIND

Farideh Hassanzadeh-Mostafavi

for my first child from my first marriage

The only flower in this world
who has no choice
but to turn into a track of a dead love
is a child of an unsuccessful marriage.

I who was your sepal
had no choice but to kill you
who was my petal.

Since your death
in the eyes of all flowers
I am nothing but the wind
with the bloody hands.

HAINT

Teri Cross Davis

no amount of dilation and suction
hemorrhaging and fever
could've erased you or
the pulp of your carved initials
made with the solid grasp
of a still forming hand

science tells me
you are still whispering
inside my bones
that years from now
cut me to the marrow
and microscopes will read
the rings of your insistent story
no matter the inconvenient
coupling of timing and desire

even now when the bloody show
disappoints our sharpening hunger
do you still cling? Or are you willing
to let another call my womb
home?

THE MEMORY OF ABORTION UNEXPECTEDLY RETURNS

Leslie Monsour

The sun has trailed its negligee across
The pinkened threshold of the globe and left
Behind a blue-gray edge around the window.
Selecting silken undies from a drawer,
She thinks of loneliness and hummingbirds.

A violet-crowned one sometimes comes to perch
In solitude against the evening sky;
It's sitting there right now, in plainest view,
Digesting nectar, waiting for the night
To settle. Suddenly it breaks away,

A tiny, falling glow, she can't retrieve—
Unlike the camisole forever sliding
Off of the lacquered bedpost to the floor—
As light as ashes, light as sighs; a small,
Bright, sleeping bird that dies and dies and dies.

GRETEL: UNMOTHERING

Lauren K. Alleyne

I'm sitting in a clinic
waiting to kill my baby.
This is what the women screamed
as I clutched my coat close.
No walk ever seemed so long,
as this march through the forest of protest;
no doorway as dangerous
as this place of endings.
There is a live thing inside me,
I know—I carry its heart.
Forgive me, little bun,
but I am no oven.

MOO AND THRALL

Dana Levin

Some people like to be
        spectacularly swayed.

By a red field
        and a glint of metal.

A surgeon's knife. A gun. A pole
        that holds up a banner . . .

I want to tell you about what I saw,
        on the quad.

Just-dead flesh-babies twelve feet high.

Monkey-head strapped in a test contraption,
        the enormous caption:
IF THIS IS ANIMAL CRUELTY THEN
        —WHAT IS THIS—
Late term.
        They looked like smashed melons. One still latched

        to the cord—

You ask what I thought. I thought,

Who am I to judge
        what another person needs?

Who am I to have to pay
      attention?—

I'd wanted coffee and walked into
      a carnival of death.

But death was always
      ho-humming it, in various forms,

all over the doomèd land—

Still, students clustered.

Young men offered to play the ballast

for the scaffolding
      from which the lurid pictures flared. I thought,

Look at that: something labeled
      "free speech board"—

At either end of the kill-display, where you could
      dig a marker
into white butcher paper—*Get Your Fucking Hands
      Off My Body*—in girlish
      curlicue.

Across the quad the clinicians waited.

Across the quad sat the rational young, offering *info*
      on colored paper, it
couldn't compete
      with lunchtime Grand Guignol—

I wanted some coffee.

I wanted some coffee and a sweet croissant.

I wanted and walked
        through the moo and thrall, how hadn't I
seen it—chalked
        underfoot, every few paces the same
smeared message:

        YOU
        ARE
        LOVED

FROM *LA NOVE DE LOS LOCOS* (THE SHIP OF FOOLS)

Cristina Peri Rossi

The girl came late when all the seats had been sold. Jose had completed the list and handed it to Ecks, who automatically checked it from top to bottom to make sure that no name appeared twice or had been omitted. The fat man was breathing noisily because of the heat, puffing away at his eternal smelly cigar. The girl had short blond hair which hardly reached her cheekbones; her complexion was white as a baby's, and her blue eyes were deep and penetrating. The color of her dress almost matched their intensity.

"Please," she told Jose. "It's imperative that I go this week. I'm already in the third month . . ."

Jose grabbed the medical certificate from her hand.

Ecks was leaning against the wall, smoking: the heat was unbearable and he was longing to turn off the neon bulbs whose milky light reminded him of the clinic in London, of ugly hospitals where old people died alone without money or memories, of barred cells in a zoo.

The fat man returned the certificate to the girl without ceremony.

"Three months and twenty-five days," he said severely. "Nothing doing. Besides, there are no seats left in tomorrow's coach, nor in the next one; we are full for the next two weeks. Why didn't you do something about it before?"

He turned his head in the direction of Ecks, seeking both his complicity and an audience for the usual theatrical pronouncements: "Plenty of speed when it comes to jumping into bed, but afterwards . . . I can't take you. We give no priorities. And as you may imagine, in this kind of journey no passenger wants to give up her place. What have you been doing the last four months? You weren't thinking of having the kid, were you?"

Ecks felt oppressed by the light: did he need glasses?

"I was looking for the money," explained the girl softly. "It hasn't been easy; I'm unemployed."

"I've heard this story before, young lady," answered Jose bluntly. "This is the way business is run. Did you expect to pay in installments?"

"Please," entreated the girl.

Jose was becoming cross.

"Utterly impossible," he said. "Off you go. Come back next time with longer notice. Next year with the next pregnancy."

(A German pharmaceutical company on several occasions requested the Nazi authorities dispatch three hundred pregnant Jewesses for experimental purposes. It was a good way of reducing numbers in the camps.

"We gratefully acknowledge receipt of your latest cargo," wrote the company director in 1938. "We have carried out tests with a new chemical substance. No survivors. However, around the end of October we are planning a new series of experiments, for which we shall require another three hundred subjects. Could they be provided on the same conditions as previously?")

The blue eyes had clouded over.

Ecks threw down his cigarette butt and crushed it underfoot.

It was too hot. Outside and inside.

Ecks overtook her before she reached the corner. She looked startled as she turned towards him.

"Excuse me," he said nervously. "There may be a way. I may be able to take you, if you'll occupy my seat by the driver. I can stand up or sit in the alleyway on top of my suitcase. Once in London, we'll be able to find another clinic. The service will be the same and so will the cost. I don't think the driver will mind. It has never happened before; he can just pocket the price of your ticket."

There was no answer: she looked down, her dress only a little paler than her eyes.

"The coach leaves tomorrow," continued Ecks softly.

"I have nowhere to stay," she confessed without emotion. "If they find out at the agency, will you lose your job?"

"I don't think so," Ecks lied. "I will pick you up somewhere on the way. No one else checks the list once we have left. I have a room near here. If you want to, you can stay there. It's not very big, but there's an old sofa."

"Thanks," she said simply.

(A month after receiving his shipment, the pharmaceutical director had written again to the German authorities:

"The women you sent this time were very thin and weak. The majority had infectious diseases. Nevertheless we managed to use all of them—no survivors. We await your next dispatch in two weeks' time. With thanks and best regards.")

When Graciela came home, Ecks was reading the paper and the girl was sleeping lightly on the sofa. Without making a sound, Graciela went to the little cooking area hidden in a cupboard. Ecks followed her and explained what was happening. Graciela made some tea in silence, anxious not to disturb the girl. She had no other luggage apart from her bag which hung from the back of the sofa.

They drank their tea without a word; Graciela showed Ecks a letter from Morris which had arrived that morning. It was addressed to both of them and related some episodes of his stay in Africa. But mainly it talked of Percival and his mother, Eve. There was a special section for Graciela in which Morris wrote about the practices of cliterodectomy and infibulation effected on young girls in various countries; he also marked the areas that Graciela should visit to see for herself and offered to accompany her. Morris described how at the age of twelve—normally after the first menstrual period—the women (or children?—he asked) were taken away from their villages and led to secluded areas where their clitoris and labia were excised by means of knife, sharp stone, or any other cutting object. The vagina was then sewn with coarse thread or thorns. This process practically sealed the girls' vulvas. The cuts would scar over within a couple of weeks, if they did not turn septic and lead to death from infection, of which there were many instances. The survivors were then returned to their villages, where they were now considered ready to be sold as brides, concubines or auctioned at the clothes and fruit markets. Infibulation was repeated whenever a girl was to be resold, or whenever the owner decided. In certain communities, Morris explained, this practice had the character of a ritual, an offering to the gods. Whoever purchased a girl had the right to test the effectiveness of the infibulation before paying the price.

Graciela was choking on her tea, something she often did when she tried to eat too many biscuits with it.

"A delicate business," whispered Ecks mockingly. "Coach-loads of pregnant women, infibulated girls, and whales committing suicide on the Atlantic shores where they should know the fish are all poisoned."

"I think I'll go," said Graciela, playing with the edge of her paper napkin.

"Let us infibulate," continued Ecks with his tendency to repeat the things that disgusted him, either to exorcise or accustom himself to them.

"It was kind of Morris to invite you," he added in a tone of voice which Graciela was unable to interpret. "But why didn't he invite me? I could leave my job as abortion guide and become the official infibulator in some African kingdom. I would insert the thorns with extreme delicacy and even paint them bright colors to incite fresh buyers.

"If you go, don't forget your great-grandmother's chastity belt, the charming iron one with spikes. And mind you close it well with two turns of the key. Doña Zacarías would be very happy in her tomb, knowing that her favorite belt was coming to the aid of her great-granddaughter."

When the girl woke up—she said her name was Lucía—they offered her tea and biscuits. Ecks played some music and then went to bed because the journey the following day promised to be uncomfortable as well as long. But he was unable to sleep. Whenever he shut his eyes he saw huge thorns or soldiers in uniform.

Translated from the Spanish by Psiche Hughes

ABORTION

Bobbie Louise Hawkins

Dr. Gore was an abortionist. Hearts broke before his eyes. Young women sat in his office with their faces blanked as they thought of their altered future. Given that face and the mother who had learned about him from a friend who was a nurse and who didn't know whether he would help but who knew he was all she had, he was an abortionist.

Contempt and blame was the commonplace response to knocked-up girls in 1948 boondocks America. I expected it. I was ashamed. I had been a fool and I had been caught. He ignored my mother, who sat crying. It wasn't her fault—it was mine, and he despised me for it.

He rode a dangerous edge. Every time he agreed to save this latest mess, he put himself and his own future in the balance. All those girls and women left bleeding and butchered by the clothes-hanger brigade made him someone for the authorities to benignly neglect. They could change their mind without notice. Every girl like me put him into jeopardy. He would say so to supplicants who were in no position to hear it. He saved us despite our inability to see his humanity in it.

He looked at me and growled, "It'll cost a hundred dollars and I don't want her to pay it, I want you to pay it."

I said I would. I felt the hope in it, that my life might be salvaged. I would have promised anything. I would have promised even more hundreds of dollars I didn't have.

The abortion was done in his examining room on his half day. He couldn't use anesthetic because I had to walk out when it was over, looking as normal as I could manage. His nurse was in the reception room. My mother was in his office. I lay on his examining table with my feet in the stirrups and my knees straddled. I did yell once and my mother came through his door, her face twisted with fear, straight into the sight of my spread legs and the bloody mess. Dr. Gore and I both yelled at the same time, telling her to get out.

At home, I cramped and moaned and my mother hovered in the small hallway outside my door, calling to ask whether I was all right. I didn't want her in the room where I hugged my pillow and lay in a tight knot. I was not all right and I was graceless enough to not keep it to myself.

My stepfather was remote, negligible, resentful. The couple would have quick flaring exchanges. She wished now she hadn't found the doctor. She was sure that something was very wrong, that I might die. My stepfather, a man with a usually gentle nature, was sure I wouldn't die and told her so, fiercely. No such luck, they'd have me forever.

One sunny afternoon I was being driven to Santa Fe by a friend. As we passed Dr. Gore's street, he said, "I have to stop here for a minute," turned left, and stopped in front of Dr. Gore's office.

"I won't be long," and he was gone.

I sat waiting, feeling anxious, and, as I had feared, the doctor walked my friend back out to the car. We were formally introduced. He recognized me but didn't let on.

We left, continued driving north.

One of the things I thought was that I hoped he didn't think this particular friend was responsible for my pregnancy.

On the drive to Santa Fe I learned that Dr. Gore was admirable, that he went regularly to the scattering of houses in Tesuque Canyon, alongside Route 66, and doctored the Mexican families there without charge. I don't know whether it was then that I learned he had been badly wounded during the Second World War and, like many who were given morphine for their pain, he had become addicted.

His addiction finally caused him to lose his license. He was arrested for misuse of drugs, found guilty, sentenced, and put in prison. I knew about all this because Albuquerque was still a small town in those days. The local newspaper was bound to be moral about a doctor discovered to be a criminal.

When he came out of prison he got a job in a mental institution. He was hired as an "orderly" but used as a doctor. That might have given him some consolation, that he was needed. I hope it did.

He deserved better than that.

FROM *COME IN SPINNER*

Dymphna Cusack and Florence James

Dallas looked at her questioningly.

"It's about a girl who I know. Well . . . I don't exactly know her, but her sister works with me, and she's got into trouble, and"—the words came out with a rush—"I thought you might be able to tell me the name of some doctor who did that sort of thing."

A professional mask slid over Dallas's face. "I presume you mean an abortion?"

Deb nodded. She felt her face flush under Dallas's keen glance.

"When did this happen?"

"I . . . I can't tell you exactly,"

Dallas looked at her professionally. "Deb, if you want me to help you, it's no good beating around the bush."

Deb looked at her blankly. It took a few seconds before Dallas's meaning penetrated her mind. "Good heavens," she gasped, "why Dallas, surely you don't think . . . whatever could put such an idea into your head?"

"You mean that it is not for yourself?"

"Of course it's not. Why . . . how could you think such a thing."

Dallas shrugged her shoulders. "Have a cigarette and we'll get this business clear."

Deb puffed furiously, virtuously, indignation mounting. She felt like walking straight out of the place. That Dallas should think that of her. Dallas of all people!

Dallas went on with infuriating calm. "You'd better tell me what you know."

Deb controlled her indignation. "It's an AWAS, Mary Parker's the name—her sister's the hairdresser over at the salon."

"Won't the man marry her?"

"He can't. He's already married and his wife refuses to divorce him. Mary and he have been on the same station for two years, and then he was sent to the Islands. It was his final leave."

Dallas sighed. "'Final leave.' How often I've heard that."

"But you can't help being sorry for her."

"You'd be less than human if you weren't. In the ridiculous social set-up we have, it's always the girl who's penalized. Nobody worries about the man."

"He seems to be a decent enough fellow."

"But he hasn't got to take the consequences. He'll go on serenely to promotion while the girl gets a dishonorable discharge, and when the war's over he'll return to the bosom of his wife. I can never see why, when they regard VD as an occupational disease for men in the army, they shouldn't regard pregnancy in servicewomen in the same light."

Deb felt more and more depressed.

"What do you expect me to do?" Dallas asked briskly.

"Well . . . I thought maybe . . . you might . . . you could suggest something."

"If you mean you hoped I might do something, I'm sorry, my dear, that's quite out of the question. I'm not afflicted with the particular brand of sentimentality that regards it as murder to remove an unwanted fetus and at the same time applauds mass slaughter in war, but I can't afford to risk my future in a profession for which I have worked very hard, for the sake of one or even one hundred little AWAS, however sorry I feel for them."

Deb was silent, fidgeting with the spoon on her saucer.

Dallas got up and leaned on the railing. "I'm so sorry for women. Whichever way they turn, most of them are caught. It doesn't matter whether they're driven by love or lust, they're the ones who fall in. If I had a daughter—as I won't, because society says unless I'm prepared to tie myself up to some man legally, I have no right to bear a child—but if I did have a daughter, I'd teach her very early that the only real salvation for women is work."

"It's all very well for you to talk like that, you've got brains and ability and you can stand on your own feet. You don't seem to need a man permanently, though goodness knows you always have plenty of them around.

But what is there for the average woman if she doesn't get married? Only an underpaid job and a back room in some cheap boardinghouse. And anyway most women are romantic and if you gave them their choice they'd rather have love than a career any day of the week."

"You misunderstand me. I have nothing against marriage or love, but love as we know it is too wild and unpredictable a passion on which to build a whole life. And even marriage, unless love develops into something more lasting than the most thrilling romance—for instance, into a partnership such as Tom and Nolly have—destroys itself and usually the woman with it."

"Well, I can think of a lot more attractive things than what Tom has reduced Nolly to," Deb replied with heat.

Dallas smiled and looked round at her. "It may surprise you, Deb," she said, "but do you know, if I weren't so fond of being myself, I'd choose to be Nolly. She's that person so rare in the world today—a fulfilled woman."

"Well, if that's your idea of fulfillment, it certainly isn't mine, and so far as I'm concerned, you can have it on your own."

Dallas went on without answering her. "When I see a happy woman, I generally find that she is good at something outside of romantic love. How I've come to loathe those words, *romantic love*! Boiled down all they mean is that women have let themselves be sold the idea that sex is a substitute for life, instead of seeing it in its right proportion as only one part of living. There comes a time for everyone when sex, merely as sex, fails you. And then, when your heart's shattered into little bits, there's no better cement for putting it in usable shape again than the knowledge that you're really cracker-jack at something else besides love."

She stood silent for a few minutes looking out over the harbor, her eyes the same sparkling grey as the water under the western sun.

"And now," she said, turning back to Deb, "what are we going to do about your little AWAS? Has she got any money?"

"Her sister and she can rack up the twenty-five pounds between them."

"Hasn't the man sent her any?"

"He doesn't know yet."

"I'm afraid there's not a reliable doctor about town who'll do it for under forty these days."

"Forty pounds!" gasped Deb. "Someone said twenty-five."

Dallas shrugged her shoulders. "Supply and demand, my dear. The price has gone up—wartime inflation, like everything else. But even then the only man I really could guarantee has retired and bought a property somewhere in the wilds!"

"Is there anyone else at all you can recommend?"

"I'm afraid there isn't. But perhaps I could find out. Is it urgent?"

"Yes, I'm afraid it is. She's got less than a week's leave left in Sydney."

"That certainly complicates things. I'll tell you what I'll do, Deb. I'll make a few discreet inquiries tomorrow, and if you ring me between six and seven in the evening, I'll probably have found someone. I have surgery at seven so don't ring then. And for heaven's sake don't mention my name to a soul if I do find anyone."

FROM "STANDING GROUND"

Ursula K. Le Guin

They were coming: two of them. The trembling began in Mary's fingertips and ran up her arms into her heart. She must stand her ground. Mr. Young had said stand your ground. He might come. If he came, they would never get past him. She wished Norman would not shake his sign like that. The shaking made the trembling worse. The sign was something Norman had made himself, not one Mr. Young had approved, even. Norman had no right to do everything himself that way. "This is a war," Mr. Young said, "and we are the army of the Right." We are soldiers. They were coming closer, and the trembling ran down into her legs, but she stood firm, she stood her ground.

An old man standing on the sidewalk ahead of them was holding up a sign on a stick, and when he saw them he began to shake it up and down. It had some dark words on it and a picture of what looked like a possum. "What's that?" Sharee asked, and Delaware said, "Road kill." A woman popped up beside the man. Delaware thought she might be an escort. She was calling out to them. Sharee asked, "Who's she?" and Delaware said, "I don't know, come on," because the man was making her nervous. He had started making a kind of chopping motion with the sign, as if he was going to cut them down with the dead possum. The woman was pretty and nicely dressed, but instead of talking softer as they came close she yelled louder—"I'm praying! I'm praying for you!" "Why doesn't she go to church?" Sharee asked. She and Delaware were holding hands now, and they walked faster. The woman danced in front of them like a basketball player trying to stop a shot. Her voice had gone up into a scream, shrill, in Sharee's face: "Mom, Mom! Stop her! Stop her, Mom!" To shut out the screaming woman Sharee put her free arm up over her eyes and ducked her head down between her shoulders as they hurried up the four steps of the building. The man was also shouting now. Delaware felt the edge of his signboard strike her shoulder, a terrible feeling, not a pain but a shock, an invasion. It seemed like she had expected it, had known it would happen, but it was so terrible it stopped her and she could not move. Sharee tugged her forward to the metal-framed pebble-glass door of the clinic and pushed at the door. It did not move. Delaware thought it was locked and they were trapped, outside. The door opened outward fast, forcing them back. An angry woman stood there saying, "There's an injunction against you getting on this property and you'd better not forget it!" Sharee let go Delaware's hand and ducked way down and hid her head in both arms. Delaware looked around and saw where the angry woman was looking. "She's talking to them," she said to Sharee. "It's okay." She took Sharee's hand again, and they went inside, past the angry woman, who held the door for them.

They were in there now. They had got in. And Pitch Defilement was laughing at him inside the door, standing there laughing. Mary was talking in her squealy voice. Screaming and squealing and devil laughter. Norman raised up his sign and swung it down, driving it edgewise into the grass along the sidewalk in front of the Butcher Shop. Squealy Mary jumped aside and stood staring at him. He pulled the sign out and stood it upright. He felt better. "I'm going for a cup of coffee," he told Mary. Walking to the coffee shop, five blocks, carrying his sign erect, he thought all the time of what was going on inside the Butcher Shop. How they laid the girl down and gassed her and spread her legs and reached inside and found him and pried and pulled him out with the instruments. Stuck them into her, farther and farther in, grasped and pulled him out quivering and bloody. Stuck the knives up in between her legs and she writhed and moaned, showing her teeth, arching her back, gasping, panting. They pulled him out and he lay limp and little, dead. "God is my witness," he said aloud, and struck the stick of his sign against the pavement. He would find a way in. He would get in there and do what must be done.

The fat woman was behind the counter at the coffee shop. Young but fat, flaunting white, freckled arms. He didn't like the place but it was the only place to get coffee near the clinic. Lists of stuff with foreign names stood on the counter. People in expensive clothes came in and ordered the foreign names. Norman said, "I want a cup of plain American coffee," as he always did, and Lard Arms nodded. When he made the sign and started bringing it into the coffee shop, she had stopped speaking to him or smiling, and looked at him warily. That was how he wanted it. She put the filled cup on the counter. He put down exact change, took the cup to a table by the window, propping his sign up against the glass, and sat down. He felt tired. His hip hurt again, the grinding ache, and the coffee tasted weak and bitter. He stared at his sign. A long, curling hair, caught in the rough wooden edge, shimmered bright as gold wire in the sunlight coming through the glass. He reached out to pull it off. He could not feel it between his fingers, stiff and half-numbed from carrying the sign all morning.

*　　*　　*

They went in front of the reception desk and the angry woman went behind it. She said to Delaware, "You're Sharee."

"I'm Sharee," Sharee said.

"It's for her," Delaware said. She moved her head and shoulders, moved forward a little, to get the receptionist to look at her instead of at her mother. "I made the appointments for her. She saw Dr. Rourke."

The receptionist looked from one to the other. After a while she said, "Which one of you is pregnant?"

"Her," Delaware said, holding Sharee's hand.

"Me," Sharee said, holding Delaware's hand.

"Then she's Sharee Aske? Who are you?"

"Delaware Aske."

After a moment of silence the receptionist, whose name tag said she was Kathryn, accepted that, and turned to Sharee. "Okay, now there's one more form to sign," she said with professional firmness, "and you for sure didn't eat anything this morning, did you?" Sharee responded at once to the institutional tone. "No," she said, shaking her head. "And I can sign the form to sign."

Delaware saw but did not acknowledge the receptionist's sudden, understanding glance at her. It was her turn to be mad. "How come you let those people yell at us out there?" she asked in an abrupt, trembling voice.

"There isn't anything we can do," the receptionist said. "They can't come onto the property. The sidewalk's free, you know." Her voice was cool.

"I thought there were escorts."

"The volunteers usually come Tuesdays, that's the regular day. Dr. Rourke put you in today because he's going on vacation. Right there, see, honey?" She showed Sharee where to sign.

"Are they going to be there when we go out?"

"Where's your car?"

"We came on the bus."

Kathryn frowned. After a pause she said, "You ought to have a taxi going home."

Delaware had no idea what it cost to ride in a taxi. She had eleven dollars and Sharee probably had around ten dollars in her bag. Maybe they could ride the taxi part way. She said nothing.

"You can call it from here. Tell it to come to the back entrance, the doctors' parking lot. Okay, that's it. If you'll just sit down over there, Nurse will be with you in a minute." Kathryn gathered up the papers and went into some inner office.

"Come on," Delaware said, and went over to the sofa, two chairs, table-with-magazines arrangement. Sharee did not follow her for a while, but stood at the reception desk, looking around. Delaware still felt angry. "Come on!" she said.

Sharee came over, sat down on the sofa, and looked around from there. She had dressed for the occasion in her new jeans skirt, white cowboy boots, and blue satin cowboy jacket. Debi at the Head Shop had given her a wet-look curl in Daffodil Gold a week ago; sometimes she let it get too tangled up, but this morning it looked good, like a lion's golden mane, wild and full. Fear and excitement made her dark eyes shine. Looking at her, Delaware felt strange and sad. She picked up a magazine and stared at it.

It was kind of a pretty place. The sofa and chairs were aqua, her favorite color. Delaware was staring at a magazine and looking mad. Sometimes Delaware acted like she knew everything. She knew a lot but she wasn't the mama, she wasn't a mama at all. That was the thing she didn't know.

And Sharee did know. She remembered all of it, how she stuck out in front like a piano and had to pee all the time, and how her own mama had been so mad. Mama was always mad. It was a lot easier ever since she went to Alaska with David, it was a lot easier without her, just Sharee and Delaware in the apartment like it was meant to be. She remembered Delaware right from the first. That deep, deep softness and so small, like everything good in the world there where you can hold it and hug onto it and the milk came and it felt so good you didn't know if you were the baby or the baby was you. Delaware didn't remember that. But she did.

This time she had known right away, next morning. With Delaware she hadn't known because she wasn't thinking about babies then, she wasn't a mama, she was just thinking all the time about Donnie and loving him. Then when she started sticking out in front and her mama asked her about it, she and Donnie had broken up and she was going with Roddy. And then her mama had got so mad she had to stop going with Roddy or anybody. But this time, this was different. This time she was mad herself. She and Donnie had been in love. But this was different. What Mac did, in the car, at the drive-in, like that, like some zoo monkey, and then made her watch the rest of the movie. When he finally brought her home, she took a long shower, and in the shower she thought, something's happening. Next morning, she thought, something's happening. And then in two days when her period hadn't started she knew. She knew it wouldn't. And she was really mad. People thought she never got mad, but she did. It was like it started right there in her stomach, the same place, and spread out around her like a ball of hot red light. She didn't say, but she knew. She didn't know everything but she knew what was hers. What was inside her was hers. Mac had bent her arm and covered her mouth and stuck his thing into her just like some zoo monkey, but what happened inside her was hers, and she made it happen or not happen. Delaware had happened because she was hers, her own, she made her happen. This was different. This was a piece of her like a wart, like a scab you pick off. Like Mac had hurt her, cut her, made this wound inside her. There was a scab over the wound, and she was going to get it off and be whole. She wasn't some zoo monkey or some kind of wound, she was the person she was. That was what Linda always said when she was in the special class. Be the person you are, Sharee. You are a whole person, a lovely person. And you have a lovely daughter. Aren't you proud of her? You're a good mother, Sharee. I know, Sharee always said to Linda, and she said it in her head now. Sometimes Delaware thought she was the mama, but she wasn't. Sharee was. As soon as she said she wanted an abortion, Delaware got mad-looking and bossy and kept saying are you sure, are you sure, and Sharee couldn't explain to her why she was sure. You have to be a mama to understand, she said. Sometimes I think I am, Delaware said. Sharee knew what she meant. But that wasn't the kind of mama she meant. See, you were me until you were you, she told Delaware. I did you. I made you. But this one isn't like that. It isn't me, it's just like this wrong piece of me I don't want, like a hangnail. Jeez, Mama! Delaware said, and Sharee told her don't swear. Anyway, Delaware knew she knew what she was doing, and stopped asking are you sure, are you sure, and got the appointment with Dr. Rourke. Now she was sitting on the aqua sofa looking sad again. Sharee took her hand. "You are my knight in shining armor," she said. Delaware looked really surprised and then said, "Oh, jeez, Mama," but not mad. "Don't swear," Sharee said.

A nurse came in from the hall, a white woman in nurses' ugly pale green slacks and smock. She looked at them both and smiled. "Hi!" she said.

"Hi!" Sharee said, and smiled.

The nurse looked at the papers in her hand. "Okay, just checking," she said. "You're Sharee," she said to Delaware. "How old are you, Sharee?"

"Thirty-one," Sharee said.

"Right. And how old are you, honey?"

"I just came here with her," Delaware said.

"Yeah," the nurse said, looking confused. She stared at the papers and then at Delaware. "Then it isn't you that's here for the procedure?"

Delaware shook her head.

"But we need to know your age."

"What for?"

The nurse went official. "Are you a minor?"

"Yes," Delaware said, nasty.

The nurse turned and went off without saying anything.

Sharee picked up a magazine with Kevin Costner on the cover. "That man looks mad," she said, studying the photograph. "There's a man comes into the Frosty that looks mad like that all the time. He's really cute, though. He always gets the burger, no fries, and a strawberry softie. I don't like softies. They don't taste like anything. I like the hard ice cream. The old fashion. Old fashion hard ice cream. That's what you like too, isn't it?"

Delaware nodded, and then said "Yes," because Sharee needed you to say things. She had found that she wanted to cry, that is, that she was ready to cry, but didn't want to. The cause was the place on her shoulder where the man's sign had hit her. She wanted to cry because it hurt. She wasn't hurt. There was no mark on her jean-jacket. There would be nothing but a little bruise on her, something she'd see tonight when she undressed, or maybe nothing. But the place where the wooden edge of the sign had hit felt separately alive and hurtful. It made her heart cold and her throat swollen. She took deep breaths. The nurse came back.

"Okay, honey!" she said to the air between Sharee and Delaware.

Sharee jumped right up, her turn to dance. She got hold of Delaware's hand and tugged her up. "Come on!" she said, looking excited and pretty.

Norman had no right to just walk off like that. He was rude and selfish. His sign had not hit the girl in the shoulder, but if it had, if it had happened to, it could quite well have gotten both of them into trouble again. He had absolutely no right to do that. Swinging the sign around that way. He could have hit her. He had no right. He never obeyed orders. She would have to tell Mr. Young if Norman was so unreliable.

It was past nine and no one else would be coming. She looked down the block, but there was no one on foot, and none of the cars that came by slowed down. The terrible woman in her boots and a satin jacket like some circus performer, dragging the girl, her own daughter, you could see how alike they looked. That poor girl, she should pray for her. Only she was so angry, it was hard to pray. She could pray for the baby. And the father. Some poor boy, maybe a serviceman, a soldier, and no doubt he didn't even know, what did they care about *his* rights, nothing. Nothing but self, self, self. They had no right. They were animals.

Her throat was sore and her hands were trembling again. She hated it when her hands trembled. They said soldiers were afraid on the battlefield. But the trembling made her feel that she was like Grandpa Kevory sitting in the dark room that smelled of urine, his big, white hands trembling and shaking, you'll have to help me hold that cup, Mary, and then his head would jerk on purpose, and the water would run down his chin and he would shake Mary with his horrible shaking hands. No one would come.

They had no right to expect her to stand here alone. Norman was supposed to be here. He had volunteered. She had only come because she had missed last Tuesday because she had to substitute for the secretary at the school and always made up for time she missed. She had promised Mr. Young. Promises were important to her. No one else really cared. They came when they felt like it and never thought a thing about not being there if it was the least bit inconvenient. He had no right to walk off like that, leaving her alone without a sign or anything, thinking of nothing but himself. She had thought that maybe Mr. Young would happen to drive by and see her standing there keeping guard, keeping the faith. But there were no cars coming down the street. No one was coming. No one would come.

I am a soldier, she thought, and as always the thought moved through her making her strong. The brave boys were there defending the flag: she saw the flag waving bright and clean over clouds of oily blackness. She would ask Mr. Young if she could carry an American flag when she was on duty. American flags were on sale now at the mall, with yellow bows. I am a soldier of life. I am on guard. She stood straight and walked up and down the sidewalk in front of the clinic, turning on her heel at the end of the lawn. She was glad and proud to be a soldier.

Going down the hall Delaware said to the nurse, "Can I come in?" She had blown it not saying how old she was. The nurse walked right on and said, "Ask Doctor," in an eat-shit voice.

Why did they talk baby talk, anyhow, wait for Nurse, ask Doctor?

Dr. Rourke greeted her, "Hi Della." Pretty close. She asked him if she could stay with Sharee and he explained that they found it better not to

let relatives or significant others stay with the patient during the procedure. Sharee let go her hand with a big smile. She liked Dr. Rourke, a
handsome ruddy redhead, and had told Delaware several times that she
thought he was cute. She followed the nurse eagerly through a swinging
door. Dr. Rourke stayed in the hall with Delaware. "She'll be fine," he
said. Delaware nodded. "Aspiration is about as big a deal as a haircut," he
said in his pleasant voice. He waited for her to nod, and then said, "You
know I can do that tubal ligation. It's not a big deal, she won't know the
difference."

"That's the trouble," Delaware said.

He didn't get it.

"She understands this," Delaware said.

"I can explain the ligation to her so that she'll understand that she won't
have to worry about prevention anymore." He was warm, urgent with
generosity.

"Can you untie it?"

"She shouldn't be having," then a pause.

"She was brain damaged during birth," Delaware said. She had said it
fairly often. "It isn't genetic." Living proof, she stared at the doctor. He
began to look angry, like Kevin Costner, like everybody.

"Yes, all right," he said. Doctors never make mistakes. "But isn't it pretty likely that she'll forget to use the diaphragm again?"

"She didn't. She doesn't forget. This jerk she knows took her to a drive-
in and came on her in the car. So like she doesn't want some date-rapist's
side effects." She stared at the doctor, who looked impatient, so that she
hurried her words. "Maybe like someday she'd want to have another baby.
I can't choose that for her. How could I do that?"

He took a deep breath and let it out heavily.

"All right," he said. He turned away. "She'll be fine," he said again.
"Piece of cake." He went through the swinging doors.

Delaware stood a while in the hall and then thought it was stupid to
wait there. She went to ask the receptionist where the bathroom was. She
had begun to need to pee while they were on the bus, even before they
changed to the westside bus at Sixth.

Norman waited till he was sure Squealy Mary would be gone, but when he came back she was prissing up and down in front of the Butcher Shop as if she owned the place, straight-backed, turning around at each end of the lawn like some wind-up toy. What did her husband think he was doing letting her show herself on the street like that? They were all the same, showing their wares, prissing on their stick legs. Sucking up to Young. Oh, Mr. Young says this. Mr. Young says that. He knew what Young said. "Though I speak with tongues of men and angels." He knew what Young said and he knew his own business. None of their business. They ought to be home, keeping house and keeping out of the way. He started to turn back, to go around the next block hoping she would be gone when he came back to the corner. When he realized what he was doing, he stopped short. He strode down the block straight to her. "All right," he said, "I'll take over now."

"I'm on duty," she said in her high, shaking voice.

"I said I'm taking over," he said, and watched her head bobble and tremble. But she did not move. "I'm going to tell Mr. Young about your behavior," she squealed.

"I stand here," he said.

"All right, stand there," she said, and she started parading up and down again. He stood holding up his sign. Again and again she came past him, from the left, then from the right, heels clicking on the pavement, hands by her sides, shoulders held narrowed in. He thought to shove the stick of his sign up into her, keep her back straight! He never looked at her. He stood at his post in front of the steps of the Butcher Shop and held up his sign. God was his witness.

Sitting in the very clean green stall, Delaware decided to cry, to get the tears and the snot out in private while her mother was busy elsewhere, but of course they wouldn't come; she just made her throat feel sore. She unbuttoned her shirt and slipped it down to look at her right shoulder, between the neck and the shoulder cap, where she could feel the hurt of the blow of the man's sign. Nothing showed except some redness that was probably because she'd kept rubbing it with the hand Sharee wasn't holding.

Back on the sofa in the waiting room she picked up the magazine to hide behind. She read some words about something, but saw with great clarity all the time the legs and feet of the woman who had shouted about praying. She was wearing tan pantyhose and navy shoes with trim little heels. Her skirt was navy and white, white dots on navy, with pleats. Above that Delaware could not see her. She could only hear the screaming, "Mom, Mom." The man was wearing slacks, brown slacks and brown shoes, and a striped shirt. He had a saggy belly because he was old, but he had no face, because he was shaking the possum sign in front of it with that chopping motion, as if it was an ax, first up and down, then closer and closer to Sharee and Delaware, as they came closer and closer, till he hit.

She flinched.

"Delaware is a pretty name," Kathryn said behind the reception desk, and after a while the words came across to Delaware. "Where did you get that name?"

"My mother just liked how it sounded."

"It's unusual."

"There's Indiana Jones."

Kathryn laughed and nodded. She sorted papers in a file. "Just you and her live together?"

Delaware didn't mind, because Kathryn's voice was easy, or because her sugar-brown face looked tired now that it didn't look angry. "Yeah," she said.

"You in high school?"

"Yeah."

"Job?"

"Summers. She works at the Frost-T-Man. She always works."

"That's good," Kathryn said softly. She sorted some more and after a while said, "You doing okay in high school," not a question but as if she knew.

"Yeah."

"I bet you do. Go on to college?"

"Yeah I guess."

"That's good," Kathryn said again. "You'll do it."

The tears arrived suddenly and quietly and poured out and dried up. Delaware read reviews of a movie about a man who killed twenty women and a movie about children possessed by demons. The nurse came to the end of the hall and said, "Your friend's in recovery now, honey."

Delaware followed her down the hall. The nurse talked to her without turning around. "She was a little nervous so Doctor gave her a tranquilizer. She'll be a little woozy for half an hour, maybe. Then she can get dressed." She led Delaware into a clean, green, windowless room with three beds in it, two of them empty. Sharee was tucked into one, her curly, thick hair pulled back and her face without makeup, so that she looked like a kid. She focused on Delaware and smiled sleepily. "Hi, baby!" she said.

DEAR ELEGY THE SIZE OF A BLUEBERRY

Katy Day

Did I ever tell you how scared I was to swallow a watermelon seed?
Even as a child I knew the pit of me was no place to take root,
no sunlight penetrated my walls, and how could I let anything grow
hostile as me? You were never more than the size of a blueberry.
Dear elegy, that is all you'll ever be. I watch your sister watch
your sister watch your sister. She is mortified by what we've done
to the planet. Seal pup on a sheet of ice is someone's dinner on TV.
I watch your sister watch the pup get eaten alive. How she cries.
Is this real? Is this all real? And I don't lie. There is nothing we can do
to save you. Dear elegy, if I could, would I wind you back up
into the size of a blueberry? Dear elegy, dear, dear, the predator
needs to eat too. When she was two, your sister called them bluebabies.
I fed them to her in a small dish. Before she swallowed, she held each one
to her lips, gave it a kiss, soothed it with her little finger, told it she was sorry.
I didn't know the cherry blossom petals falling was beautiful too.
I wish I could show you snow in April, elegy, the way I wish I could show
you the cormorants flying in again, giving spring a second chance.

"FAREWELL, MY LOVE," FROM
THE SACRAMENT OF ABORTION

Ginette Paris

When I awoke that morning with a prickly feeling in the tip of my breasts and a subtle heaviness in my lower belly, I already knew I was pregnant. It was the first time it had happened when I didn't want it to happen. I thought about nothing else night and day for two weeks. I wanted to weigh everything, think of everything, all the alternatives, all the angles, taking into account the energy, the support, and the money that was available or even possible. No matter how I looked at it I came to the same conclusion: *alone with your children, with no help from their father,* I could accept a third child only through some dubious and costly form of heroism on my part. I would be giving life at the cost of swallowing up what little energy is left over from my job. I would be giving life to the detriment of my two small children who still need me a lot. And finally, I would lose the creative momentum in the work that I adore, the work that nourishes me, the work that was then and still is my contribution to the world. So the decision was clear, the appointment was made, and yet I was inconsolable. Several times a day, at the most unexpected moments, I was overcome with tears that I had more and more difficulty hiding from or justifying to my two children who are too young to understand. My heart was broken.

Paradoxically, during this period of reflection and calculation, my heart went about doing what it had done for my other children, loving this little creature curled up somewhere in my belly. I had long silent conversations with it. Why had it come? Why the absurd contraceptive failure? And above all why these waves of love for it, just as I was getting ready to refuse it a place, and thereby a life? The waves of love were so physical they were beyond my control; they submerged me every day in a painful and sensual way, like inflows of milk. I could only let myself glide along, feverish and amorous, full but without roundness yet, a little intoxicated as at the beginning of an affair. So why refuse all that? The absurd tearing apart of the abortion process seemed intolerable. I had to find an answer in the deepest part of my being.

During one of those inexplicable loving conversations I felt as if I was carrying in me someone who had previously died in the complete oblivion, anonymously, far from loved ones. And that it had come this time to refashion its departure from life. Just the departure. But this time in full and loving consciousness. And I could give that. I don't know where the idea came from, nor is it important; it gave meaning to what I was going through and allowed me to commit myself wholeheartedly to my decision and to my love.

Which I did, right up to the night before the appointment. The separation approached and wrung my heart. I cried so much that evening I thought a dam had burst. I asked myself: "What am I crying about? the death of a fetus? my own cruelty? a child I'll never know?" The friend who offered me a shoulder to cry on assured me the answer was not important, that I just needed to let myself feel the pain. But I felt I might find a clue in that answer.

I suddenly realized through my tears that I was afraid of being a bad mother to this baby. But bad mothers, if they exist at all, don't worry about harming their little ones. No, I wasn't a bad mother. On the contrary I was giving this creature the best of me, as I had done for the other two. All of this came to me with such certainty that a great sense of peace ran through me, and I went to sleep with only a few leftover sobs.

I woke up in the same frame of mind, calm, sad, and serene.

When my turn came I stretched out on the table, feet in the stirrups, ready to let my little darling go. But as soon as the doctor touched my cervix with the first metal instrument, I became terribly nauseated and drenched in sweat; everything toppled over backwards, the whole room went dark. They began to throw cold water in my face, check my blood pressure, call out to me, while I put my total effort into each breath so as not to lose contact. I was in a state of clinical shock, my body reacting violently to what it perceived as mortal danger. I wondered for a long time afterward why that had happened when I had been so at peace with my decision. I realized that, even if my head and my heart accepted the loss, my uterus still saw it as a mortal threat and was protesting with all its strength in an effort to protect its little lodger. I was very proud of my uterus for doing its job so well!

After everything calmed down the procedure moved gently ahead. One instrument, then another. Breathe, breathe, breathe. Say yes, say yes. And when the machine made its horrible, absurd noise I talked to it: "Farewell. Goodbye, my beautiful little love." And I cried. Then the machine shut off. It was over. My baby was really gone. The rest of the day went by smoothly, my hands on my belly for warmth, and a kind of muted pain or the memory of pain. A few tears of sorrow now and then. Only sorrow.

The next day life went back to normal. But curiously several friends I met asked me: "What's going on with you? You're so radiant today, you're absolutely glowing." What's going on is that I've just had an abortion and lived an impossible love and accomplished a great reconciliation with myself. But it was my secret and my gift.

Now, seven years later, I cry as I write this. Not with regret or remorse or guilt. Just tears of sadness. My darling is still alive but he is far away. And I am his mother.

Translated by Joanna Mott

AFTERLIFE

Joan Larkin

I'm older than my father when he turned
bright gold and left his body with its used-up liver
in the Faulkner Hospital, Jamaica Plain. I don't
believe in the afterlife, don't know where he is
now his flesh has finished rotting from his long
bones in the Jewish Cemetery—he could be the only
convert under those rows and rows of headstones.
Once, washing dishes in a narrow kitchen
I heard him whistling behind me. My nape froze.
Nothing like this has happened since. But this morning
we were on a plane to Virginia together. I was seventeen,
pregnant and scared. Abortion was waiting,
my aunt's guest bed soaked with blood, my mother
screaming—and he was saying kids get into trouble—
I'm getting it now: this was forgiveness.
I think if he'd lived he'd have changed and grown
but what would he have made of my flood of words
after he'd said in a low voice as the plane
descended to Richmond in clean daylight
and the stewardess walked between the rows
in her neat skirt and tucked-in blouse
Don't ever tell this to anyone.

WILL

THROUGH THE BLOOD

Busisiwe Mahlangu

At night, I hug my body to sleep
just to feel like it belongs to me.

Body has been dragged through mud
with a million hands grabbing their own pieces.
Body has been talked down into a hole
by a thousand mouths each taking a bite.
Body is exhausted of searching for ways to be mine.

There are many ways I whisper *I love you* to it.
Sometimes the whisper is a loud bang of protest.
Other times the whisper is just silence.
In this ugly world,
any whispering Black woman is a danger to herself.

You should swallow a storm.
You should eat the wind.
Any way to lock the voice in your throat.

Somewhere, a law is written against my body.
Here, I give my body all the love I have.
I eat as much fried chips as I can.
I stay up all night watching movies.
I walk into a hospital and terminate a pregnancy I don't need.

I don't explain to anyone why I did it.
There are only few words to say I did it for life.
I don't explain to anyone why I did it.

There isn't enough time for them to see
that the life I speak of is mine.

That I was alive before the abortion
and I am alive now—
That too is a life blessing.

When the world crumbles with their insults again,
I whisper to the empty space in my womb,
This is love
This is love
This is love, too.

RIGHT TO LIFE

Marge Piercy

A woman is not a pear tree
thrusting her fruit in mindless fecundity
into the world. Even pear trees bear
heavily one year and rest and grow the next.
An orchard gone wild drops few warm rotting
fruit in the grass but the trees stretch
high and wiry gifting the birds forty
feet up among inch long thorns
broken atavistically from the smooth wood.

A woman is not a basket you place
your buns in to keep them warm. Not a brood
hen you can slip duck eggs under.
Not a purse holding the coins of your
descendants till you spend them in wars.
Not a bank where your genes gather interest
and interesting mutations in the tainted rain.

You plant corn and you harvest
it to eat or sell. You put the lamb
in the pasture to fatten and haul it in
to butcher for chops. You slice
the mountain in two for a road and gouge
the high plains for coal and the waters
run muddy for miles and years.
Fish die but you do not call them yours
unless you planned to eat them.

Now you legislate mineral rights in a woman.
You lay claim to her pasture for grazing,
fields for growing babies like iceberg
lettuce. You value children so dearly
that none ever go hungry, none weep
with no one to tend them when mothers
work, none lack fresh fruit,
none chew lead or cough to death and your
foster homes are empty. Every noon the best
restaurants serve poor children steaks.

At this moment at nine o'clock a *partera*
is performing a tabletop abortion on an
unwed mother in Texas who can't get Medicaid
any longer. In five days she will die
of tetanus and her little daughter will cry
and be taken away. Next door a husband
and wife are sticking pins in the son
they did not want. They will explain
for hours how wicked he is,
how he wants discipline.

We are all born of woman. In the rose
of the womb we suckled our mother's blood
and every baby born has a right to love
like a seedling to sun. Every baby born
unloved, unwanted is a bill that will come
due in twenty years with interest, an anger
that must find a target, a pain that will
beget pain. A decade downstream a child
screams, a woman falls, a synagogue is torched,
a firing squad is summoned, a button
is pushed and the world burns.

I will choose what enters me, what becomes
flesh of my flesh. Without choice, no politics,
no ethics lives. I am not your cornfield,
not your uranium mine, not your calf
for fattening, not your cow for milking.
You may not use me as your factory.
Priests and legislators do not hold
shares in my womb or my mind.
This is my body. If I give it to you
I want it back. My life
is a nonnegotiable demand.

FROM *ZAMI: A NEW SPELLING OF MY NAME*

Audre Lorde

Two weeks later I discovered I was pregnant.

I tried to recall half-remembered information garnered from other people's friends who had been "in trouble." The doctor in Pennsylvania who did good clean abortions very cheaply because his daughter had died on a kitchen table after he had refused to abort her. But sometimes the police grew suspicious, so he wasn't always working. A call through the grapevine found out that he wasn't.

Trapped. Something—anything—had to be done. No one else can take care of this. What am I going to do?

The doctor who gave me the results of my positive rabbit test was a friend of Jean's aunt, who had said he might "help." This help meant offering to get me into a home for unwed mothers out of the city run by a friend of his. "Anything else," he said, piously, "is illegal."

I was terrified by the stories I had heard in school from my friends about the butchers and the abortion mills of the *Daily News*. Cheap kitchen-table abortions. Jean's friend Francie had died on the way to the hospital just last year after trying to do it with the handle of a number one paintbrush.

These horrors were not just stories, nor infrequent. I had seen too many of the results of botched abortions on the bloody gurneys lining the hallways outside the emergency room.

Besides, I had no real contacts.

Through winter-dim streets, I walked to the subway from the doctor's office, knowing I could not have a baby and knowing it with a certainty that galvanized me far beyond anything I knew to do.

The girl in the Labor Youth League who had introduced me to Peter had had an abortion, but it had cost three hundred dollars. The guy had paid for it. I did not have three hundred dollars, and I had no way of getting three hundred dollars, and I swore her to secrecy telling her the baby wasn't Peter's. Whatever was going to be done I had to do. And fast.

Castor oil and a dozen Bromo Quinine pills didn't help.

Mustard baths gave me a rash, but didn't help either.

Neither did jumping off a table in an empty classroom at Hunter, and I almost broke my glasses.

Ann was a licensed practical nurse I knew from working the evening shift at Beth David Hospital. We used to flirt in the nurses' pantry after midnight when the head nurse was sneaking a doze in some vacant private room on the floor. Ann's husband was a soldier in Korea. She was thirty-one years old—and *knew her way around,* in her own words— beautiful and friendly, small, sturdy, and deeply Black. One night, while we were warming the alcohol and talcum for p.m.-care back rubs, she pulled out her right breast to show me the dark mole which grew at the very line where her deep-purple aureola met the lighter chocolate brown of her skin, and which, she told me with a mellow laugh, "drove all the doctors crazy."

Ann had introduced me to amphetamine samples on those long sleepy night shifts, and we crashed afterward at her bright kitchenette apartment on Cathedral Parkway, drinking black coffee and gossiping until dawn about the strange habits of head nurses, among other things.

I called Ann at the hospital and met her after work one night. I told her I was pregnant.

"I thought you were gay!"

I heard the disappointed half-question in Ann's voice, and remembered suddenly our little scene in the nurses' pantry. But my experience with people who tried to label me was that they usually did it to either dismiss me or use me. I hadn't even acknowledged my own sexuality yet, much less made any choices about it. I let the remark lay where Jesus flang it.

I asked Ann to get me some Ergotrate from the pharmacy, a drug which I had heard from nurses' talk could be used to encourage bleeding.

"Are you crazy?" she said in horror. "You can't mess around with that stuff, girl; it could kill you. It causes hemorrhaging. Let me see what I can find out for you."

"Everybody knows somebody," Ann said. For her, it was the mother of another nurse in surgery. Very safe and clean, foolproof and cheap, she said. An induced miscarriage by Foley catheter. A homemade abortion. The narrow hard-rubber tube, used in postoperative cases to keep various body canals open, softened when sterilized. When passed through the cervix into the uterus while soft, it coiled, all fifteen inches, neatly into the womb. Once hardened, its angular turns ruptured the bloody lining and began the uterine contractions that eventually expelled the implanted fetus, along with the membrane. If it wasn't expelled too soon. If it did not also puncture the uterus.

The process took about fifteen hours and cost forty dollars, which was a week and a half's pay.

I walked over to Mrs. Muñoz's apartment after I had finished work at Dr. Sutter's office that afternoon. The January thaw was past, and even though it was only 1:00 p.m., the sun had no warmth. The winter grey of mid-February and the darker patches of dirty Upper East Side snow. Against my peacoat in the wind I carried a bag containing the fresh pair of rubber gloves and the new bright-red catheter Ann had taken from the hospital for me, and a sanitary pad. I had most of the contents of my last pay envelope, plus the five dollars Ann had lent me.

"Darling, take off your skirt and panties now while I boil this." Mrs. Muñoz took the catheter from the bag and poured boiling water from a kettle over it and into a shallow basin. I sat curled around myself on the edge of her broad bed, embarrassed by my half-nakedness before this stranger. She pulled on the thin rubber gloves, and setting the basin upon the table, looked over to where I was perched in the corner of the neat, shabby room.

"Lie down, lie down. You scared, huh?" She eyed me from under the clean white kerchief that completely covered her small head. I could not see her hair, and could not tell from her sharp-featured, bright-eyed face how old she was, but she looked so young it surprised me that she could have a daughter old enough to be a nurse.

"You scared? Don't be scared, sweetheart," she said, picking up the basin with the edge of a towel and moving it onto the other edge of the bed.

"Now just lie back and put your legs up. Nothing to be scared of. Nothing to it—I would do it on my own daughter. Now if you was three, four months, say, it would be harder because it would take longer, see? But you not far gone. Don't worry. Tonight, tomorrow, maybe, you hurt a little bit, like bad cramps. You get cramps?"

I nodded, mute, my teeth clenched against the pain. But her hands were busy between my legs as she looked intently at what she was doing.

"You take some aspirin, a little drink. Not too much though. When it's ready, the tube comes back down and the bleeding comes with it. Then, no more baby. Next time you take better care of yourself, darling."

By the time Mrs. Muñoz was finished talking she had skillfully passed the long slender catheter through my cervix into my uterus. The pain had been acute but short. It lay coiled inside of me like a cruel benefactor, soon to rupture the delicate lining and wash away my worries in blood.

Since to me all pain was beyond bearing, even this short bout seemed interminable.

"You see, now, that's all there is to it. That wasn't so bad, was it?' She patted my shuddering thigh reassuringly. "All over. Now get dressed. And wear the pad," she cautioned, as she pulled off the rubber gloves. "You start bleeding in a couple of hours, then you lie down. Here, you want the gloves back?"

I shook my head, and handed her the money. She thanked me. "That's a special price because you a friend of Anna's," she smiled, helping me on with my coat. "By this time tomorrow, it will be all over. If you have any trouble you call me. But no trouble, just a little cramps."

I stopped off on West 4th Street and bought a bottle of apricot brandy for eighty-nine cents. It was the day before my eighteenth birthday and I decided to celebrate my relief. Now all I had to do was hurt.

On the slow Saturday local back to my furnished room in Brighton Beach the cramps began, steadily increasing. Everything's going to be all right now, I kept saying to myself as I leaned over slightly on the subway seat, if I can just get through the next day. I can do it. She said it was safe. The worst is over, and if anything goes wrong I can always go to the hospital. I'll tell them I don't know her name, and I was blindfolded so I couldn't know where I was.

I wondered how bad the pain was going to get, and that terrified me more than anything else. I did not think about how I could die from hemorrhage, or a perforated uterus. The terror was only about the pain.

The subway car was almost empty.

Just last spring around that same time one Saturday morning, I woke up in my mother's house to the smell of bacon frying in the kitchen, and the abrupt realization as I opened my eyes that the dream I had been having of giving birth to a baby girl was in fact only a dream. I sat bolt upright in my bed, facing the little window onto the air shaft, and cried and cried and cried from disappointment until my mother came into the room to see what was wrong.

The train came up out of the tunnel over the bleak edge of south Brooklyn. The Coney Island parachute jump steeple and a huge grey gas storage tank were the only breaks in the leaden skyline.

I dared myself to feel any regrets.

That night about 8 p.m., I was lying curled tightly on my bed, trying to distract myself from the stabbing pain in my groin by deciding whether or not I wanted to dye my hair coal black.

I couldn't begin to think about the risks I was running. But another piece of me was being amazed at my own daring. I had done it. Even more than my leaving home, this action which was tearing my guts apart and from which I could die except I wasn't going to—this action was a kind of shift from safety towards self-preservation. It was a choice of pains. That's what living was all about. I clung to that and tried to feel only proud.

I had not given in. I had not been merely the eye on the ceiling until it was too late. They hadn't gotten me.

There was a tap on the alley door, and I looked out the window. My friend Blossom from school had gotten one of our old high school teachers to drive her out to see if I was "okay," and to bring me a bottle of peach brandy for my birthday. She was one of the people I had consulted, and she wanted to have nothing to do with an abortion, saying I should have the baby. I didn't bother to tell her Black babies were not adopted. They were absorbed into families, abandoned, or "given up." But not adopted. Nonetheless I knew she was worried to have come all the way from Queens to Manhattan and then to Brighton Beach.

I was touched.

We only talked inconsequential things. Never a word about what was going on inside of me. Now it was my secret; the only way I could handle it was alone. I sensed they were both grateful that I did.

"You sure you're going to be okay?" Bloss asked. I nodded.

Miss Burman suggested we go for a walk along the boardwalk in the crisp February darkness. There was no moon. The walk helped a little, and so did the brandy. But when we got back to my room, I couldn't concentrate on their conversation anymore. I was too distracted by the rage gnawing at my belly.

"Do you want us to go?" Bloss asked with her characteristic bluntness. Miss Burman, sympathetic but austere, stood quietly in the doorway looking at my posters. I nodded at Bloss gratefully. Miss Burman lent me five dollars before she left.

The rest of the night was an agony of padding back and forth along the length of the hallway from my bedroom to the bathroom, doubled over in pain, watching clots of blood fall out of my body into the toilet and wondering if I was all right, after all. I had never seen such huge red blobs come from me before. They scared me. I was afraid I might be bleeding to death in that community bathroom in Brighton Beach in the middle of the night of my eighteenth birthday, with a crazy old lady down the hall muttering restlessly in her sleep. But I was going to be all right. Soon it was going to be over, and I would be safe.

I watched one greyish mucous shape disappear in the bowl, wondering if that was the embryo.

By dawn, when I went to take some more aspirin, the catheter had worked its way out of my body. I was bleeding heavily, very heavily. But my experience in the OB wards told me that I was not hemorrhaging.

I washed the long stiff catheter and laid it away in a drawer, after examining it carefully. This implement of my salvation was a wicked red but otherwise innocuous-looking.

I took an amphetamine in the thin morning sun and wondered if I should spend a quarter on some coffee and a danish. I remembered I was supposed to usher at a Hunter College concert that same afternoon, for which I was to be paid ten dollars, a large sum for an afternoon's work, and one that would enable me to repay my debts to Ann and Miss Burman.

I made myself some sweet milky coffee and took a hot bath, even though I was bleeding. After that, the pain dimmed gradually to a dull knocking gripe.

On a sudden whim, I got up and threw on some clothes and went out into the morning. I took the bus into Coney Island to an early-morning food shop near Nathan's, and had myself a huge birthday breakfast, complete with french fries and an english muffin. I hadn't had a regular meal in a restaurant for a long time. It cost almost half of Miss Burman's five dollars, because it was kosher and expensive. And delicious. Afterward, I returned home. I lay resting upon my bed, filled with a sense of well-being and relief from pain and terror that was almost euphoric. I really was all right.

As the morning slipped into the afternoon, I realized that I was exhausted. But the thought of making ten dollars for one afternoon's work got me wearily up and back onto the weekend local train for the long trip to Hunter College.

By mid-afternoon my legs were quivering. I walked up and down the aisles dully, hardly hearing the string quartet. In the last part of the concert, I went to the ladies' room to change my Tampax and the pads I was wearing. In the stall, I was seized with a sudden wave of nausea that bent me double, and I promptly and with great force lost my $2.50-with-tip Coney Island breakfast, which I had never digested. Weakened and shivering, I sat on the stool, my head against the wall. A fit of renewed cramps swept through me so sharply that I moaned softly.

Miz Lewis, the Black ladies'-room attendant who had known me from the bathrooms of Hunter High School, was in the back of the room in her cubby, and she had seen me come into the otherwise empty washroom.

"Is that you, Autray, moaning like that? You all right?" I saw her low-shoed feet stop outside my stall.

"Yes ma'am," I gasped through the door, cursing my luck to have walked into that particular bathroom. "It's just my period."

I steadied myself, and arranged my clothes. When I finally stepped out, bravely and with my head high, Miz Lewis was still standing outside, her arms folded.

She had always maintained a steady but impersonal interest in the lives of the few Black girls at the high school, and she was a familiar face which I was glad to see when I met her in the washroom of the college in the autumn. I told her I was going to the college now, and that I had left home. Miz Lewis had raised her eyebrows and pursed her lips, shaking her grey head. "You girls sure somethin'!" she said.

In the uncompromising harshness of the fluorescent lights, Miz Lewis gazed at me intently through her proper gold spectacles, which perched upon her broad brown nose like round antennae.

"Girl, you sure you all right? Don't sound all right to me." She peered up into my face. "Sit down here a minute. You just started? You white like some other people's child."

I took her seat, gratefully. "I'm all right, Miz Lewis," I protested. "I just have bad cramps, that's all."

"Jus' cramps? That bad? Then why you come here like that today for? You ought to be home in bed, the way your eyes looking. You want some coffee, honey?" She offered me her cup.

"Cause I need the money, Miz Lewis. I'll be all right; I really will." I shook my head to the coffee, and stood up. Another cramp slid up from my clenched thighs and rammed into the small of my back, but I only rested my head against the edge of the stalls. Then, taking a paper towel from the stack on the glass shelf in front of me, I wet it and wiped the cold sweat from my forehead. I wiped the rest of my face, and blotted my faded lipstick carefully. I grinned at my reflection in the mirror and at Miz Lewis standing to the side behind me, her arms still folded against her broad, short-waisted bosom. She sucked her teeth with a sharp intake of breath and sighed a long sigh.

"Chile, why don't you go on back home to your mama, where you belong?"

I almost burst into tears. I felt like screaming, drowning out her plaintive, kindly, old-woman's voice that kept pretending everything was so simple.

"Don't you think she's worrying about you? Do she know you in all this trouble?"

"I'm not in trouble, Miz Lewis. I just don't feel well because of my period." Turning away, I crumpled up the used towel and dropped it into the basket, and then sat down again, heavily. My legs were shockingly weak.

"Yeah. Well." Miz Lewis sucked her teeth again, and put her hand into her apron pocket.

"Here," she said pulling four dollars out of her purse. You take these and get yourself a taxi home." She knew I lived in Brooklyn. "And you go right home, now. I'll cross your name off the list downstairs for you. And you can pay me back when you get it."

I took the crumpled bills from her dark, work-wise hands. "Thanks a lot, Miz Lewis," I said gratefully. I stood up again, this time a little more steadily. "But don't you worry about me, this won't last very long." I walked shakily to the door.

"And you put your feet up, and a cold compress on your tummy, and you stay in bed for a few days, too," she called after me, as I made my way to the elevators to the main floor.

I asked the cab to take me around to the alley entrance, instead of getting out on Brighton Beach Avenue. I was afraid my legs might not take me where I wanted to go. I wondered if I had almost fainted.

Once indoors, I took three aspirin and slept for twenty-four hours.

When I awoke Monday afternoon, the bed-sheets were stained, but my bleeding had slowed to normal and the cramps were gone.

I wondered if I had gotten some bad food at the foodshop Sunday morning that had made me sick. Usually I never get upset stomachs, and prided myself on my cast-iron digestion. The following day, I went back to school.

On Friday, after classes, before I went to work, I picked up my money for ushering. I sought out Miz Lewis in that auditorium washroom and paid her back her four dollars.

"Oh, thank you, Autray," she said, looking a little surprised.

She folded the bills up neatly and tuck them back into the green snap-purse she kept in her uniform apron pocket. "How are you feeling?"

"Fine, Miz Lewis," I said jauntily. "I told you I was going to be all right."

"You did not! You said you *was* all right and I knew you wasn't, so don't tell me none of that stuff, I don't want to hear." Miz Lewis eyed me balefully.

"You gon' back home to your mama, yet?"

THE SPRING OF LIFE

Ann Townsend

The newts swam agitated in the jar
he cradled in his hands and held
toward three girls on the bank,
while I crouched on the hotel bathroom's
cold tile, bile on my tongue.
What a terrible painting, I thought,
then threw up in the sink.
The newts jostled against the glass
until water dampened and feathered
the lace of his cuff.
From my vantage point on the floor,
the painting felt filled with PRESSURE.
The title, seen from an angle:
"The Spring of Life."
His shoes were wet with mud,
spring water quickening at his feet.
These girls, their dresses
pin-tucked across the bodice—

One looked unhappy.
One looked enraptured.
One looked stupid but perhaps
the bathroom light failed to flatter her.
That day the newt on the ultrasound
was no larger than a peppercorn.
Five weeks along, the sonographer said,
scrolling the wand across my belly
as she scanned what swam inside.
It's so small, I said.

My voice had love in it.
Still at 1:50 I swallowed the pills.
I could throw them up—I could—
was the thought minutes past.
You'll expel the uterine contents
eventually, the doctor said
from far behind her desk.
It took four days,
then into my hand you swam,
faceless face curled in a puddle,
sliding against the placental blood,
the cord a length of thread quivering.
Grapeskin, mucosal smear I cradled
in my palm. Look, he said,
at the newts in their jar
swimming briskly in their orbit.
One girl held her skirts in fists.

One girl reached for them.
Look, he said. The water swirled
and eddied with the motion
of his wrist. Naked in your blood
you curled, asking your impossible question.
I weighed you in my hand,
slipped you into a soft wrapper,
kissed the wrapper,
tucked you beneath the roots of a tree.
What tree I will not say—
let them look and never find you.
I pressed my foot down
to close your door.
Of course I loved you,
even as I set my heel against the dirt.

FROM *for colored girls who have considered suicide when the rainbow is enuf*

Ntozake Shange

lady in red
these men friends of ours
who smile nice
stay employed
and take us out to dinner

lady in purple
lock the door behind you

lady in blue
wit fist in face
to fuck

lady in red
who make elaborate mediterranean dinners
& let the art ensemble carry all ethical burdens
while they invite a coupla friends over to have you
are sufferin' from latent rapist bravado
& we are left wit the scars

lady in blue
bein betrayed by men who know us

lady in purple
& expect
like the stranger
we always thot waz comin

lady in blue
that we will submit

lady in purple
we must have known

lady in red
women relinquish all personal rights
in the presence of a man
who apparently cd be considered a rapist

lady in purple
especially if he has been considered a friend

lady in blue
& is no less worthy of being beat within an inch of his life
bein publicly ridiculed
havin two fists shoved up his ass

lady in red
than the stranger
we always thot it wd be

lady in blue
who never showed up

lady in red
cuz it turns out the nature of rape has changed

lady in blue
we can now meet them in circles we frequent for companionship

lady in purple
we see them at the coffeehouse

lady in blue
wit someone else we know

lady in red
we cd even have em over for dinner
& get raped in our own houses
by invitation
a friend

     [The lights change, and the ladies
     are all hit by an imaginary slap, the
     lady in red runs off up left.]

lady in blue
eyes

lady in purple
mice

lady in red
womb

lady in blue & lady in purple
nobody

     [The lady in purple exits up right.]

lady in blue
tubes
tables
whitewashed windows
grime from age wiped over once
legs spread
anxious
eyes crawling up on me

eyes rollin' in my thighs
metal horses gnawing my womb
dead mice fall from my mouth
i really didn't mean to
i really didn't think i cd
just one day off . . .
get offa me alla this blood
bones shattered like soft ice-cream cones

i cdnt have people
lookin' at me
pregnant
i cdnt have my friends see this
dyin danglin' between my legs
& i didn't say a thing
not a sigh
or a fast scream
to get
those eyes offa me
get them steel rods outta me
this hurts
this hurts me
& nobody came
cuz nobody knew
once i was pregnant & shamed of myself.

[The lady in blue exits stage left.]

FROM "INTRODUCTION TO 'THE IDEA' AND 'THE IDEA'"

Hilde Weisert

INTRODUCTION TO THE IDEA

"Hello, Flower." It's my aunt in a late-night phone call, drinking, ready to talk. Last week it was about her sister in Rye mistakenly baking the rat in the oven. This week, it's about me. Or not me. What she has decided she needs to tell me, before she passes on, before the memory is gone, is what my mother said back when all the wives (sisters, sisters-in-law) lived together in the big apartment on the North Side of Chicago and the husbands were all at war. I've always thought of it as a sort of paradise for them, independent, unencumbered, going to work and having martinis and taking care of each other's babies.

I've heard a lot of the stories of that golden time. Now here's another one. "You know, you weren't always so special. Actually, you weren't even wanted. You should know this. I'm sure your mother never told you. About how she cried. She told me, she just didn't know if she could go on with it. With your father. He was gone, and she felt like she could breathe for the first time in ten years. She didn't want him back.

"She had a good job, actually quite glamorous, you know, she'd tell us about it when she came home after work, stories about Dave Garroway and Hugh Downs and the other men at the radio station. Your mother liked men. She was the center of attention there, the only woman. 'How can I go through it all again?' she said. I bet you didn't know any of that."

"No, I didn't." As I listen, I'm skeptical. All I ever heard were stories about what a beautiful baby I was, how beloved. "Angel child," my grandfather called me. But listening to my drunk aunt ramble, I think, maybe. Maybe she did think about bailing on it all, bailing out of committing another lifetime to my father. She'd told me about the other pregnancy, my brother, years before me, when she stood on the Wabash Avenue Bridge and thought about throwing herself into the river. I'd ask her, but I can't, because she's dead.

"Right, you had no idea, did you? Everyone thought she was so perfect. You have no idea the things she told me."

I think my aunt is crying softly on the other end of the phone, a signal that the conversation is almost over. "I don't, I know I really don't. Don't worry about it, whatever it was, it's okay. You should get some sleep." Some snuffles, something more about Flower, the line clicks off. Interesting, I think. Here's the trump card in every right-winger's anti-choice deck—"How would you feel if. . . ?" Well, this is how I feel.

THE IDEA
Why would this be the worst thing?
That you held me as an idea you could turn
into one thing, or the other? Mother,
I can almost imagine it.

NOT YOURS

Angelique Imani Rodriguez

> *No woman has an abortion for fun.*
>
> —Elizabeth Joan Smith

I sat on the toilet for so long that my legs fell asleep. The three pregnancy tests I had taken were on the white tiled floor, originally all in one box, the third packaged as a bonus test, as if the company that made them knew I would need all three to confirm what I already recognized in my body. My period hadn't come and though I had experienced irregularity with my cycle in the past, this time felt different. I could feel it in the cramps low and dull in my belly, in the way my stomach churned in the morning, the lightheadedness.

I fucking knew it. But I still took all three tests.

I sat there afterwards, staring at them, lined up in a row, six blue lines telling me that I was pregnant.

How the fuck did I let this happen?

The guy I slept with was the guy everyone in my family wanted me to stay away from but who I harbored such an infatuation for that I kept going back, rebounding after breakups by rolling around in his bed. I got pregnant after one of those he-always-makes-me-feel-better rebound moments when the condom broke. We stared at each other as if the world were ending.

"I pulled out in time. You should be okay." His voice was soft, reassuring.

I thought I would be. I was wrong.

I didn't tell him I was pregnant. I justified it with, "Well, he ain't looking for me," or "He's chilling with that other chick now, so who cares?" The reality was that I was afraid to tell him because I was afraid of what his reaction would be. I didn't want to hear "Are you sure it's mine?" I didn't want to hear him say I should keep it.

Because I knew I was going to have an abortion.

Not my proudest moment, no. He deserved to know.

Years later, he confessed his love for me over a candlelit table. I could see the love in his eyes, the hope of a brilliant future fluttering in his eyelashes. I could hear his voice trembling with nervousness as he said it.

"When I kiss you, I feel it in my stomach. I have loved you for a long time. I can't see anyone else having my children, Angie."

I put my hand over his and said, "I have something to tell you."

Our relationship was never the same after that, the rebound moments ended, though a warm friendship remained. He has a son now. His son looks just like him.

I made the choice to have an abortion with the knowledge that I had put myself in a place I didn't want to be. I was twenty-two, completely unprepared for a child both mentally and emotionally, not to mention being financially incapable of supporting a new life. I was just starting a new job, I had no degree under my belt, no plan of action for my life, no dreams. I didn't want to start a family with a dude who I thought didn't know I existed outside of my vagina and what I could make him feel in bed. I didn't want to have a child knowing that I could not provide it with the life it deserved, with the support it deserved.

I was reeling from a life not yet faced. I hadn't even begun to work on the layers of shit I had to unlearn because I was in the midst of creating more fucking layers.

I was not ready, and I didn't want to be a mother.

That was my reasoning and I have been damned to hell and judged for it by people in my life.

By myself.

* * *

My mother was diagnosed with breast cancer the summer I found out I was pregnant. I cried when I found out because I knew that me confessing to her would be a burden for her to carry during such a delicate time for her. She didn't need this.

And I was the one who had done this.

I told her I was pregnant over the phone while I was on a break from working in a cell phone store. I walked into a CD store and browsed the

stacks of CDs as I dialed her number. We chatted for a few minutes before I said anything.

"Mami, I haven't gotten my period yet."

"What are you telling me?"

"I . . . I took a test and . . ."

"Imani, are you pregnant?"

I let the words slam into me, a gavel coming down. An explanation
rushed out of me, an urge to plaster the holes, to solve the issue before she
could say anything.

"I am. But don't worry, I am going to set up an abortion. It's the only
thing I can do right now. I'm not doing well at work because I've been so
sick. I don't have a degree. I don't have anything together for my future. I
can't have a kid, Mami . . . and now with you being sick, I . . ."

"Don't use that as a reason for what you decided to do. You should've
been smarter, Imani," she said.

The moment froze, suspended in the air, a judgment and a reprimand.

The day I had my abortion, my mother poked her head in my bedroom
when she got home from work. She sat on the edge of the bed as I cried. I
don't remember what was said. I don't remember crying in her lap or her
putting her hand on me.

I remember her sitting at the edge of the bed, a heavy sigh leaving her.
I remember thinking to myself that I wanted her to not have that look
on her face, the one where her hopes for me died. I remember wanting to
apologize.

But I didn't.

Instead, after she left, when I was alone, I wrote in my journal that I
wanted to die in the folds of my bedsheets.

* * *

When a friend became pregnant with her second child, she didn't tell me.
It was a year or so after I had my abortion. She asked me to talk to her
about it one day as we chatted on the phone. She told me she wanted to
hear all of the specifics.

So, I did. I told her every single detail, from the man handing me a paper that said I was a murderer at the entrance, to the hours of waiting in rooms with uncomfortable chairs covered in faded burgundy fabric, to the ultrasound and the cashew-sized baby on the screen I couldn't look at, to the fear and the shame I carried. All of it. I was honest, my previously bottled emotions spilling out. I wouldn't want to be forced to make that decision again but I told her that it was the smartest decision for me to make.

When I found out she was pregnant, it wasn't even from her, it was from another friend. The pregnancy was mentioned casually over a phone call.

"Wait, she's pregnant? Is she keeping the baby?"

"Yeah. She told me that she could never do what you did."

I held on to the shame of that for years before we spoke about it.

Her beautiful daughter is eleven years old now, a vibrant shiny spirit and I am so happy to know her. Her mother and I remain friends, learning from each other that every woman has her own journey to follow, and every woman has a right to her own choice.

BEING A WOMAN

Jennifer Goldwasser

A woman must
Choose
When met with
The male counterpart
Of her warrior-self
To take life or to give.
She must remember
Death is also a
Woman who plows the fields

AN ABORTION DAY SPELL FOR TWO VOICES*

Annie Finch

As I turn your blood back to the earth,
I am life, you are death, and we kiss
Through the fire that is my freedom's birth.

By the womb of our love's endlessness,
As you turn my blood back to the earth,
I am death, you are life. And we kiss

As we move *through the deep*, giving forth
To the web that is love-woven bliss,
By *the fire that is* our freedom's birth.

---

* Those interested in ritual healing may be interested in the ritual I wrote and used success-
fully to heal after my own abortion. It is available on my website and as an appendix to
my book *Among the Goddesses: An Epic Libretto in Seven Dreams* (Red Hen Press, 2010).

I THINK SHE WAS A SHE

Leyla Josephine

I think she was a she.
No.
I know she was a she, and I think that she would have looked just like
me:
full cheeks, hazel eyes, and thick brown hair that I could have plaited
into dreams at night.
I would have stuck glow-up stars on her ceiling
and told her they were fireflies to protect her from the dark.
I would have told her stories about her grandfather.
We could have fed the swans at the park.
She would have been like you too, long limbs
with a sarcastic smile and the newest pair of kicks.
She would have been tough, tougher than I ever was,
and I would have taught her all that my mother taught me,
and I would have taken her to all the museums
and there she could see the bone dinosaurs,
and look to them and wonder about all the things that came before
she was born.
She could have been born.
I would have made sure that we had a space on the wall to measure her
height as she grew.
I would have made sure I was a good mother to look up to.
But I would have supported her right to choose.
To choose a life for herself, a path for herself.
I would have died for that right, just like she died for mine.
I'm sorry, but you came at the wrong time.
I am not ashamed. I am not ashamed. I am not ashamed.
I am so sick of keeping these words contained.
I am not ashamed.

I was a teenage girl with a boy she loved between her thighs that felt
very far away.
Duvet days and dole don't do family planning well.
I am one in three. I am one in three. I am one in three.
I had to carve down that little cherry tree that had rooted
itself in my blood and blossomed in my brain.
A responsibility I didn't have the energy or age to maintain.
The branches casting shadows over the rest of the garden.
The bark causing my thoughts, my heart to harden.
I am not ashamed. I am not ashamed. I am not ashamed.
It's a hollowness? that feels full, a numbness that feels heavy.
Stop trying to fit how this feels on an NHS bereavement brochure
already.
I am allowed to feel it all, I am allowed to feel.
I am woman now, I am made of steel,
and she wasn't a girl and she wasn't a boy.
That's just the bullshit you receive to keep you out of parliament
and stuck on maternity leave.
Don't you mutter murder on me.
70,000 per year. 70,000 per year. 70,000 per year.
Dead.
That's 192 per day
from coat hangers, painkillers, the back-alley way.
Don't you mutter murder on me.
Worldwide performing abortion like homework,
looking for the answer in the groves in our palms, the bulges on our
bellies,
the whispers in our ears,
only to be confronted with question marks.
Women have been hidden away in the history books.
After all it's history:
His story.
Well this is herstory, ourstory, goddamn it.
This is my story,
and it won't be written in pencil and erased with guilt.

It will be written in pen and spoken with courage.

You will hear it on the radio on your way to work, you will study it in English.

You will read it on the coffee shop's bulletin boards next to the flyer about yoga for babies.

Because I am not ashamed, I am not ashamed, I am not ashamed.

I am woman now.

I will not be tamed.

I have determination that this termination will still have a form of creation.

It will not be wasted.

This is my body. This is my body. This is my body.

I don't care about your ignorant views.

When I become a mother, it will be when I choose.

REGARDING CHOICE

Alexis Quinlan

be all you
can be* you
can be all
you can be
you (who) you
can you can
you can can
be all you
be
you
can

---

* "Be All You Can Be" was the advertising slogan of the United States Army from 1980
to 2001.

WE WOMEN

Edith Södergran

We women, we are so near the brown earth.
We ask the cuckoo what he expects from the spring,
we throw our arms around the cold pines,
we search in the sunset for signs and advice.
I loved a man once, he didn't believe in anything . . .
He came one cold day with empty eyes,
he went one heavy day with forgetfulness on his brow.
If my baby doesn't live, it's his . . .

Translated from the Swedish by Samuel Charters

"DON QUIXOTE'S ABORTION," FROM *DON QUIXOTE*

Kathy Acker

When she was finally crazy because she was about to have an abortion, she conceived of the most insane idea that any woman can think of. Which is to love. How can a woman love? By loving someone other than herself. She would love another person. By loving another person, she would right every manner of political, social, and individual wrong: she would put herself in those situations so perilous the glory of her name would resound. The abortion was about to take place:

From her neck to her knees she wore pale or puke-green paper. This was her armor. She had chosen it specially, for she knew that this world's conditions are so rough for any single person, even a rich person, that person has to make do with what she can find: this's no world for idealism. Example: the green paper would tear as soon as the abortion began.

They told her they were going to take her from the operating chair to her own bed in a wheeling chair. The wheeling chair would be her transportation. She went out to look at it. It was dying. It had once been a hack, the same as all the hacks on Grub Street: now, as all the hacks, was a full-time drunk, mumbled all the time about sex but now no longer not even never did it but didn't have the wherewithal or equipment to do it, and hung around with the other bums. That is, women who're having abortions.

She decided that since she was setting out on the greatest adventure any person can take, that of the Holy Grail, she ought to have a name (identity). She had to name herself. When a doctor sticks a steel catheter into you while you're lying on your back and you do exactly what he and the nurses tell you to; finally, blessedly, you let go of your mind. Letting go of your mind is dying. She needed a new life. She had to be named.

As we've said, her wheeling bed's name was "Hack-kneed" or "Hack-neyed," meaning "once a hack" or "always a hack" or "a writer" or "an attempt to have an identity that always fails." Just as "Hackneyed" is the glorification or change from nonexistence into existence of "Hack-kneed," so, she decided, "catheter" is the glorification of "Kathy." By taking on such a name which, being long, is male, she would be able to become a female-male or a night-knight.

Catharsis is the way to deal with evil. She polished up her green paper.

In order to love, she had to find someone to love. "Why," she reasoned to herself, "do I have to love someone in order to love? Hasn't loving a man brought me to this abortion or state of death?"

"Why can't I just love?"

"Because every verb to be realized needs its object. Otherwise, having nothing to see, it can't see itself or be. Since love is sympathy or communication, I need an object which is both subject and object: to love, I must love a soul. Can a soul exist without a body? Is physical separate from mental? Just as love's object is the appearance of love; so the physical realm is the appearance of the godly: the mind is the body. This," she thought, "is why I've got a body. This's why I am having an abortion. So I can love." This's how Don Quixote decided to save the world.

What did this knight-to-be look like? All of the women except for two were middle-aged and dumpy. One of the young women was an English rose. The other young woman, wearing a long virginal white dress, was about nineteen years old and Irish. She had packed her best clothes and jewels and told her family she was going to a wedding. She was innocent: during her first internal, she had learned she was pregnant. When she reached London Airport, the taxi drivers, according to their duty, by giving her the run-around, made a lot of money. Confused, she either left her bag in a taxi or someone stole it. Her main problem, according to her, wasn't the abortion or the lost luggage, but how to ensure neither her family nor any of her friends ever found out she had had an abortion, for in Ireland an abortion is a major crime.

Why didn't Don Quixote resemble these woman? Because to Don Quixote, having an abortion is a method of becoming a knight and saving the world. This is a vision. In English and most European societies, when a woman becomes a knight, being no longer anonymous she receives a name. She's able to have adventures and save the world.

"Which of you was here first?" the receptionist asked. Nobody answered. The women were shy. The receptionist turned to the night-to-be. "Well, you're nearest to me. Give me your papers."

"I can't give you any papers because I don't have an identity yet. I didn't go to Oxford or Cambridge and I'm not English. This's why your law says I have to stay in this inn overnight.

"As soon as you dub me a knight—by tomorrow morning—and I have a name, I'll be able to give you my papers."

The receptionist, knowing that all women who're about to have abortions're crazy, assured the woman her abortion'ld be over by nighttime. "I, myself," the receptionist confided, "used to be mad. I refused to be a woman the way I was supposed to be. I traveled all over the world, looking for trouble. I prostituted myself, ran a few drugs—nothing hard—exposed my genitalia to strange men while picking their pockets, broke-and-entered, lied to the only men I loved, told the men I didn't love the truth that I could never love them, fucked one man after another while telling each man I was being faithful to him alone, fucked men over, for, by fucking me over, they had taught me how to fuck them over. Generally, I was a bitch.

"Then, I learned the error of my ways. I retired . . . from myself. Here . . . this little job . . . I'm living off the income and property of others. Rather dead income and property. Like any good bourgeois," ending her introduction. "This place," throwing open her hands, "our sanctus sanitarium, is all of your place of safety. Here, we will save you. All of you who want to share your money with us." The receptionist extended her arms. "All night our nurses'll watch over you, and in the morning," to Don Quixote, "you'll be a night." The receptionist asked the knight-to-be for her cash.

"I'm broke."

"Why?"

"Why should I pay for an abortion? An abortion is nothing."

"You must know that nothing's free."

Since her whole heart was wanting to be a knight, she handed over the money and prayed to the Moon. "Suck her, Oh Lady mine, this vassal heart in this my first encounter; let not Your favor and protection fail me in the peril in which for the first time I now find myself."

Then she lay down on the hospital bed in the puke-green paper they had given her. Having done this, she gathered up her armor, the puke-green paper, again started pacing nervously up and down in the same calm manner as before.

She paced for three hours until they told her to piss again. This was the manner in which she pissed: "For women, Oh Woman who is all women who is my beauty, give me strength and vigor. Turn the eyes of the strength and wonderfulness of all women upon this one female, this female who's trying, at least you can say that for her, this female who's locked up in the hospital and thus must pass through so formidable an adventure."

One hour later they told her to climb up pale green-carpeted stairs. But she spoke so vigorously and was so undaunted in her bearing that she struck terror in those who were assailing her. For this reason they ceased attacking the knight-to-be: they told her to lie down on a narrow black-leather padded slab. A clean white sheet covered the slab. Her ass, especially, should lie in a crack.

"What's going to happen now?" Don Quixote asked.

The doctor, being none too pleased with the mad pranks on the part of his guest (being determined to confer that accursed order of knighthood or nighthood upon her before something else happened), showed her a curved needle. It was the wrong needle. They took away the needle. Before she turned her face away to the left side because she was scared of needles, she glimpsed a straight needle. According to what she had read about the ceremonial of the order, there was nothing to this business of being dubbed a night except a pinprick, and that can be performed anywhere. To become a knight, one must be completely hole-ly.

As she had read—which proves the truth of all writing—the needle when it went into her arm hardly hurt her. As the cold liquid seeped into her arm which didn't want it, she said that her name was Tolosa and she was the daughter of a shoemaker. When she woke up, she thanked them for her pain and for what they had done for her. They thought her totally mad; they had never aborted a woman like this one. But now that she had achieved knighthood, and thought and acted as she wanted and decided, for one has to act in this way in order to save this world, she neither noticed nor cared that all the people around her thought she was insane.

AMERICAN ABORTION SONNET #7

Ellen Stone

For Rebekah in St. Louis

Missouri, I thought you were a woman.
Must be the way your name curls round me.
Just like a river carries travelers home,
your arms should keep your people safe—and free.

Missouri, you cannot have my daughter.
She is not bound to God by apron strings,
views this hard world with a clear-eyed manner,
makes her choices, no matter what life brings.

Missouri, you know a woman's body
is like soil. Her fertile ground is cursed
when men force her to bloom. So now, if she
decides to not bear fruit, you'll say she must?

Missouri, she loves you, and she will grieve,
but, like that river, she will also leave.

AFTER THE ABORTION, AN OLDER WHITE PLANNED PARENTHOOD VOLUNTEER ASKS IF MY HUSBAND IS HERE & SQUEEZES MY THIGH AND SAYS, "YOU MADE THE RIGHT DECISION," AND THEN "LOOK WHAT COULD HAPPEN IF TRUMP WERE PRESIDENT, I MEAN, YOU MIGHT NOT EVEN BE HERE."

Camonghne Felix

What else could   I say   except I   agree with you   really am bulldozed with grief

my strength a whistle in this cold parabola   everything an archnemesis   all of my self a bowl

Instead I said   yes   he is here I mean my fiancé   I know   I made   the right decision   of course

he is okay   we already   agreed on this plan   I mean look what could   happen   she says Hillary is

our only option   I say I know   Look   I haven't told anyone this   I am quitting my job   she says   my

god   I think I   understand your   geography no   not really   I mean I'm   leaving my good

god government job   I work for   the   governor   she says are you running   I say   sort of I

mean   I'm   going to work   for Hillary   for   America   because   we're looking at a critical   fault

otherwise

they need

my colloquial   criticalities my   totalizing   abnormalities my   compounds and constructs of trajectory this is the only how I know to be had   I belong to the   people but not your   people I mean

I'm saying   my people   you wouldn't understand this   I'm stealthy and svelte   I can

counter-swell   any tide   I   am   prepared   she holds my hands   says thank you

you must know that it   matters all of it   matters

in the bed next to me a   woman solid with   anguish and sleep   is ruby with the wash of   bleeding out

and   no one is   tending   I look down at myself, curried

with the same deep pink   realize no one is   tending in the taxi cab   my husband I mean fiancé

holds my hands his fingers   all lead   a dying creek at the pitch of   a sword   he   says I'm okay   when

you're okay   you have to be okay   remember they're waiting   on you   for days I slept like this

my open submission   to the cosmic opacities   of time   my body shedding its just-built

mouth   he lies awake   meters between   us

steady   documenting a   decay   my black studies professor said   what are you here for

if   you're not   willing   to die for it   I   Get   It   I'm   skunked with   the fear of   what

I'm willing to kill for it   where do I file this nuance   to whom do I spare this   complaint

When I woke   he'd been fed   watered   wanted for   realized he

didn't need my indecision   or   his inability to travel   time   or   the   bottomless   glamour of

conquering the unknown   I know now the octane faults of our   ontological   duties

the war between becoming and the formal   unbecoming of   being called and they said they   needed me   they

did so I went   we bellied the hole   I did what my   mother asked of me   stepped into the heavy quilt of her   ill-drawn life   I did   my fucking   job I did   what I was told in the end all my

chemistry a performance of gratitude   all my insides turned   purple with storms   on election

           night I flipped from   the

channel to channel   neurosis in practice   as   weighted predictions balance

draw I think   no oh please   don't

you know what I've bled   for this in the distance a lone   voice is soprano with cheer and the silence

settles in   succeeds with   bare platitudes

I swear my love   I did my best I worked with   what I know I tilled   I paved I

foraged labored a land

got us   some   growth settled   my currents*   left   all of us

famished bloody   hungry at   war.

---

* and somehow, as I don't remember, I got out the pool.

NEW WORLD ORDER

Lisa Alvarado

They call us criminals
as they stand in front of clinics.
They call us criminals
and sit in judgment on Capitol Hill.
They call us criminals
because we do what is forbidden.
We say women are not receptacles.
We say women are not breeders.
In their world,
they would pass sentence on us.
In their world,
we will kneel with coat hangers,
darkness covering us;
the dark flow of life
running down open legs.
In their world,
we will climb the narrow stairs
meeting shadowy men.
Men with scalpels
that sing with fear and old blood;
who will take our money
and promise to keep silent.
In their world,
I have done what is forbidden.
I am a criminal.
My crime is that I chose myself instead of a child.
My sin is that I am not sorry.
My sentence is I know I am not safe.

FROM *DAUGHTER OF EARTH*

Agnes Smedley

Then I knew something was wrong—something that drowned the music of "work, money, school." I complained to my landlady of a sickness each morning. She laughed coarsely. Sex and birth were huge indecent jokes to her.

"Yer goin' to have a baby!"

I turned and left the room when she said that. Fear, bitterness, hatred, gone from me for weeks, swept through me again like a hurricane. Everything that was hopeful vanished—I saw myself plunged back into the hell from which I was struggling—the hell of nagging, weeping women, depending for food and clothing upon my husband, with study but a dream. I looked upon my baby with concentrated hatred.

"I won't have a baby!" I announced to my landlady, as if it were her fault. "I won't. I'll kill myself first .... tell me what to do."

I rode along the desert roads, madly, alighted, and ran until exhausted. Wept and hated, wept and hated. Still the sickness came each morning. I stopped eating, thinking in my ignorance that the enemy within me would stop growing. The doctor who had his office above the pool room told me that he could do nothing to help me—it was illegal; I could go to a drugstore and get something. He instructed me verbally. If things went wrong, he said, I could call him and he would have the legal right to finish the operation.

"How much will it cost?"

"I'll make a special price for you of one hundred dollars."

All the money I had saved! Still it would be cheaper. I paid his consultation fee of ten dollars, and stopped at the drugstore. But I did not even know how my own body was constructed. In secret and blind terror I tried to learn. I could not—my mind was unclear, terror-stricken. I had not the least idea of the nature of the workings of my body, of the conception or nature of growing life.

"This is your fault," I wrote at last to Knut. "Come and get me out of this or I shall kill myself."

Days passed and no reply came. One night I lay face downward in the bath tub, but could not hold myself under the water. My landlady, hearing the splashing and choking, ran in and pulled me out.

But Knut came—he had traveled for days. He went to the doctor. "You either operate or we go to the city and have it done," he told him. "My wife will kill herself within a week if something is not done."

The doctor gravely examined my lungs and heart and said it was as he suspected—I had tuberculosis and the operation was necessary! Childbirth would be most dangerous.

When I came back to consciousness Knut was sitting by my bedside, smiling. I lay gazing at him and hating the smile—hating it, hating it, hating it! How dared he smile when my body was an open wound, when I had stood before eternity . . . how dared he smile when a child had been taken from my body, and now my body and mind called for it . . . how dared he smile when I felt alone in space . . . how dared he . . . he a man who knew nothing, nothing, nothing!

All my money was gone and Knut had returned to the desert. I would not let him pay for the operation . . . it was my body and I would let no man pay for it, I said. He had become very pale at that.

Then I learned of a normal school beyond the mountains and I wrote to ask if I could not work my way through. The answer came after a month, and it said yes, I could make some money but not enough. I wrote Knut a letter and said, "Now I am going and I am not coming back . . . if you ever want to see me you must come where I am."

THE ABORTION

Anne Sexton

Somebody who should have been born
is gone.

Just as the earth puckered its mouth,
each bud puffing out from its knot,
I changed my shoes, and then drove south.

Up past the Blue Mountains, where
Pennsylvania humps on endlessly,
wearing, like a crayoned cat, its green hair,

its roads sunken in like a gray washboard;
where, in truth, the ground cracks evilly,
a dark socket from which the coal has poured,

Somebody who should have been born
is gone.

the grass as bristly and stout as chives,
and me wondering when the ground would break,
and me wondering how anything fragile survives;

up in Pennsylvania, I met a little man,
not Rumpelstiltskin, at all, at all . . .
he took the fullness that love began.

Returning north, even the sky grew thin
like a high window looking nowhere.
The road was as flat as a sheet of tin.

Somebody who should have been born
is gone.

Yes, woman, such logic will lead
to loss without death. Or say what you meant,
you coward . . . this baby that I bleed.

CONFESSION #1

Yesenia Montilla

If I knew back then that I'd one day be a poet,
that one day my words would matter,
that one day I might mean something to someone,
I might not have had that abortion in '93. Or maybe
I would have, but under a different name. Anne
Sexton taught me everything about lust and shame
but nothing about regret. No matter, when they ask
why I did it, I'll tell them I was young
& I desperately wanted the fruit to fall far
from the tree, that is to say, my mother's face
is a red stone and I wanted to be a diamond—

FROM *FROG*

Mo Yan

Every woman of childbearing age in Dongfeng Village who had given birth twice had had their tubes tied off if one of them had been a son. If they'd had only girls, Gugu said she'd taken village customs into consideration and chosen not to force the women to have their tubes tied; however, they were required to insert IUDs. After a third pregnancy, even if they were all girls, the tubes had to be tied. Zhang Quan's wife was the only woman in any of the more than fifty commune villages who had neither had her tubes tied nor used an IUD, and she was pregnant again. Gugu's boat had traveled to Dongfeng Village during a downpour expressly to get Zhang Quan's wife to go to the health center for an abortion. While Gugu was on her way, Party Secretary Qin Shan phoned the branch secretary of Dongfeng Village, Zhang Jinya, ordering him to take all steps and use any force necessary to deliver Zhang Quan's wife to the health center. When Gugu reached the village, Zhang Quan was standing guard at his gate with a spiked club; eyes red, he was shouting almost insanely. Zhang Jinya and a team of armed militiamen were watching from a distance, not daring to get close. Zhang's three daughters were kneeling in the doorway, noses running, tears flowing, as they cried out in what seemed to be practiced unison: Merciful elders and uncles, mothers and aunts, brothers and sisters, spare our mother . . . she has a rheumatic heart. If she has an abortion she will die for sure—if she dies, we will be orphans.

Gugu said the effects of Zhang Quan's sympathy-seeking ruse were excellent—many of the women watching were in tears. Of course, some were resentful. As women with two children and IUDs, or three without a son, had had their tubes tied, they had no sympathy for Zhang Quan's wife. A bowl of water must be carried level, Gugu said, and if we let Zhang Quan's wife have a fourth child, those women would skin me alive. If Zhang Quan prevailed, the red flag would be lowered, but that would be nothing compared to halting the progress of family planning. So I gave the signal, Gugu said, and walked up to Zhang Quan with Little Lion and Huang Qiuya. Smart, courageous, loyal Little Lion moved in front of me in case Zhang used his club. I pulled her back behind me. The petty bourgeois intellectual, Huang Qiuya, was fine for a bit of technical help, but when push came to shove, she was so scared she nearly fell apart.

Gugu strode straight up to Zhang. The language he used on me, she said, was worse than you could imagine, and if I repeated it, the words would dirty your ears and my mouth. But my heart was hard as steel then, and my personal safety was not a concern. Go ahead, Zhang Quan, call me any insulting thing you want—whore, bitch, murderous devil—I don't care. But your wife is going with me. Going where? To the health center.

With eyes fixed on Zhang's savage face, she walked right up to him. His three daughters rushed up to her, cursing like their father, the two smaller ones holding on to Gugu's legs, while their older sister rammed her head into Gugu's midsection. All three were on her like leeches, and she tried to fight them off. A sharp pain in her knee, she knew, meant she'd been bitten. Another head to her midsection knocked her flat on her back. Little Lion grabbed the oldest girl by the neck and flung her to the side; but the girl came right back at her, driving her head into the Little Lion's midsection, where her belt buckle hit her on the nose, which started to bleed. Seeing the blood on the back of her hand a moment later produced a mixture of terror and dread. As Zhang rushed to club Little Lion like a raving maniac, Gugu ran up and put herself between them. The club hit her forehead. She fell again. Are you people dead? Little Lion screamed at the onlookers. Zhang Jinya and his militiamen ran up and wrestled Zhang Quan to the ground, pinning his arms behind him. His daughters looked like they wanted to come to his aid, but they too were wrestled to the ground by Party women. Little Lion and Huang Qiuya wrapped a bandage from the medicine kit around Gugu's head; blood seeped through the wrapping almost at once. They wrapped it some more. Gugu's head was spinning and her ears rang; she saw stars and everything took on the color of blood; people's faces were as red as cockscomb, even the trees seemed to blaze like torches.

Hearing what was happening, Qin He came over from the river and froze when he saw Gugu's injury. Then a howl burst from his lips, followed by a mouthful of blood. When people rushed up to help him, he pushed them away and staggered forward as if drunk, picking up the club, now stained with Gugu's blood, and raised it over Zhang's head. Put that down! Gugu shouted as she struggled to her feet. You're supposed to be watching the boat. What are you doing here? Making things worse. With a sheepish look, Qin He dropped the club and walked slowly back to the riverbank.

Gugu pushed Little Lion away and walked up to Zhang Quan. Qin He was still howling as he walked towards the riverbank—Gugu was too focused on glaring at Zhang Quan to look behind her. The man was still cursing, but there was fear in his eyes now. Let him go, she said to the militiamen who held him by the arms. When they hesitated, she repeated herself. Let him go!

Give him back his club! she demanded.

One of the militiamen dragged the club up and tossed it down in front of Zhang.

Pick it up! Gugu said with a sneer.

Zhang mumbled, I'll fight anyone who tries to end the Zhang family line!

Fine! Gugu said. You're a brave man. She pointed to her head. Hit me here, she said, right here! She took a couple of steps closer. Me, she shouted, Wan Xin. This is the day I put my life on the line! Back when a little Japanese soldier came at me with a bayonet, I wasn't afraid, so why should I be afraid of you today?"

Zhang Jinya came up and shoved Zhang Quan. Apologize to Chairwoman Wan!

I don't need his apology, Gugu said. Family planning is national policy. If we don't control our population, there won't be enough to feed and clothe our people, and a failure in education will lower the quality of our population, keeping the country weak. Sacrificing my life for national family planning is a small price to pay!

Zhang Jinya, Little Lion said, get on the phone and send for the police.

Zhang Jinya kicked Zhang Quan. On your knees! he demanded, and ask Chairwoman Wan for forgiveness.

Forget it! Gugu said. Zhang Quan, you could get three years in prison for hitting me, but I won't lower myself to your level, and I'm willing to let you go. There are two paths open to you now. You can have your wife go with me to the health center for an abortion, where I will personally perform the procedure and guarantee that she comes through it safely. Or I can turn you over to the police for punishment; then, if your wife goes with me willingly, fine. If not—she pointed to Zhang Jinyan and the militiamen—they will take her there.

Zhang Quan was in a crouch, holding his head in his hands and sobbing. Three generations have had only one son each. Will I be forced to see that line ended? Open your eyes, Heaven . . .

Zhang Quan's wife walked out of the yard; she was weeping, and had straw in her hair. Obviously, she'd been hiding in a haystack.

Chairwoman Wan, be kind, forgive him. I'll go with you.

Gugu and Little Lion were heading east on the riverbank behind our village, probably to make a report at brigade headquarters. But as they entered the lane that would take them there, the woman on the boat—Zhang Quan's wife—came out of the cabin and jumped into the river.

Translated from the Chinese by Howard Goldblatt

GETTING INTO TROUBLE

Jacqueline Saphra

Mr. Giles said he didn't want the school used as a political jousting ground and made me take the pro-abortion poster down, although I explained patiently that the ancient Romans didn't mind it, that the church was okay with it in the thirteenth century until quickening (when, they said, the soul enters the body), and the statute books condoned it.

Michelle, who was a Born Again, insisted life was ensouled even before conception, Clare believed that once the fetus was viable it had a right to exist, my mother said she didn't believe in the primacy of the unborn, and I sat in biology wondering if I had a soul, and if I did, where it was. I daydreamed of knitting needles, coat hangers, and permanganate.

After my mother came back from hospital—unharmed, grateful, and political, only to find that my stepfather had spent her emergency money on canvasses and Carlsberg and dinner with that woman in Portobello Road—she sent me straight to the doctor to get myself a Dutch cap.

My boyfriend who was stupid but useful told all his friends I was a virgin and forced me to see *Close Encounters of the Third Kind* three times and listen to nothing but Genesis, which I preferred to the Sex Pistols, because I never believed there was No Future, not when my mother was, at least for now, empty-wombed and full of soul, as she stirred a pot of her famous lentil soup, not yet tied by blood to the man she loved.

THE CHILDREN'S CRUSADE

Ana Blandiana

In 1966, Nicolae Ceaușescu of Romania issued Decree 770, a law that criminalized all family planning, enforced monthly gynecological exams, and required women to birth at least four children. First published in 1984 in the student magazine Amfiteatru, *the legendary poem below was at first hand-copied and shared in secret.*

An entire people
still unborn,
but condemned to be born,
lined up before being born,
fetus by fetus,
an entire people
that cannot see, or hear, or understand,
but marches on
through the aching bodies of women,
through the blood of mothers
who are never asked.

Translated from the Romanian by Chrisula Stefanescu

A PROMISE

Gloria Steinem

When I was in high school, the greatest shame was to get pregnant. It was the worst thing that could happen to you. It was most likely to get you banished from your family, disapproved of by your neighborhood, turned into somebody who was clearly not a "nice girl." And in my neighborhood growing up—a very working-class, factory-working neighborhood in Toledo—there were clearly only two types of girls: nice and not nice. There was also very little knowledge about reliable contraception, so most of the people who I knew got married either before they graduated from high school or immediately afterwards—and most of them got married, at least in part, because they had to.

As a senior in college, I was engaged to a wonderful man, but not somebody I should have married. That would have been a disaster for both of us. So I broke off the engagement with him and that was part of my motivation for taking the fellowship and going to India. He and I were together again just before I left, and soon I kind of knew—or feared—that I was pregnant. I was living in London, waiting for my visa to India, which took a very long time, working as a waitress with no money, no friends, dark winter days, trying to figure out what to do.

You know, in a way, ambivalence about abortion is a function of its legality. I was not ambivalent. I was desperate. I did not want to see any way that I could possibly give birth to someone else and also give birth to myself. It was just impossible. So there was not one moment, not one millisecond, of me thinking it would be a good idea to have a child.

In London at the time (the mid-1950s) if you got two physicians to say that having a child would endanger your health or your mental health, then it was possible to get a legal abortion—not easy, but it was possible. After many weeks of fear, confusion, and magical thinking that I would somehow have a miscarriage, I found this wonderful doctor who had many writers and poets as his patients, and he said, "All right, I'll help you. But you must promise me two things. You must never tell anyone my name and you must promise me to do what you want with your life."

So he signed what was necessary and sent me to a woman surgeon, who gave me an anesthetic, so I was not conscious for the actual procedure. Afterwards, she gave me pills and told me to be aware of the amount of bleeding, but it wasn't much. So I just went home and stayed in bed for the weekend and went back to work as a waitress—but with such a feeling of lightness and freedom and gratitude.

I thought everybody was supposed to feel guilty, so I used to sit and think and think and think; but I could not make myself feel guilty for even a moment. Far from feeling guilty, it was the first time I had taken responsibility for my own life. It was the first time I hadn't been passive. That I had said, *No, I'll take responsibility for my own life, I am going to make a decision*. And you know, to this day, I would raise flags on all public buildings to celebrate the chance I had to make that decision.

SPIRIT

POEM FOR MYSELF AND MEI: CONCERNING ABORTION

Leslie Marmon Silko

Chinle to Fort Defiance, April 1973

The morning sun
        coming unstuffed with yellow light
        butterflies tumbling loose
        and blowing across the Earth.
They fill the sky
        with shimmering yellow wind
        and I see them with the clarity of ice
        shattered in mountain streams
                where each pebble is
                speckled and marbled
     alive beneath the water.

All winter it snowed
mustard grass
and springtime rained it.

Wide fancy meadows
warm green
        and butterflies are yellow mustard flowers
                spilling out of the mountain.

There were horses
     near the highway
     at Ganado.
And the white one
        scratching his ass on a tree.

They die softly
against the windshield
and the iridescent wings
                    flutter and cling
                              all the way home.

A GOOD WOMAN WOULD NEVER

Sylvia Beato

for years you told no one
how you cried yourself to sleep
after the doctor held your hand
"are you sure about this?"

how you cried yourself to sleep
while blood poured down your legs
"are you sure about this?"
and protestors booed outside the clinic

while blood poured down your legs
you stopped believing in god
and protesters booed outside the clinic
because a good woman would never

you stopped believing in god
"are you sure about this?"
because a good woman would never
for years you told no one

ABORTION ISN'T BEAUTIFUL

Nicole Walker

It is hard to write anything beautiful about abortion. I can see the beauty in snapping off a couple of yellow flowers to give more energy for the current tomato plant to grow. I can see the beauty in pulling off the dead petals of geranium. I can see the beauty in cutting off a branch that sucks too much water from the main trunk of the apple tree, but it's hard to see the beauty in the suctioning out of fetal tissue. Perhaps the image becomes too medical right off the bat. Make it narrative? Is there beauty in a waiting room? Beauty in stirrups? Beauty in ultrasounds?

I've had two abortions. One when I was eleven and one when I was twenty-one. The one when I was twenty-one was much more beautiful than the first. In Portland, Oregon, there is some kind of advanced thought about abortion. The doctor inserts flags of seaweed inside your cervix to let it expand naturally. The lights are dimmed. It's still not beautiful but it's not punitive.

Perhaps it's that abortion is not natural that makes it hard to find beauty, but the flower snapping, the petal pulling, the branch cutting isn't natural either, and petals and branches are supposedly natural. A skirt can be beautiful. A blanket. A bowl.

If we called abortion "miscarriage," or maybe "optional miscarriage," would it be more beautiful? If you had to opt in to a pregnancy or you would automatically be opted out, like registering for the health benefits you may not have which might cause you to opt out of the pregnancy, would that make the choice easier or harder? If nature stopped pregnancy's "progressing" and instead stayed still until you checked the "go-ahead pregnancy" box, would the choice seem as sinister? Why is choosing an ending morally more troubling than choosing a beginning?

I don't think it is death that robs abortion of its beauty. Many deaths have poignancy and significance. To sit beside your mother as you hold her hand while her breathing slows and slows and stops is beautiful. Beautiful that you got to be there. Beautiful that the moment was charged with meaning. But the fetus doesn't know it's alive. Its hands are not holdable.

Is the choice "yes" always more beautiful than the choice "no"? Did I choose to have my current children? I mean these very children? I chose to try to get pregnant, or at least not try very hard not to. I didn't know that a fetus would be Zoe. I didn't know a fetus would be Max. They are beautiful to be sure but was the choice itself beauty? I can't pinpoint the moment of choice so it's hard to say. There were beautiful moments being pregnant, but I think I may have borrowed that beauty from a TV show I once watched, and who Zoe and Max are has very little to do with what beauty I pregnantly fantasized.

I cannot make abortion beautiful even when I think of my children that I would not have had had I not had the abortions I did. It's still not beautiful that I went to college and that I went to PhD school or that I am writing this right now. It's not beautiful that I was eleven years old. It was not beautiful at all when the doctor said, you are too young to be having sex, and I was like, yes, that's true, you should tell the guy who molested me, but she was right. I was too young. Maybe there's something beautiful there?

If nature is beautiful then so is rain and snow and slippery snakes. Grass and gases and tardigrades and fluke worms and flat worms and round worms. How, if fluke worms are beautiful, can abortion not be? It's not because it signals absence—vacuums and sleep and silence, space and time and free lunch are beautiful. It's not the non-baby that makes abortion not beautiful.

It might be the stirrups and the blood that make abortion not beautiful but that is the stuff of women and some women are found to be beautiful even while lying back in stirrups and while bleeding. Perhaps beauty here just means fuckable but indeed every abortion signals some level of fuckability. Whether the fucking was by consent or by rape, the sex itself still worked.

Rape and abortion are two unbeautiful things that go together in many sentences. Some people won't even let a raped refugee in the custody of ICE get an abortion. Those people might become Supreme Court justices. I would like to know those people's opinion on beauty.

Maybe abortion cannot be beautiful because beauty is not something you can do. You can possess beauty and be beautiful. You can look for beauty and call truth beauty but you cannot beauty your day away. Choice is about verbs, and beauty does not move. Beauty is permanent, memorialized, stuck in a place. Choice winds its way through canyons and through fluttering trees, cutting down mountains and making mulch for next year's buds. What a gift it is to be able to move like wind.

MAGDALEN

Amy Levy

All things I can endure, save one.
The bare, blank room where is no sun;
The parcelled hours; the pallet hard;
The dreary faces here within;

The outer women's cold regard;
The Pastor's iterated "sin";—
These things could I endure, and count
No overstrain'd, unjust amount;

No undue payment for such bliss—
Yea, all things bear, save only this:
That you, who knew what thing would be,
Have wrought this evil unto me.

It is so strange to think on still—
That you, that you should do me ill!
Not as one ignorant or blind,
But seeing clearly in your mind

How this must be which now has been,
Nothing aghast at what was seen.
Now that the tale is told and done,
It is so strange to think upon.

You were so tender with me, too!
One summer's night a cold blast blew,
Closer about my throat you drew
That half-slipt shawl of dusky blue.

And once my hand, on summer's morn,
I stretched to pluck a rose; a thorn
Struck through the flesh and made it bleed
(A little drop of blood indeed!)

Pale grew your cheek you stoopt and bound
Your handkerchief about the wound;
Your voice came with a broken sound;
With the deep breath your breast was riven;
I wonder, did God laugh in Heaven?

How strange, that you should work my woe!
How strange! I wonder, do you know
How gladly, gladly I had died
(And life was very sweet that tide)

To save you from the least, light ill?
How gladly I had borne your pain.
With one great pulse we seem'd to thrill,—
Nay, but we thrill'd with pulses twain.

Even if one had told me this,
"A poison lurks within your kiss,
Gall that shall turn to night his day:"
Thereon I straight had turned away—
Ay, tho' my heart had crack'd with pain—
And never kiss'd your lips again.

At night, or when the daylight nears,
I hear the other women weep;
My own heart's anguish lies too deep
For the soft rain and pain of tears.

I think my heart has turn'd to stone,

A dull, dead weight that hurts my breast;
Here, on my pallet-bed alone,
I keep apart from all the rest.

Wide-eyed I lie upon my bed,
I often cannot sleep all night;
The future and the past are dead,
There is no thought can bring delight.

All night I lie and think and think;
If my heart were not made of stone,
But flesh and blood, it needs must shrink
Before such thoughts. Was ever known
A woman with a heart of stone?

The doctor says that I shall die.
It may be so, yet what care I?
Endless reposing from the strife?
Death do I trust no more than life.

For one thing is like one arrayed,
And there is neither false nor true;
But in a hideous masquerade
All things dance on, the ages through.

And good is evil, evil good;
Nothing is known or understood
Save only Pain. I have no faith
In God, or Devil, Life or Death.

The doctor says that I shall die.
You, that I knew in days gone by,
I fain would see your face once more,
Con well its features o'er and o'er;

And touch your hand and feel your kiss,
Look in your eyes and tell you this:
That all is done, that I am free;
That you, through all eternity,
Have neither part nor lot in me.

THE YEAR THE LAW CHANGED

Carol Muske-Dukes

Waiting hours, each of us in a curtain-stall.
Two men outside, mopping the floor and hall,
Shouting "Murderers!" at us. Were they janitors?
Or medics who'd read our charts & diagnosed?
If men could get pregnant, it would end up
a sacrament, Gloria said. Simone said, We
know that no woman takes it lightly. *So*
could both be true. In class in San Francisco
our teacher spoke of his wife who lost
a child to leukemia, haunted by her ghost
& told by her shrink to write about blood.
She wrote about a vampire and her book shot
to fame so maybe she forgot the one who
never grew into her name. When my name
was called I went to have it done and then knew
I had my life back but covered myself with blood—
mine and some not—but still of me. I don't know
what I mean by "of me," it's undefined & even
the shouting accusers won't cross that line. I had to
swear I was clinically mad to have it done. What's
madness to the men in white: they clean the world
of residue like me and all the blood from both of us.

I BLOOMED

Angie Masters

In my womb
freedom bloomed,
Intoxicated with blood
With the glow of the moon.

My veins burned,
My heart beat fast
A thousand fingers aimed at my forehead.

My wings are not white,
From deep within
I birthed myself anew.

I loathed that which was established for me,
I was born again, tearing up the earth.

Let the rose become violet,
Let the tender find strength.

I reemerged fertile
I am the mother of my ideas,
I am the mother of my works.

I renounced the idea
of an obligation that must be fulfilled
That instead of giving me wings
made me suffer against my will.

I accept my nature

and my ovulation
I take it back
and I take back my decision.

FROM "CORONA AND CONFESSION"

Ellen McGrath Smith

III
I was sixteen and chosen to deliver the Word,
one of a handful of city spies reporting
to the Human Life Group in the suburbs.
Some students played music, some sports—

but we did more: We were concerned
for the unborn child. On meeting nights,
I'd have them drop me off before the turn
onto my street, then take my flight

into the dark, not wanting them to see
where I lived (not split-level,
scruffy lawn). They took my energy
with them, in their smart cars, out to Bethel
Park, a wholesome place for wholesome families.
I was one of them, not one of these.

IV
I was one of them, not one of these
hard girls who sprayed their hair stiff,
lugged large combs, let their feet freeze
waiting for some guys to drive by. If

I noticed them at all, it was
by way of contrast. There was one
I'd heard had two abortions, in my class,
and with that knowledge my eyes ran

over her as she came in to morning roll
call. At one of our assemblies,
as we showed the cacciatoried, pulled-
apart fetuses on the wide and trembling
portable screen, I thought of D with a cruel
precision, gloried in the anguish of her soul.

V
They glory in the anguish of the souls
who try to quickly enter clinics
ten years later. Children fed full
of venom damn them passing, mimics

of their parents and their pastors.
It is not a grand conversion, how I left them.
I was in college, no longer ruled by my father,
no longer cowed by my church, when D came

into focus as a living, feeling woman
(that I'd failed to see is hardest to confess):
dim auditorium, her long legs on platforms,
the nun stepping from the aisle to let her pass;
then, minutes later in the girls' room,
sobbing, her friends murmuring *Come on.*

VI
A sob in the midst of friends—how commonly
a woman's body melts to this in labor,
sorrow, grief. But the Virgin had been summoned
from the circle and cycles of her neighbors,

set apart from her gender's company.
I'd been praised by my parish priest
for my efforts, my unwitting complicity
in an ages-old patriarchal contest.

In art class, I drew a full-figured body
on her knees praying—to God, to the moon—
for her period to come, a blue hooded
sweatshirt pulled over a bloated abdomen.
That frightened young woman was me,
and I understood what I had done.

THE PROMISE

Tara Betts

we had a talk pregnant with pauses
about what I could not write about
while still able to pray and breathe.
I agreed to that small silence since
she wanted my moment to dodge
judgment, gossip about mothering.
I promised on Catholic-school skirt
communion dress dragged deep
into dreams, I would not say a word.

FROM "A HEALING ABORTION CEREMONY"

Jane Hardwicke Collings and Melody Bee

ALL journeys of the womb deserve tending,
each and every one.
When we feel forced to split off from our stories as women,
be they stories of joy or pain,
love or fear, hope or despair, we split off from the fullness of our power,
our beauty, our wisdom.

And so, may all women,
everywhere, be supported to be in the fullness of their stories.
Around the world may we all be supported to be safe and whole,
in both body and heart,
may we be supported to be heard,
and may we be honoured always as the wise shapers and crafters
of these our own Sacred Lives.

Let's stand in a big circle
Hold hands
Big breath in, and out with a sigh
say a tone together
Feel your sister's hand in yours
Feel all the sisters' hands in yours
send love, send healing, send hope
and now let's put our hands on the earth
and send healing love to all the women in the world
who cannot access safe legal abortion . . . may they be safe and held.
Hug each woman beside you,

Thanks for coming
Blessèd Be.

A BIRTH PLAN FOR DYING

Hanna Neuschwander

A week before my daughter was born, I typed up her birth plan. Reading it now, it sounds strange and stilted. "If the baby is born alive, we would like both a birth and death certificate. . . . I have fears that laboring will be painful without the joy of knowing we will be giving birth to a healthy baby who will come home with us. I have fears that I will be deeply sad during labor/at birth instead of happy to meet our daughter."

How do you organize anguish? How do you bureaucratize grief and fear into bullet points?

River's birth was scheduled for September 26. She would be born in the same hospital where I had given birth to our daughter, whom I'll call M, two years before. The staff were ready for us. A kind nurse checked us in at noon and led us to a delivery room with a small sign on the door—a leaf with droplets of water that looked like tears. It's a secret code. It alerts everyone who comes in the room that your baby is going to die, so people don't accidentally congratulate you for being there.

It's hard to know how to give birth under these circumstances. While you wait for the Pitocin to kick in and get labor started, do you read? Do you make small talk with your husband? Can you will yourself to disappear? I had trouble sitting still. I went out into the bright afternoon sun and walked a paved labyrinth in the courtyard. As I circled toward the center of the labyrinth I imagined I was coming to meet her. As I unwound, I prepared to say goodbye.

Once the Pitocin-induced contractions got going, they were intense bursts of knotty pain with just twenty or thirty seconds' rest in between, very different from the long, rolling waves I recalled from my first delivery. It was tiring. I paced around the room, tried to lie down, paced again. As the sun was setting, we went for another walk. Twilight had painted a dark rainbow at the edge of the sky, and Mars or Jupiter or some planet was twinkling just above it. It would have been beautiful except for the ugly parking lot we were walking through. I remember being confused and then excited about the large silhouette I took to be a horse statue at the end of the sidewalk—what is that amazing statue doing in this ugly parking lot, I wondered—arriving at it only to realize it was a dumpster.

* * *

When I was around twenty weeks pregnant, after an abnormal ultrasound made it clear that something was wrong but not exactly what, my struggle with language began in earnest. First there was the fog of her diagnosis, what amounted to a cavernous hole in her brain, surrounded by a bunch of misshapen junk. When the genetic counselor first called to give us the results—there was a "large midline cyst," some "nodularity," "agenesis" (lack of formation) of a structure called the corpus callosum, which connects the left and right hemispheres—each word she spoke was a fragment, unmoored from any meaning I could discern.

We had a follow-up ultrasound appointment in which the perinatologist flipped through a diagnostic textbook, looking for clues to help her identify what she was seeing. She had no idea. Meanwhile, the wobbly underwater music of River's fetal heart tones played in the background. There was back-and-forth with the radiologist. I had an amniocentesis. I was sent for an urgent fetal MRI. The fragments multiplied. There were frantic, dissatisfying conversations with specialists, endless PubMed searches for scientific papers that might contain clues (there were none), calls with genetic counselors. River didn't have a nameable disease, something straightforwardly awful like Trisomy 13, just a mounting pile of abnormalities in her brain.

It was all so vague that for a few days, I teetered frantically between a profound optimism—perhaps she would read below grade-level—and crushing despair that her life would be an unimaginable cascade of suffering that my love would not be large enough to break.

No one could give us a concrete prognosis, not even an educated guess about whether she would live, or how long she might live, or what her quality of life would be. We did receive a lot of grim looks. At some point, it became clear that we were expected to make a decision. No one named the decision. When my doctor called with the MRI results, the first thing she said was "It's worse than we thought."

* * *

In the delivery room, at midnight, I called for an epidural. Sitting with my back curled so they could slip the needle next to my spine, I furiously rubbed a small stone in my hand and tried to breathe through an icy terror. Soon my legs felt like big, dumb stumps—the way your lips feel an hour after getting a cavity filled. The relief was immediate, but not being able to walk off my jitters was distressing. I felt marooned on that small metal bed—just me and the reality of what I was there to do. So I slept, as hard and as long as I could. A thick, empty, opioid sleep.

The room was empty of sound. There were no monitors on, none of the maniacal beeping that usually accompanies a hospital birth. It took me a while to realize why. Fetal monitors allow the hospital staff to search for signals of something gone awry. They search so they can rescue, so they can intervene if anything goes wrong. We were there for River's birth and her death. It was her life that was wrong. There wasn't any point in monitoring us. That night, I remember gliding up through my oblivion to the surface and hearing only my ragged breath, John rustling under a blanket on the bench beside me, someone padding quietly down the hall outside the door. I felt I could hear River, swimming quiet laps inside me.

* * *

The day we got the MRI results was fourteen days before the legal cutoff for pregnancy termination in Oregon. The soundscape of my pregnancy became a clock grimly ticking.

It's one thing to decide to pull life support after watching your baby repeatedly suffer broken bones from resuscitations in the NICU, or endless failed surgeries. It's one thing to be given a fatal diagnosis like Trisomy 18, and to know that death is certain. It's one thing to know your pregnancy could kill you.

It is another to be told, "It's worse than I thought," but to have no prognosis whatsoever. To peer desperately into the medical literature and glean that it was almost equally likely that your child would be healthy with functional disability; would suffer excruciating, uncontrollable seizures and be physically and mentally incapacitated; or would be born without the ability to breathe and would die immediately anyway. The scales appeared to be tipped toward catastrophe, but certainty was a vapor.

The next night, sitting on the floor of our bedroom, facing John, the magnitude of it hit me. We had the responsibility of transmuting this meaningless horror into some kind of medical decision.

The first choice you have to make is whether or not to choose at all. I contemplated this deeply. It was the most alluring possibility of all, to abdicate choice. To say very simply: I cannot end my child's life and I am willing to accept whatever that entails. But every time I tried this idea on, it closed like a corset around me. My heart would seize up then race forward; I kept not being able to breathe.

We made lists. What outcomes did we feel we were prepared to handle? Physical incapacitation? There were mechanical fixes for that. Learning disabilities, even severe ones? We knew how to navigate systems. Seizures, the only outcome we were certain of? They posed a problem. Some kinds were controllable. Others were not. We spoke with a pediatric neurosurgeon—there was no way of knowing in advance how severe they would be. We spoke with a friend whose son had begun to have grand mal seizures at age three, and was now a grown man who had been through dozens of surgeries and three times nearly died, who possessed neither the ability to talk, nor to care for himself, nor to smile.

I accept that some degree of suffering is unavoidable, that it even has value in instructing us to be more compassionate emotionally, morally, spiritually, and politically. The outcome that terrified me the most was not that River would suffer, but that she would never feel the redeeming joy that makes suffering tolerable.

As we made our list we began to realize how futile it was. The whole exercise was predicated on having some idea of what outcome River would have. I ripped the list into pieces so small they couldn't be ripped anymore.

* * *

Tick, tick, tick.

* * *

Around noon the day River was born, something changed. I was jolted out of my druggy haze by an urgent pain in my left side. I called the nurse and told her the epidural was wearing off; she called for an increase. The pain didn't go away. I felt a rising panic. I ate a popsicle. John tried to read me some poems. I felt confused, overwhelmed, cagey. After an hour or so, it sank in that she was coming.

The doctor on call, a hospitalist named Jill, came to check on me. With a tenderness that still astonishes me, she examined me and let me know that River was ready. Because I was not quite six months along and she was so small, it would probably just take one or two pushes. I nodded. My panic subsided in an instant and I felt clear, like the moment just after you slip your body into a cold lake. The next contraction was different. I looked at the doctor. I looked at John. I looked at our friend Adrian, who was with us. "She's here," I said. On the next contraction, I gave the slightest push, more like an encouragement, and she slipped out like a little fish.

* * *

Trying to peer into River's future was like standing at the edge of the ocean, scrutinizing a featureless, terrifying abyss. It was like being handed a rock and a shard of glass, and being told to use them to locate a star in another galaxy.

Hidden inside my body, I had not realized until now, was a kind of scaffolding, a haphazard architecture of beliefs and norms and values and ideas that I had cobbled together over the years, out of which I had constructed the idea of myself, and which I used to guide my decision-making.

But in the face of this horror, it collapsed entirely, leaving behind desolate rubble. Facing the man I had loved for fifteen years, with whom and against whom I had come to define myself, I said, "I am not sure if I exist."

"You exist," he reassured me.

* * *

Gut decisions are typically made in moments of crisis when there is no time to weigh arguments and calculate the probability of every outcome—or, as in our case, when there simply aren't any probabilities available. Gut decisions are made in situations where there is no precedent and consequently little evidence.

* * *

Two days after we received the MRI results, Adrian called. After listening for a long time, she asked tentatively, "Have you asked River what she wants?" My twenty-two-week-old fetus? My unborn, unconscious child? No. Then again, nobody else had answers.

I hung up the phone and lay back on the quilt my mother-in-law had given us as a wedding gift. I tried to become very quiet. I reached my mind into River's amniotic lake. I felt around the edges of her body, and I asked her what she thought about all of this. Do you want to live? I asked. I waited a long time for an answer. I told her, There is a lot of suffering out here, but we'd still have a lot of fun. I asked, Would you like that?

I waited again.

* * *

Three hundred years after the Enlightenment, bodies are still profoundly suspect—especially women's. We generally believe that information from trained medical professionals, even the Internet, is superior to what a woman says about her own physical experiences. Ironically, there is now a growing corpus of research showing how often women's reports of pain are discounted by their doctors; for poor women and women of color, this is doubly true. When I'm struggling to align how I feel with what others will think about how I feel or about how I'm acting because of how I feel, I usually tell myself, "I'm really emotional today," right before I dismiss myself.

* * *

River never answered me, of course. She couldn't. She had a giant hole in her brain. But her silence was the most complete answer anyone had been able to give me.

* * *

As soon as we decided to let River go, my panic subsided. We had eleven days left until Oregon's cutoff. We scheduled my induction for seven days later. We ejected ourselves from our normal lives and planned to spend our last week together as a family. We went to the soccer stadium and stood in the fan section next to the drums and trumpets, so River could feel the bass thrum. We went to watch a migration of Vaux's swifts. We went to the Pacific Ocean, and I waded out to a rock and let the icy water surround me. We talked with our two-year-old about what death is. We had a dance party every single morning at breakfast. In every minute we were aware not just of losing River, but also of having River. It was the most joyful week of my life.

Even so, every single morning the first thing I did was go over all of it again, step-by-step—the MRI results, the medical papers, the feeling in my gut—and every morning I made the decision all over again. I kept waiting for it to be different, but it never was. I didn't decide to end River's life once; I decided a thousand times.

"This is what parenting is," my midwife told me kindly. "It's making very difficult decisions with imperfect information, and trying to do right by them. You are River's mother, and right now, you are being her mother."

I wanted to meet her.

* * *

The minute she was born, they handed River's tiny, slippery, reddish-pink body to me, and I clutched her tightly to my chest. She was alive, as I had hoped she would be, and she was riverine. Her eyes were fused shut and her ears still pinned to her head and her skin was translucent as film and her fingers were as thin and lithe as a wraith's. She didn't look like a baby who should have been born. To almost anyone else, I think she would have looked terrifying. To me she was beautiful. I had a singular yearning to hold her in the place right between my breasts. With her there, we were still one person.

A few minutes after she was born, the nurse took her and weighed her: 1 pound, 3 ounces. She was wrapped in a tiny yellow blanket my mother had knitted for her, and placed back in my arms. She was very still, very quiet. Every five or so minutes, she took a small, gasping breath through tiny, white, caterpillar lips. Twice, her little golem hands stretched out and she resettled herself. The blanket we had wrapped her in was sticking to her skin, and I worried about how raw it might feel to her. I had read every medical paper I could find about fetal pain perception and strongly believed that at twenty-three weeks and four days she could not feel pain. Yet still I worry she felt her blanket chafing her. It is high on the list of things I play over and over in my mind, wondering if I made the right choice.

Another was our choice to have her photographed. The bereavement literature gently recommends it. It is full of stories of mothers and fathers who couldn't bear the pain of holding or looking at their dead child, and so fail to say a proper goodbye—and then live with an unresolvable regret. We were determined not to turn away from our grief, so invited our friend Morgan to come take photographs. He was profoundly respectful, moving quietly around us, camera clicking. He arrived twenty minutes after she was born and stayed a half hour. For a while, we had turned the lights on so he could shoot. We did the things we had planned to do: John and I took turns holding her and singing her songs; we flipped through a book of family photos and read aloud the names of all her relatives; we read her a children's book her sister had picked out for her. My mother arrived and walked her to the window to show her the sunlight, even though her eyes couldn't open.

Everyone left at the same time, including the hospital staff, and then it was just the three of us—John, River, and me. We turned the lights out again, and lay together on the bed, cradling one another, just looking and breathing and looking. This was what I had wanted to give her: quiet, peace, a chance for us to meet.

And that realization provoked a sharp regret. We had wasted half her precious life—forty-five minutes—with the lights on, passing her back and forth and photographing her. When I think of it now, it brings me a bitter sadness. I look at the photos sometimes and all I see are the minutes I wasn't holding her, keeping her warm. Other times, I am happy to have some physical evidence that she existed. If someone ever tried to tell me she didn't—a fear that for some reason I still harbor—I could prove them wrong.

* * *

In pregnancy, there are two protagonists—the mother and the baby. We want their stories—their need, their suffering, their joy—to be the same. But they rarely are.

I needed to give birth to River, to say hello so I could say goodbye. But I wonder often if I sacrificed something she needed for something I needed. In some hospitals, River's birth would have been impossible. Fearful of lawsuits arising from policies that require intervention to save the life of a child, most hospitals give women who choose to end pregnancies through labor and delivery a shot of potassium chloride (KCL) to stop the baby's heart twenty-four hours before induction.

After deciding to end her life, this was the decision that most distressed me: KCL was possibly the most merciful option for River, but it felt violent and harrowing to me. In the end, the thought of carrying River dead inside me was too horrific.

The problem, is there is no right way for your child to die.

* * *

At some point I realized that her tiny mouth was slack. A nurse checked her heart rate, putting a cold stethoscope to her, and I sobbed not because she was gone but because of the coldness. This would trouble me for weeks. When we received word that her body had been sent to California for a forensic autopsy, I was frantic that she was without her blanket in the belly of the airplane. When they called to tell us the cremation was complete, I held onto a mute terror that she had felt herself burning.

* * *

I held her for another two hours, lying on my side with her cradled to my chest, my cheek resting on the top of her head. It was as cool and smooth as a stone losing the heat of day after the sun goes down. Lying with her, she was not gone. I scarcely felt she had left my body. Though she was beginning to turn purplish, it was like watching a bruise form on my own skin.

I would have liked to stay in the riverbed there with her forever. I would have liked to let everyone and everything else rise while we remained, sinking to the bottom through the blue dark water, clanking and settling among the other river stones, feeling the cold rush past us down wherever water goes.

Looking up from the bottom, I felt the eyes of a bleak bird perched on the riverbank above us, wavering in the watery light. I considered it coldly. I closed my eyes and opened them again. It remained.

And this was the worst moment of my life: to be with her utterly, but to know that I had to rise, had to unfasten my cheek from her head, had to place her in a nurse's arms, had to turn and walk out the hospital doors without her, into a world that never knew her.

I am not sure how I lifted my body, heavy as a bag of rocks, from the bed. I sat on the edge holding River to my chest. John went to find a nurse. The kind doctor came back in her street clothes and held my face between her hands and kissed me tenderly on the forehead and then kissed River on the forehead, with the same wonderment and gentleness as you would kiss a living newborn. I cried at the kindness of that. The nurse came. I put River in her hands. The yellow blanket flopped down and I tucked it back under her chin to keep her warm.

It was time to turn away, to walk out the doors. But I couldn't make my body leave hers. John held me, steered me out of the room and down the hall. As soon as the doors opened and the night air came rushing at me, my legs gave out and I collapsed. A faraway sound came out of me that I think was the true sound of her body loosening itself from mine.

When I was through wailing, John lifted me up like a child and carried me in his arms to the car.

* * *

Three weeks later I realized I'd had a late-term abortion. None of our doctors had ever used the word.

I called Adrian and said, "I had an abortion, I think." She was very quiet, then tentatively offered a kind of absolution, if I wanted it: "But it's not really the same thing. You wanted her." I thought for a minute about what it would mean to take her up on the offer.

* * *

The next night on TV I watched as Donald Trump, in a presidential debate with Hillary Clinton, unintelligibly dismissed late-term abortion: "In the ninth month, you can take the baby and rip the baby out of the womb of the mother just prior to the birth of the baby. . . . You can take the baby and rip the baby out of the womb in the ninth month on the final day."

I ran into the bathroom and threw up.

* * *

If words compose a kind of map of what's possible—what it's possible to think, to feel, to do—then my map has new territories on it I couldn't have imagined before: The island called "I Held My Dead Child." The ocean called "I Killed My Daughter" (on many versions of the map, "killed" is spelled "loved.") The volcano called "I Promised Myself I Would Not Feel Regret." A new supercontinent, veined with rivers that murmur and murmur and murmur their own name.

And there are parts of the map no longer accessible to me, word-territories whose meanings have become noxious as a mining pit, leaching technicolor poison into everything that surrounds them. Words like "choice" and "life."

The worst of it is this: If you show this map to anyone, to try to give shape to the contours of the greatest, most difficult act of love you have ever committed, you will be called a murderer. To illustrate the full story of your love is to open yourself and your family to unimaginable abuse.

I don't seek pity, but to have your worst personal pain be the site of the most toxic conversation in public life is awful. It is awful every day.

* * *

Three months after River was born, I sat in a rocking chair looking at rain materialize from an endless gray cloud shrouding the Columbia River. It was a vast, stuck sky. The river could have been blue snow, or cold metal, or bruised glass. When we named her River, we put her out there, in the landscape.

Rocking, I thought about what my life would be if she were living. My left arm would be sore and strong from nursing her, carrying her everywhere. My brain would be like the washed-gray basin of sky, just a loose, watery bell jar trapping the sound of her, the smell of her. Her needs would be my needs. But she would be learning—me and not-me, self and world. Like a glass window beaded with rain, she'd be on one side, I on the other. But we'd both be the window, too. We would still be able to slip through its pores, become one another.

I imagined that if she were alive, we'd always be able to do this if the need arose. If one day she grew up and became very sick, I would slip into her hospital bed and become her again. If she needed to become me, I would slip off my self like a silk robe and she could enter.

* * *

This is hard to say: Ending River's life was the most moral decision I have ever made. Moral in the literal sense: "concerned with the principles of right and wrong behavior and the goodness or badness of human character." I grappled with my deepest being—my spiritual, my intellectual, my biological selves. I made my decision, then remade it a thousand times. I am terrified I have failed her, have failed my family, have failed my culture. But morality is no longer an abstract question for me. "Right or wrong" cannot contain the scope of my moral reckoning, my moral longing. What is an acceptable level of suffering? Whose suffering matters more? Who gets to decide? No one, not even the ablest philosophers, has been able to answer these questions to our society's satisfaction. But for some reason we like to shame and vilify the very people who have grappled most viscerally with them.

* * *

River is gone. River is not gone. She is in my cells. When she died, she was the cradle my body became, not the center that escaped.

Rocking in that chair, I cradled a still-secret knowledge in the basin of my heart: I was pregnant again. The night we conceived, I knew. The force of it rang my body like a bell. Of course, there's no medical literature to back me up.

Every day I reached my mind into the river inside me and asked, Do you want to live?

No one heard what my child whispered but me.

ON THAT DAY

Arisa White

the uniformed men told us we were coming with them.
I was too busy getting Kayana ready, I didn't notice
I was still in my pajamas, and the hairstyle you did
the other day needed to be combed.

You woke up from the anesthesia, took the train half drugged.
On that day, Jamar, me, and Ibert sat in the air-conditioned police station,
drinking apple juice. The white cops told us, *Better not see you here again.*
They laughed. We imagined Kayana alone in the hospital shaking.

On the train you fell asleep, opened your eyes
just before our stop. We wondered where you were
while rubbing goose bumps down, watching pistachio
paint peel, listening to our hunger come.

On that day the apartment was too quiet a place
for living children, you cried, and we let our minds wander.

Your head begged for bed. You called
your best friend on that day and asked her to get us.
Walked on legs withering beneath you
to Kayana in the hospital five blocks away.

Later in Angie's doorway, Ibert hugged your thighs,
rested his head between your legs. We shouted,
Where you been? On that day, without a reply,
we calmed our excitement to enter your hush.

NEW RELIGION

Mary Morris

Remove the bloody icons
from your walls.
Wrap them in white gauze.
Perform a decent burial.
Chant gospel,
play Nina Simone.
If you must, have an abortion.
Make the sign of the swan.
Lay yourself in the sun,
like a temple on a mountain.
Be sworn.
Be sworn in.

HAIL MARY

Deborah Hauser

Anonymous, among women, we wait, sharing a communal grief.
By tacit agreement, we exchange only furtive glances, denying
ourselves the comfort of direct eye contact.

A sterile nurse announces my name. I follow her down
a hollow hall to a stark room. I strip, lay myself bare
on the sacrificial altar.

This thin gown offers no protection against the chill,
steel table. Feet in stirrups, eyes pinned to the ceiling,
a water stain contorts into the face of the Virgin Mary.

My fingers ache to count the long-abandoned beads
of my first rosary. A gift for my communion, the tiny gold cross
dangling from a string of iridescent pearls.

Caressing them, I felt superior. I fell to my knees
to scoop them up when they broke. Cheap plastic
beads skittered across the linoleum floor in the First Aid

aisle of the drugstore, but Mother yanked me to my feet. "Leave
that junk," she hissed, pulling me along behind her to the checkout line.
I try to recall the prayers I used to recite, kneeling at my bed,

palms pressed tightly together, the nape of my neck glowed
beneath the heat of his gaze. Hail Mary, Mother
Mary comes to me. She disappears into the ceiling tile.

AT ADVENT, THE WAITING ROOM

Daisy Fried

We small army say if you turn time
backwards, Mary goes back to Bethlehem,
the lowing of the cattle, the comfort of straw.
Labor's just as terrible, if not worse, in reverse,
but then the swelling hurt subsides; her breasts
grow lighter, de-manufacturing the milk
that would have fed the god. Mary still
remembers the strange unraveling. Therefore
no one ever bears, no one ever
bears the whole world's weight alone again.

FROM *A BOOK OF AMERICAN MARTYRS*

Joyce Carol Oates

"M omma? Why aren't we leaving?"
"Why? Because we *are not*."
Dawn was baffled why Edna Mae, and some others, were not leaving the Cleveland County Planned Parenthood Women's Surgical Clinic. The last of the clinic staff had quickly departed, to a chorus of cries—*Murderers! Cowards!*

Edna Mae plucked at the children's arms. Hurry! Reverend Trucross was leading them.

Dawn was very tired. Dawn could not comprehend. Where were they going? The clinic was shut for the night. There was no one to pray over, or to harass or threaten. One TV camera crew remained in the street.

Only a few volunteers remained—fewer than twenty. But these appeared to be members of Reverend Trucross's church.

They were led to the rear of the clinic. In the alley behind the clinic where there were trash cans and dumpsters. It was dark here. Flashlights were lighted. Dawn could not see well. The younger children stumbled and whimpered. Edna Mae spoke in a voice trembling with excitement. One of the TV crew was speaking to Reverend Trucross. A pair of headlights flared in the alley and Dawn saw the sharply shadowed faces of volunteers. Mostly they were strangers but there was Edna Mae Dunphy among them. They had the look of persons who did not know their surroundings, where they were or why. Dawn did recognize Jacqueline, a heavyset girl with asthma, from Mad River Junction, of whom it was said that Jesus had "saved" her when her throat had closed up as a younger girl and she'd been unable to breathe. At the Pentecostal church it had happened, dozens of witnesses would testify that Jesus had "breathed" life into Jacqueline and restored her to the world.

Edna Mae had acquired a flashlight. There was a smell in the alley of rotted fruit, rotted meat. Something sour and rancid. Dawn swallowed hard, not wanting to be sick to her stomach. Edna Mae was reaching for her, gripping her hand with surprising strength. "Dawn! Come with me."

She would not come with her mother! She dug her heels into the ground.

Yet still, somehow her mother pulled her. Who would have thought that Edna Mae Dunphy was so *strong*.

In the alley behind the clinic amid the sickening stench they had overturned trash cans to poke in the debris. Boldly they had thrown open dumpster lids to poke inside and to peer with flashlights.

A cry went up—they had discovered a cache of cardboard boxes in one of the dumpsters. The first was removed and seen to be secured tight by duct tape neatly wrapped. With a knife they cut the duct tape, and opened the box. Inside were five or six Ziploc bags and in each bag a small star-shaped thing . . . More cries went up, of anguish and jubilation.

Edna Mae said fiercely, "You see? Babies—that didn't get born as you did."

Though Edna Mae was very frightened, too, Dawn could see, her face was drawn and ashen and her mouth was set in a fixed half-smile like the smile of a mannequin. Her fingers were very cold.

In the quivering flashlight beam the first of the babies was examined. For (as Reverend Trucross said) you had to determine if indeed the baby was truly *dead*.

Though it was clear, the poor thing had never lived. A tiny kitten-sized creature with a disproportionately large head. Its limbs were stunted, and one of its arms was missing.

Dawn tried to pull away from Edna Mae's grip. Her heart was beating very fast. She was close to hyperventilating. Yet she could not look away from the tiny, dead baby being removed from the stained Ziploc bag.

In a quavering voice Dawn said to Edna Mae, "The babies are dead. They don't know what you're doing for them."

(Where were Anita and Noah? Dawn hoped they were not near, and that someone was watching over them, for Edna Mae seemed to have forgotten them.)

Edna Mae looked at Dawn with disgust. "You are so ignorant! It's pathetic how ignorant you are. Why do we bury the dead?—because they are *dead*. But their souls are *not dead*. We are honoring the babies' souls, not their poor, broken bodies. For shame, *you*."

"But—they never lived . . ."

"Of course, they lived! They were all alive, in their mothers' wombs. As you were alive, before you were born." Edna Mae spoke to Dawn with a savage sarcasm? Dawn had never heard before in her mother though (it seemed to Dawn) Edna Mae was trembling too, with fear and dread.

The volunteers exclaimed in shock, pity, horror. Dawn steeled herself against what she might see. Reverend Trucross was praying loudly.

"Merciful God help us. God who taketh away the sins of the world help us in our rescue of these holy innocents . . ."

In the beam of the flashlight another tiny creature was exposed. This one had been shaken out of the Ziploc bag? in which it had been stuck. It was larger than the first baby, fleshy, meat-colored, damp with blood. You could see the tiny curved legs, the tiny fingers and toes, the misshapen head. You could see the eyes that appeared large and were tight-shut. You could see the miniature pouting mouth? that had never cried.

Other babies appeared to have been dismembered. Their overlarge heads were intact but their bodies had been broken into pieces.

All lay very still on the ground. It seemed wrong to Dawn, that even a dead baby should lie *on the ground*.

Though the eyes of the dead babies were shut tight, tight as slits, and the faces shriveled into grimaces, yet you did expect the eyes to open suddenly. You could not look away from those eyes.

Dawn begged Edna Mae to let her go.

"Let you go *where*? You will wait for me. We are all going home together in the morning."

In horror Dawn stood as Edna Mae and the others lifted boxes out of the dumpsters with their bare hands. (At Home Depot, Dawn and her coworkers, unloading merchandise, all wore gloves. And if you did not wear gloves, your supervisor would hand a pair of gloves to you!) Some of the boxes were upside down, all were toppled as if they'd been dumped hastily.

Carefully the boxes were placed in the rear of a minivan in the alley. The plan was to bury the aborted infants in a consecrated cemetery a few miles away with a proper Christian burial, Christian prayers.

As Edna May insisted, Dawn helped stack the boxes. She could not breathe for the stench, and was feeling lightheaded.

(Where was Jesus? Had it been His plan all along, for Dawn to help bury the babies?)

(He had not warned her beforehand. It had been a terrible shock!)

(Since the Hammer with the black-taped grip, that had struck the fleeing screaming boys with such power, Dawn had come to respect Jesus in another, unexpected way. Jesus was an ally but you could not take Jesus for granted as an ally; it was that simple.)

In all, there were fourteen boxes secured with duct tape, retrieved from the dumpsters. In each box, five or six Ziploc bags with aborted babies inside.

Thrown away like garbage! God have mercy on the murderers.

TUNNEL OF LIGHT

Julie Kane

Those who return report that, at the end
Of the tunnel of light, there's a receiving line
Made up of dead loved ones: relatives, not friends,
Blocking the gate to whatever lies behind.
It could be from a lack of oxygen,
A shared illusion as the brain cells die,
But it will still feel like it's genuine,
No matter if it's real or one last lie.
My mother waits there in her spider web:
No way around except by going through.
My little lost infant waits in her crib.
I don't fear dying, but I fear those two.
O holy mother, help us to forgive
Those who killed us and those who let us live.

LIZARD

Ulrica Hume

She bought a stroller for the twins, found it in a slick catalog of things she could not afford. It was from Scandinavia, all black and ergonomic, a two-seater. She assembled it herself, and when the stroller was there before her with its glitzy funereal air, she changed her mind about everything. She ended up at an abortion clinic the following rainy Tuesday.

Finn, the father of the twins, was not someone she knew well. He was a plumber who had come by that day to fix the bathroom's leaky drainpipe. Thick red hair, green starburst eyes, a schoolboy's dimples. She watched him gingerly slide down under the sink. Silence as he scrutinized. Then a long-winded prophecy about couplings and nipples. I have the gift of the gab, he joked, and she laughed along, giving away her power, yet feeling helplessly pretty. As he worked she dusted the plump leaves of her jade plant. Then he called her, Laura my dear, he said, can you fetch me that wrench from my toolbox please. She rummaged through greasy rags and rubber washers, thinking how lovely it was, someone calling to her from another room.

She gave him the wrench, and he winked a thank-you. See, here's the problem here, he said. But as she leaned in with fascination, he suddenly swung himself round, next she was pinned to the floor and he was holding the wrench as a weapon. And so it happened: a spreading damp, and she the trembling prey.

At the abortion clinic, she stared at the bad art on the waiting room wall. Then rain began, a cheerful staccato. She knew all the leaks in the world would remind her of him—a haunting. A conspiracy of unscreamed screams ratcheted up inside her as she let go the twins. After, she was sadly relieved. She stepped lightly.

Protestors were gathered outside the clinic, with signs bearing fetuses. Thou Shalt Not Kill. They also carried umbrellas. She wondered if their sixth commandment applied to war as well, or just to those who die who are not yet born.

She came home rattled. Sipped chamomile tea.

A few weeks went by. She was checking the mail when she noticed something odd on the sidewalk. A discarded cardboard box, stuffed with a blanket. She opened it cautiously.

Marble eyes—fixed, omniscient, pleading—met her blue ones. A forked tongue teased the space.

It was a lizard. Probably abandoned for having grown too large. She knew that she must help it.

She brought the lizard inside and coaxed it out of the box. It emerged majestically, sashaying across her plush carpet, tail swinging.

The lizard's skin was a primitive pattern of black, green, white, rose, and beige. She stroked it gently. So much was communicated in that feathery moment: a surreptitious beauty, which she could not trust but had to trust, or let herself be ruined.

She fed it grapes and scraps of bread. Blew soap bubbles, which it reached for in an ethereal way. Yet how needy it was. Following her around, always at her heels. Its nocturnal wanderings took some getting used to. She could hear it swishing in the dark, prompted by a secret reptilian agenda. It lurked at the edge of things, remembering its clear, clear purpose at the center of it all.

The first time she took the lizard out in the stroller, she felt a wild sense of pride. The two-seater worked perfectly if the lizard reclined sideways—this was no problem. Since the sun was quite bright, she covered its head with a bonnet.

Off they went.

Stares. Unkind words. Such as, Where'd you get that ugly baby? Lots of open mouths. It's Little Red Riding Hood! one child exclaimed.

They promenaded as far as the railroad tracks, then back again. It would be like this from now on, she supposed, just them against everyone else. Such sweet rapport they had! The lizard loved to drape itself around her shoulders and cuddle. For hours it did this, in an affectionate wrestler's hold. The scaly skin against her neck a telling veil of sweetgrass and moonwater. Giving her time to think of the twins and who they might have been. The lizard's lips turning in a fey smile as it snored. Even the cold-blooded have hearts.

BENEATH THE WORLD: TWO POEMS TO THE CHILD NEVER TO BE BORN*

Sharon Doubiago

I.
I sleep beneath a map of the world.
The world glows in the dark.
In the furthest place
the northern lights
bear down.

In the morning I will bear down.
This thing. This fish
swollen in the sea, glowing
beneath love.

Canada and Alaska yearn over me
for Asia. China, as if in flight
flees the map. You must walk
south to the dead center, the US
The eyes, the heart, the feet
must follow
the drift to the east, antipodes,
Tierra del Fuego: the delicate
fire in this painting.

O island. O little land
I see your journey
on my water's swift current.

---

* "Beneath love," comes from a poem by Loretta Manill. "*Corazón blue, corazón red, corazón negra*" comes from a song by Desiree.

Tomorrow I will open.
The axis will tilt, the earth will quake

and he and I,
two lonely gods,
will suck you
from gravity.

But I hear, little spirit,
your suck,
the great song,
Corazón.
Your heart
and the world glow.
Corazón blue, corazón red,
corazón negra.

II.
Tomorrow I'll break

I'll forsake
words altogether. I will paint
with my soul
the curvature
of Earth, the tipping of her
axis, her wobbly
pole.

This pale face, this series of faces
that comes now
a spermy cloud
to cover Her.

I will spend my life walking

your borders
these land masses broken
for you, these continents
and their drift.

I will wash you in the great mourning
in the great morning sea
of the East Pacific Rise

I will lose you
in the nightsea
of the Mid-Atlantic Ridge

You will be unknown
in the Westwind Drift

PRAYER TO THE SPIRIT

Starhawk

To release the spirit to find a new entry into life*

Spirit, spirit,
I have sent you back
across the gate.
How sorry I am
To close my womb to you,
but I am not the one
to bring you to birth.
I light this candle for you
to light your way
as you search for the womb
that is meant to bear you.
Here are wombs that are open,
here are women whose arms
ache for a child.
*[Name the women you know
who want to have a child.]*
Each will light a candle for you.
May you choose wisely.
May you come to birth in joy.

---

* The women named in this prayer do not have to be physically present but should be
asked beforehand for consent. Each one should light a candle when she is ready to call
the child into being.

the lost baby poem

Lucille Clifton

the time i dropped your almost body down
down to meet the waters under the city
and run one with the sewage to the sea
what did i know about waters rushing back
what did i know about drowning
or being drowned

you would have been born into winter
in the year of the disconnected gas
and no car we would have made the thin
walk over genesee hill into the canada wind
to watch you slip like ice into strangers' hands
you would have fallen naked as snow into winter
if you were here i could tell you these
and some other things

if i am ever less than a mountain
for your definite brothers and sisters
let the rivers pour over my head
let the sea take me for a spiller
of seas   let Black men call me stranger
always   for your never named sake

ABORTION CHILD

Jean Valentine

I thought:
You live somewhere
deeper than the well
I live down in.
Deeper than anything from me or him.

No but it took me
time to see you, thirty earth years.

"FIRE SECTION" FROM *ABORTION: A HEALING RITUAL*

Minerva Earthschild and Vibra Willow

INTRODUCTION

This ritual is intended to create a healing space for women who have had one or more abortions and to acknowledge and work with the spiritual aspects of the experience. Through our own abortion experiences, we came to reject the dichotomy of abortion politics that would require women to choose between two beliefs: that pregnancy is a miracle, the fetus's life is sacred, and therefore abortion is wrong; or that pregnancy is merely a physical event, the fetus is just a mass of tissue, and therefore abortion is insignificant. As feminists and pagans, we believe that women are literally a gateway between the worlds and that abortion is a responsible exercise of the sacred power of choice. Using Wiccan practices and feminist process, we have designed this ritual for women wishing to heal from their abortion experiences and to reclaim sacred power in their reproductive choices. . . .

. . . FIRE

After the stories have all been told, it is time to release those deeper feelings of anger, rage, shame, and judgment that have kept us bound and powerless, that have prevented our healing. The content of this phase of the ritual varies, depending on the needs of the women in the group and the common threads among the stories. If many women told of multiple abortions, perhaps this is the pattern or bond that needs to be broken. If women expressed a great deal of anger or rage against the men in their stories, this could be released.

Place the unlit cauldron in the center. Invite the women to speak or shout into the cauldron, at the same time rather than in turns, what it is that they want to release or have transformed. It is often helpful to speak the hurtful words that have been spoken to us about our abortions: "How could you be so careless, so stupid, so irresponsible, so selfish?" You've had *how* many abortions? Three? Four?" "Abortion isn't a form of birth control, you know!" "Murderer! Baby-killer!" And so on. Just as each of us has our own story, we each have experienced different (but similar) forms of condemnation for our abortions.

When all of the women have completed this speaking, their voices will rise and blend into wailing, keening, moaning, and or sounds of fury and rage. Let this build and fall. Be sure to ground this energy, dropping down and touching the floor or earth. Next bind the wrists of each woman snugly with one or two strands of the thread. As you are binding each woman's wrists, talk about the meaning of bonds, both the negative and positive. Bonds can keep us caught in patterns of thinking or behavior that do not serve us, that inhibit our creative energies. Bonds can also connect us to other women who have had the same experiences we have had and who can help us in our healing. Many of us have felt bound in some way to "choose" abortion.

When all of the women have been bound, light the cauldron. When each woman is ready, she can break her bonds and throw them into the cauldron, perhaps shouting what it is that she is releasing. Begin a chant and wild dance around the cauldron, transforming the negative messages, thoughts, and patterns into power. Raise a cone of power over the cauldron. Ground the energy. The women may experience changes in their feelings about their abortion stories, so some time should be allowed for sharing these shifts.

AN ABORTION

Frank O'Hara

Do not bathe her in blood,
the little one whose sex is
undermined, she drops leafy
across the belly of black
sky and her abyss has not
that sweetness of the March
wind. Her conception ached
with the perversity of nursery
rhymes, she was a shad a
snake a sparrow and a girl's
closed eye. At the supper, weeping,
they said let's have her and
at breakfast: no.

Don't bathe
her in tears, guileless, beguiled
in her peripheral warmth, more
monster than murdered, safe
in all silences. From our tree
dropped, that she not wither,
autumn in our terrible breath.

FROM "PRINCIPLES OF MIDWIFERY,"
FROM *MY NOTORIOUS LIFE*

Kate Manning

I went along now on Mrs. Evans's good days when she took me out to help her in the bedrooms of the city, where women labored and dropped their infants worse than rabbits, night and day. The Bible says in sorrow she shall bring forth children, but sorrow is a quiet humor and my apprenticeship was not quiet. I heard noises from girls like cats being killed. Worse. The battle of Gettysburg where boys was gored through by swords and felled by cannons was surely a match for the sounds of agony as came from these rooms of mothers laboring, and the slicks of blood was so equally sanguinary that you would expect Morrigan, the fairy of war, to land on dark crow's wings by the side of every female in confinement. Before I reached the age of seventeen, I knew the rudiments of my trade just by watching and listening and placing my hands where Mrs. Evans tutored me to place them. I reached in and helped along a breech boy to be born, his little red feet emerging and his chin stuck somewhere up the chimney so I worried would his head snap off. I seen mothers give birth drunk as sots and I seen them quaff the Sanative Serum like it was cider. I seen twins delivered, and an infant born with a caul, filmy as the skin off steamed milk, veiling the face. Its mother put that filament aside in a tobacco tin saying she would sell it to a sailor.

—A caul will save you from drowning, said Mrs. Evans.

She tutored me always. While I was helping out with the births I wasn't yet allowed to assist her in the premature deliveries for the Obstruction, but she had me observe and listen to her narration as she scraped a blocked woman called Mrs. Torrington who had eight children already and observed again as she de-obstructed another broken-down nag, Mrs. Selby, who had seven boys. Neither one could afford another squalling child, and both of these ladies no matter how much My Teacher hurt them only thanked her in the end. It was my sorry task to empty the bowl and on one of these occasions I seen amidst the gore a pale delicate outline of a form such as what you see in the smashed egg of a sparrow, not bigger than a thumbnail.

—What's wrong with you? cried Mrs. Evans when she seen my woeful face.

—It's been killed.

—It was never alive, said she quite firmly, and dragged me home to her Bible where she pointed me out a lesson from King Solomon and said,—Ponder it.

> If a man fathers a hundred children and lives many years, but his soul is not satisfied with good things, and he does not even have a proper burial, then I say, Better the miscarriage than he, for it comes in futility and goes into obscurity; and its name is covered in obscurity. It never sees the sun and it never knows anything; it is better off than he.

And she ordered me to go look in the street at the poor wee bundles of rags having their childhood in the alleyways of the Bend and ask myself what was meant by Charity and to read the verses of Ecclesiastes again, so I did:

> Behold I saw the tears of the oppressed and that they had no one to comfort them; and on the side of their oppressors was power, but they had no one to comfort them. So I congratulated the dead who are already dead more than the living who are still living. But better off than both of them is the one who has never existed, who has never seen the evil that is done under the sun.

Under sun and moon both, Mrs. Evans schooled me about evil and good and the practicalities of administering them and all remedies in between. A few drops of opium will save the mother pain. Palpation of the belly will determine a breech presentation. A glassful of spirits will restart a stopped labor. If by feel you determine the head is rotated wrongly coax the mother on her side and push with the hands to turn the child. If the face is presenting place one hand within and the other without, and push inside to tuck the chin, while outside pressing the head forward by a stroking motion across the belly. Small hands is a blessing. A steady hand is a blessing. A firm hand is a blessing. A warm heart is and so is a soft voice. Mrs. Evans had these all, whereas my heart was guarded and my voice was mostly silent. I watched and listened and did what I was told.

—You will see mothers die of prolapse where the u****s falls right out, Mrs. Evans said. You will see them die when the child is stuck in the canal. Mothers will die of fever and they will die of hemorrhage. Their soft parts will rip and tear. They will die just of exhaustion.—And remember, she said,—till you have a child of your own, no woman will accept you for a midwife alone.

I went along to thirty births. Sixteen boys and fourteen girls. The mothers moaned and carried on but when they were through most of them smiled and looked down at their raw new infants with wet eyes glinting.—It's a beautiful gift of God, Mrs. Evans said, her own eyes crinkled with wonder.—Such a wonder.

And it was. As disgusting as the Blessed Event seemed to me at first, I soon was dumbstruck at the power and workings of the female machine and never got tired of the drama and the miracle, even when I seen Mrs. Kissling die in her husband's arms, her newborn wailing, not even when I seen a mongoloid. I saw all manner of effluvia manufactured by the feminine anatomy, including blood, the Liquor amnii, p*** and s***, vernix and vomit. Plus, all manner of womanly afflictions, swellings, growths, lacerations, fistula, bruises, and the burns of a cigar. But the worst I ever saw was left on the doorstep.

CHRISTMAS CAROLS

Margaret Atwood

Children do not always mean
hope. To some they mean despair.
This woman with her hair cut off
so she could not hang herself
threw herself from a rooftop, thirty
times raped & pregnant by the enemy
who did this to her. This one had her pelvis
broken by hammers so the child
could be extracted. Then she was thrown away,
useless, a ripped sack. This one
punctured herself with kitchen skewers
and bled to death on a greasy
oilcloth table, rather than bear
again and past the limit. There
is a limit, though who knows
when it may come? Nineteenth-century
ditches are littered with small wax corpses
dropped there in terror. A plane
swoops too low over the fox farm
and the mother eats her young. This too
is Nature. Think twice then
before you worship turned furrows, or pay
lip service to some full belly
or other, or single out one girl to play
the magic mother, in blue
& white, up on that pedestal,
perfect & intact, distinct
from those who aren't. Which means
everyone else. It's a matter

of food & available blood. If motherhood is sacred, put
your money where your mouth is. Only
then can you expect the coming
down to the wrecked & shimmering earth
of that miracle you sing
about, the day
when every child is a holy birth.

NICOLETTE

Colette Inez

Nicolette, my little carrot,
I pull you out of the dark ground
of Pennsylvania
where they blasted my thighs
and scraped your seed away.

You are twelve, my counterpart child
breathlessly running into rooms
with acorns and leaves
you want to arrange
for the most senseless beauty.

I have married your father.
We are reconciled to minus signs.

The moist kiss you give me
comes from the forest
of a dark time;

anthracite in the earth,
old signals from the stars
when I walked away from the kill,
blood on my legs, a phrase to caulk
the falling walls in a universe
moving light years away
from our promises.

Nicolette, we will meet
in my poem and when the light

calls your name
you will rise like a fern
to live all summer long,
a green integer
in a pure equation of song.

FROM "LILY'S ABORTION IN THE ROOM OF STATUES," IN *AMONG THE GODDESSES*

Annie Finch

[. . .] So those statues were my companions
two more nights, and three more days,
as my hunger and sickness kept me
weak but wakeful. I could see them,

dozens, watching me with eyes,
squatting goddesses, with children or alone,
alabaster, or dark burned stone,
mouths sometimes open, sometimes in pain,
chipped out hollows shadowing distance,
inset eyes of turquoise staring
from attenuated heights.
And the queen of heaven, Inanna,
never left my eyes alone;

hard on the beams of her eyes I went downward
till that day passed, and evening came,
and into the second night's solitude
there rose another, terrible queen.
She stood over me with the height of a murderer,
her hand on my belly, her voice in my blood,
while Inanna watched me without one movement.
Till the dawn came, I felt that hand
burning, and I knew the flame

was spinning, heavy, out from her forehead,
resting between my eyes like new wisdom,
as my pregnancy shrank and contracted.

Inanna had taken me to the vision,
and she held me there till it was over,
under Ereshkigal's hand. They all saw me
as death moved through me, and I took a life,
so many of them, without pity or fear,
massed on the shelves with their eyes wide open.

By the third morning, weak and thirsty,
no longer nauseous, I lay in a daze,
waiting for Kali. I waited till evening,
with Inanna's eyes on me, steady
as the sun she ruled ruled the day,
and stopped at dusk. All I wanted was there,
day and its lover, night and its lover,
brought by Inanna. They healed the pain.
In the gray light, I left the room.

CHAPEL OF FORGIVENESS

Cathleen Calbert

In San Francisco, my mother goes
to Chinatown for tea or ginseng,
silk change purses, black canvas shoes.

She stops in to pray at Old St. Mary's
if she's tired, so it wasn't surprising
she proposed doing so with me.

After our stacks of saucers had been
assessed by the waitress, and we'd paid
for our dim sum, the little bits of heart

we ate in the shape of shrimps
rolled in white rice dough, slippery
pork baos, and sweet black seed cakes,

we ascended the steps, feeling our way
in the dark entry to those dual chapels:
"Of Forgiveness," "Of Repentance."

She dipped her fingers in holy water
and sighed how she likes to choose
"Forgiveness" for everybody.

"Hold on," I said. "Aren't we the ones
who're supposed to need forgiving?"
I laughed until she laughed, and we collapsed

on the cement steps, tossing leftover pieces
of Chinese dumpling to the city pigeons as
they descended like a blessing upon us.

FROM *SURFACING*

Margaret Atwood

I knew when it was, it was in a bottle curled up, staring out at me like a cat pickled; it had huge jelly eyes and fins instead of hands, fish gills, I couldn't let it out, it was dead already, it had drowned in air. It was there when I woke up, suspended in the air above me like a chalice, an evil grail, and I thought, Whatever it is, part of myself or a separate creature, I killed it. It wasn't a child but it could have been one, I didn't allow it.

Water was dripping from me into the canoe, I lay in a puddle. I had been furious with them, I knocked it off the table, my life on the floor, glass egg and shattered blood, nothing could be done.

That was wrong, I never saw it. They scraped it into a bucket and threw it wherever they throw them, it was traveling through the sewers by the time I woke, back to the sea, I stretched my hand up to it and it vanished. The bottle had been logical, pure logic, remnant of the trapped and decaying animals, secreted by my head, enclosure, something to keep the death away from me. Not even a hospital, not even that sanction of legality, official procedures. A house it was, shabby front room with magazines, purple runner on the hall floor, vines and blossoms, the smell of lemon polish, furtive doors and whispers, they wanted you out fast. Pretense of the non-nurse, her armpits acid, face powdered with solicitude. Stumble along the hall, from flower to flower, her criminal hand on my elbow, other arm against the wall. Ring on my finger. It was all real enough, it was enough reality forever, I couldn't accept it, that mutilation, ruin I'd made, I needed a different version. I pieced it together the best way I could, flattening it, scrapbook, collage, pasting over the wrong parts. A faked album, the memories fraudulent as passports; but a paper house was better than none and I could almost live in it, I'd lived in it until now.

He hadn't gone with me to the place where they did it; his own children, the real ones, were having a birthday party. But he came afterward to collect me. It was a hot day, when we stepped out into the sun we couldn't see for an instant. It wasn't a wedding, there were no pigeons, the post office and the lawn were in another part of the city where I went for stamps; the fountain with the dolphins and the cherub with half a face was from the company town, I'd put it in so there would be something of mine.

"It's over," he said, "feel better?"

I was emptied, amputated; I stank of salt and antiseptic, they had planted death in me like a seed.

"You're cold," he said, "come on, we'd better get you home." Scrutinizing my face in the light, hands on the wheel, tough, better this way. In my deflated lap there was a purse, suitcase. I couldn't go there, home, I never went there again, I sent them a postcard.

They never knew, about that or why I left. Their own innocence, the reason I couldn't tell them; perilous innocence, closing them in glass, their artificial garden, greenhouse. They didn't teach us about evil, they didn't understand about it, how could I describe it to them? They were from another age, prehistoric, when everyone got married and had a family, children growing in the yard like sunflowers; remote as Eskimos or mastodons.

I opened my eyes and sat up. Joe was still there beside me; he was holding on to the edge of my canoe.

"You all right?" he said. His voice came to me faintly, as though muffled.

He said I should do it, he made me do it; he talked about it as though it was legal, simple, like getting a wart removed. He said it wasn't a person, only an animal; I should have seen that it was no different, it was hiding in me as if in a burrow and instead of granting it sanctuary I let them catch it. I could have said No but I didn't; that made me one of them too, a killer. After the slaughter, the murder, he couldn't believe I didn't want to see him anymore; it bewildered him, he resented me for it, he expected gratitude because he arranged it for me, fixed me so I was as good as new; others, he said, wouldn't have bothered. Since then I'd carried that death around inside me, layering it over, a cyst, a tumor, black pearl; the gratitude I felt now was not for him.

I had to go onto the shore and leave something: that was what you were supposed to do, leave a piece of your clothing as an offering. I regretted the nickels I'd taken dutifully for the collection plate, I got so little in return: no power remained in their bland oleo-tinted Jesus prints or in the statues of the other ones, rigid and stylized, holy triple name shrunken to swearwords. These gods, here on the shore or in the water, unacknowledged or forgotten, were the only ones who had ever given me anything I needed; and freely.

The map crosses and the drawings made sense now: at the beginning he must have been only locating the rock paintings, deducing them, tracing and photographing them, a retirement hobby; but then he found out about them. The Indians did not own salvation but they had once known where it lived and their signs marked the sacred places, the places where you could learn the truth. There was no painting at White Birch Lake and none here, because his later drawings weren't copied from things on the rocks. He had discovered new places, new oracles, they were things he was seeing the way I had seen, true vision; at the end, after the failure of logic. When it happened the first time he must have been terrified, it would be like stepping through a usual door and finding yourself in a different galaxy, purple trees and red moons and a green sun.

I swung the paddle and Joe's hand came unstuck and the canoe went towards the shore. I slipped on my canvas shoes and bundled up the sweatshirt and stepped out, looping the rope to a tree, then I climbed the slope towards the cliff, trees on one side, rockface on the other, balsam smell, underbrush scratching my bare legs. There was a ledge, I'd noticed it from the lake, I could throw my sweatshirt onto it. I didn't know the names of the ones I was making the offering to; but they were there, they had power. Candles in front of statues, crutches on the steps, flowers in jam jars by the roadside crosses, gratitude for cures, however wished-for and partial. Clothing was better, it was closer and more essential; and the gift had been greater, more than a hand or an eye, feeling was beginning to seep back into me, I tingled like a foot that's been asleep.

MOURNING SICKNESS

T. Thorn Coyle

A sense of losing something
In the darkness
Before light
Opens your eyes.
   Raspberry. Comfrey. Valerian. Yarrow.
A woman's way
To heal herself.
A woman's way to mourn.
Ways to stop the bleeding.
Blood flows so easily sometimes.
This as winter sap.
   I sacrificed my son today.
Dark, fertile earth,
too cold to grow
such tender seeds.
Shifting into nether world.
Preparing land to bury
is tilling land for birth.
Dirt black, bloody fingernails.
Powerful hands.
   Hoe. Break. Carry. Cover.
Walk the knowledge of the Dead.
Wrap the spiral
shoulders broad
in starshot mantle.
Pressing soft the loam,
my feet walk true.
   I face the dawn.

LULLABY

Claressinka Anderson

I do not know if it is ink or blood
running down my thigh,
like the bird on my windowsill—
it escapes me.

How could I know that the simple act
of moving a candle from one room to the next
and smelling it unlit
would return me abruptly
to the place where I once held my belly
and thought I was home?

I was given a brown swan for a flower,
long and graceful with a beak of fur.
Its wings are green stalks,
its legs are leaves
falling around mine.

ACKNOWLEDGMENTS

Editing an anthology of this scope, and over such a long period of time, necessitates the help of many, many people. I am immensely grateful that in this case the people were so wonderful.

Over the two decades it took the project to become a book, innumerable helpful and well-informed people helped me locate works to include. Early members of the Discussion of Women's Poetry Listserv were the first to hear and respond to my calls for abortion writing in 1999, and a number of those useful recommendations are included here. Richard Peabody kindly shared research from his 1995 coedited literary anthology about abortion, *Coming to Terms*. Poets Joy Harjo, Barbara Hemming, Charlotte Mandel, Ellen Moody, Meg Reynolds, and Susan Tichy each recommended contributors or contributions that made their way into the book. Ellen Bass, Moira Egan, Rusty Morrison, Smita Sahay, and the Binders of Women Poets Facebook group all helped by sharing the announcement and spreading the word.

Dr. Karen Weingarten shared a rich list of abortion literature. Kit Bonson graciously connected me with winners of the abortion rights poetry contest organized by Split This Rock in Washington, DC. Dr. Rochelle Davis educated me about Saniyya Saleh and Leila Aboulela. Adrienne Pine traced down powerful contemporary writings from Latin America, and Sarah Leister offered her translation skills at short notice. Dr. Kristen Ghodsee, Dr. Agnieszka Mrozik, and Ursula Phillips led the way to Zofia Nałkowska's *Granica (Boundary)*. Mary Pradt at the St. Francis College Library used her considerable research skills to track down obscure texts. When herbalist Susun Weed heard about this book, she gifted me with a rare copy of Deborah Maia's extraordinary *Self-Ritual for Invoking Release of Spirit Life in the Womb: A Personal Treatise on Ritual Herbal Abortion*.

Deep thanks to Shikha Malaviya for connecting me with writers from India and Pakistan—including those for whom reproductive autonomy is more a matter of the freedom *not* to have an abortion than it is a matter of the freedom *to* have an abortion. Many thanks to Mo'afrika Mokgathi-Mvubu and her organization Hear My Voice, which is devoted to developing young spoken-word artists in South Africa, for assistance in curating poetry from South Africa. Thanks to Georgia Saxelby and Glenys Livingston for their invaluable aid in finding the texts from Australia. Thanks to Julie Wark for wonderful help with translation and for connecting me with Indigenous writers. Thanks to Leyla Josephine for urging me to include work from Northern Ireland and setting me on the path to connect with writers there. Thanks to Sarah Clark, T. Thorn Coyle, Althea Finch-Brand, Josh Davis and Elliot Long, Mason Hickman, Joy Ladin, and Trace Peterson for their help with my repeated efforts to track down transgender contributors.

Dr. Lauren Margaret MacIvor and Dr. Cornelia Dayton generously helped with finding and understanding early American texts: Martha Ballard's *Midwife's Diary* and Abigail Nightingale's deposition in Rex vs. Harrison (these fascinating pieces had to be cut in the end for space, but I list them here as a resource for those interested in the history of abortion).

I am also grateful to all those who have supported the book in other ways. While I was directing the Stonecoast MFA Program, my research assistant, Teal Gardella, did top-notch research work for the anthology; it would never have gotten off the ground without her help. Another Stonecoast writer, poet Autumn Newman, helped get the book moving after a hiatus and provided powerful moral support as I intuited its structure.

Connecting with feminist sheroes was a wonderful side benefit of this project. Thanks to Gloria Steinem for her staunch belief in the book's value at the beginning, for emailing me in the wee hours, and for putting me in touch with potential backers for the book. And thanks to Jennifer Baumgardner, Alicia Ostriker, and Robin Morgan for their kindness and to Faye Wattleton for her good words of support.

Thanks to poet and editor Mahogany L. Browne for connecting me with the fabulous Haymarket Books community. My editors there, Nisha Bolsey, Julie Fain, and Maya Marshall, brim with professionalism, great ideas, sound judgment, patience, and inspirational enthusiasm. I feel blessed to work with you. Also, thanks to Fred Courtright for stellar and steadfast permissions support.

Thank you is not enough of a word to acknowledge my beloved husband Glen Brand's contributions to this project. Glen's incredible support included donating weekends to help set up the Kickstarter, keeping an eye out for relevant articles and news, gracing my prose with high-level editorial feedback, pitching in with data entry, providing yeoman duty in the kitchen, offering a shoulder to cry on when things got overwhelming, and reminding me to put out a call for much-needed volunteers—and then coming through once more after I woke up on the morning the manuscript was due and realized the book needed a timeline. Thank you, Glen, for your many extraordinary gifts.

Kate Carey, Alicia Cole, Kai Karpman, Lauren Korn, Alexis Quinlan, and Savannah Slone were the generous volunteers who stepped forward in response to my call for help with the manuscript. You are amazing people for doing that. I'd especially like to acknowledge three of the volunteers whose cheerful enthusiasm and generous willingness to help reminded me continually of the importance of our goal and kept me aware that a project like this is really about community. Kate Carey donated her lunch hours for many weeks and did a stellar job coordinating contributor information. Savannah Slone volunteered her brilliant design, production, and social media skills with extraordinary energy over numerous aspects of the project; please check out the *Choice Words* Facebook, Instagram, and Twitter for Savannah's beautiful and inspiring pro-choice memes. Last but not least, Alexis Quinlan stood with me through the difficult last stages of manuscript preparation, sharing her eagle eye for copyediting, kind patience through some aggravating formatting situations, and a number of fabulously creative and helpful editing suggestions. I couldn't have imagined better help than the three of you, and every reader of this book is in your debt.

Without Kickstarter, this book would not exist. Immense thanks to Margot Atwell for superb advice and guidance, and to the 487 Kickstarter backers who literally made this book possible. Your generous donations will fund the permissions costs to enable the book to be published and to attain the stretch goal of donating copies of *Choice Words* to clinics in states where abortion rights are under attack. An especially warm, hearty, and loud shout-out goes to the Kickstarter donors who went the extra mile for this book: A. B., Claressinka Anderson, Brautigam, Kate Baldwin, Pat Benson, Amelie Brown, Rebecca Burton, Desiree Cooper, Carolyn Dille, Jessica Epperson-Lusty, Luise Erdmann, Michael Herron, Paula Kamen, Erin Keogh, Jennifer MacKenna, Amanda Maystead, M. McDermott, Adele Ryan McDowell, Sue Jones McPhee in honor of Julia G. Kahrl, Ph.D., Alice Liddington Moore, Carol Muske-Dukes, Anita Nalley, Patti Niehoff, Deborah O'Grady, Maria Carra Rose, Seth M. Rosen, Sharon Shula, F. Omar Telan, Joyce Tomlinson, Toni, Waffles, Kate Warren, and Elizabeth Wrigley-Field.

Finally, I would like to thank the *Choice Words* contributors, an extraordinary community I was delighted to get to know during the editing process. Many of you shared writing you had never shown to anyone before. Others wrote new pieces for this anthology, sometimes telling stories you had waited years or decades to tell. Some of you came back with repeated drafts, considering my suggestions and patiently revising until the piece was finished. It's been wonderful getting to know you, and I hope to meet you at the launch readings. And to the many writers who sent work that couldn't be included, I want to thank you also; your courage and creative energy are part of this book as well.

CREDITS FOR REPRINTED TEXTS

CONTRIBUTORS

Leila Aboulela is the author of the novels *The Kindness of Enemies, The Translator* (longlisted for the Orange Prize), *Minaret*, and *Lyrics Alley*, which was Fiction Winner of the Scottish Saltire Literary Prize. Her work has been translated into fifteen languages, and she is the first-ever winner of the Caine Prize for African Writing.

Kathy Acker (1948–1997) was a postmodernist writer and performance artist whose books include *Blood and Guts in High School; Don Quixote; Literal Madness; Empire of the Senseless; In Memoriam to Identity; My Mother: Demonology; Pussy, King of the Pirates; Portrait of an Eye*; and *Rip-Off Red, Girl Detective.*

Ai (1947–2010) was an American poet and educator. Her ten books of poetry include *Cruelty, Sin,* and *Greed.* Her work is known for its innovative use of dramatic monologue to explore the shadow side of human nature. She won numerous awards including the National Book Award for *Vice: New and Selected Poems.*

Josette Akresh-Gonzales was a finalist in the 2017 Split Lip Chapbook Contest and has been Pushcart nominated; her poems are in *The Pinch, Breakwater, [PANK] Magazine*, and elsewhere. She lives in the Boston area with her husband and two boys and bikes to work at a nonprofit medical publisher. @Vivakresh

Lauren K. Alleyne, author of *Honeyfish* and *Difficult Fruit*, is a poet and educator. Her award-winning work appears in venues such as the *Atlantic, New York Times, Tin House*, and *Ms. Muse.* She is assistant director of the Furious Flower Poetry Center at James Madison University.

Lisa Alvarado Chicana. Jew. Poet. Inside agitator. Eldest daughter of an eldest daughter. "New World Order" was written as a cautionary tale. It is now news. lisaalvarado.net

Amy Alvarez's poems have appeared in *Sugar House Review, Rattle, New Guard Review,* and elsewhere. Her poem "Alternative Classroom Senryu" was nominated for a Pushcart Prize. She is an alumna of the Stonecoast MFA program at the University of Southern Maine. She teaches at West Virginia University.

Claressinka Anderson lives and works in Los Angeles. Originally from London, she founded Marine Projects, which presents an adaptable model for engaging with contemporary art. Some of her writing can be found at *Autre Magazine, Contemporary Art Review Los Angeles, Artillery Magazine* and *The Chiron Review.*

Anonymous balladeers in the Scottish border country are believed by scholars to have been mostly women. They passed their ballads on orally over centuries, so the words exist in many different versions. The earliest reference to "Tam Lin" occurs in 1549, but the ballad itself may be far older.

Judith Arcana writes poems, stories, essays, and books—including *Grace Paley's Life Stories, a Literary/Political Biography; Announcements from the Planetarium*, a recent poetry collection; and, coming soon, *Hello. This Is Jane* is a collection of linked fictional stories seeded by Judith's pre-Roe underground abortion work in Chicago. juditharcana.com

Linda Ashok is a poet from India. Author of *whorelight* (Hawakal, 2017), she runs the annual RL Poetry Award, directs RLFPA Editions, and edits the Best Indian Poetry series. For more about her published works, fellowships, press, and media, visit lindaashok.com.

Margaret Atwood is the author of more than forty books of fiction, poetry, and critical essays, including *The Blind Assassin*, winner of the Booker Prize, and *The Robber Bride, Cat's Eye,* and *The Handmaid's Tale.* She is the winner of the National Book Critics Circle and PEN Center USA Lifetime Achievement Awards.

Sylvia Beato is a writer and educator whose poems have appeared in *Split This Rock, Calyx Journal, Tupelo Quarterly*, and elsewhere. Her chapbook, *Allegiances*, is available from Ghostbird Press.

Melody Bee is an advocate and facilitator for both the lived and liminal experiences of having a womb. She works for grassroots reproductive knowledge and culture reclamation as an operative to reimagine the dominant paradigm. She lives with her family on Arakwal Country in Northern NSW, Australia.

Tara Betts is the author of *Break the Habit* and *Arc & Hue.* She's a co-editor of *The Beiging of America: Personal Narratives about Being Mixed Race in the Twenty-First Century* and editor of the critical edition of Philippa Duke Schuyler's memoir *Adventures in Black and White.*

Ana Blandiana has published fourteen books of poetry, two books of short stories, nine books of essays, and one novel. Her work has been translated into twenty-four languages and published in fifty-eight books of poetry and prose to date. She was awarded the European Poet of Freedom Prize for her book of poems *My Native Land A4.*

Gwendolyn Brooks (1917–2000) authored many books of poetry, including *Annie Allen, A Street in Bronzeville*, and *The Bean Eaters,* and two volumes of memoir. Poet Laureate of Illinois for thirty-two years and the first African American to receive the Pulitzer Prize for poetry, she was honored on a US postage stamp.

Rita Mae Brown is the bestselling author of the Sneaky Pie Brown series; the Sister Jane series; the Runnymede novels, including *Six of One* and *Cakewalk*; as well as the Mags Rogers novels, including *A Nose for Justice* and *Murder Unleashed*; *Rubyfruit Jungle, In Her Day,* and many other books. She is a poet and an Emmy-nominated screenwriter.

Mahogany L. Browne is a writer, organizer, and educator. She is author of *Woke Baby, Black Girl Magic, Kissing Caskets, Dear Twitter*, and the forthcoming *Woke: A Young Poet's Call to Justice*. Artistic director of Urban Word NYC, Browne has received fellowships from Cave Canem, Poets House, and Rauschenberg. She resides in Brooklyn.

Debra Bruce's most recent book is *Survivors' Picnic*. She has published several poems on the subject of unwanted pregnancy and abortion in *Evansville Review, Salamander, Shenandoah*, and *Women's Studies Quarterly*. "(Amber)" first appeared in *Mezzo Cammin: An Online Journal of Formal Poetry by Women*. debrabrucepoet.com

Sue D. Burton is author of *BOX* (Two Sylvias Press Prize, 2018) and *Little Steel* (Fomite, 2018). Her heroic crown "Box Set" (sections 1–5 in *Choice Words*) was awarded Fourth Genre's Steinberg Prize. She apprenticed as a physician's assistant at the Vermont Women's Health Center, and worked as a physician's assistant for over twenty-five years.

Cathleen Calbert's writing has appeared in many publications, including *Ms. Magazine, New Republic, New York Times*, and *Paris Review*. She is the author of four books of poetry: *Lessons in Space, Bad Judgment, Sleeping with a Famous Poet*, and *The Afflicted Girls*.

Emily Carr's newest book, *Whosoever Has Let a Minotaur Enter Them, Or a Sonnet—*, is available from McSweeney's. It inspired a beer of the same name, now available at the Ale Apothecary. Carr's tarot romance, *Name Your Bird Without a Gun*, is forthcoming from Spork.

Wendy Chin-Tanner is the author of *Turn*, which was an Oregon Book Awards finalist, and *Anyone Will Tell You*. She serves as poetry editor at *The Nervous Breakdown* and is published at such journals as the Academy of American Poets' Poem-a-Day, *RHINO, Denver Quarterly,* and *The Rumpus*.

Lucille Clifton (1936–2010), author of *Good Woman: Poems and a Memoir* (1987), *Next* (1987), and *Two-Headed Woman* (1980), among others, served as Poet Laureate of Maryland, was twice a finalist for the Pulitzer Prize, and won numerous poetry awards including the National Book Award, Ruth Lilly Prize, and Frost Medal.

Lisa Coffman has published two collections of poetry: *Likely* and *Less Obvious Gods*. Her poems and articles have been featured in *Writer's Almanac*, *Oxford American*, *BBC News*, *Village Voice*, and numerous literary journals. Coffman has earned fellowships from the National Endowment for the Arts and the Pew Charitable Trusts.

Jane Hardwicke Collings is an Australian midwife, writer, and teacher. Founder of the School of Shamanic Womancraft, she gives workshops internationally on sacred and shamanic dimensions of pregnancy, birth, and menopause. Her books include *Thirteen Moons: How to Chart Your Menstrual Cycle* and *Ten Moons: The Inner Journey of Pregnancy*.

Julia Conrad is a writer from Brooklyn. She holds an MFA in nonfiction from the University of Iowa, and her essays are published in *Massachusetts Review, Vol. 1. Brooklyn*, and *Revista Nexos*, among others. She believes in countering shame with humor, pastrami sandwiches, and unswerving love.

Desiree Cooper is a 2015 Kresge Artist Fellow, Pulitzer Prize–nominated journalist, and the award-winning author of the flash-fiction collection *Know the Mother*. Her short film based upon "The Choice" won awards at the Berlin Flash Film Festival, and the Los Angeles Best Short Film Festival. She resides in coastal Virginia.

T. Thorn Coyle is the author of multiple spirituality books—including *Evolutionary Witchcraft* and *Kissing the Limitless*—and two contemporary fantasy series—The Witches of Portland and The Panther Chronicles. As a genderqueer person, they want to remind us that reproductive justice affects everyone: cis, trans, and nonbinary.

Teri Cross Davis's poetry collection *Haint* (Gival Press) won the 2017 Ohioana Book Award for Poetry. Her work has appeared in many anthologies and journals including *Not Without Our Laughter: Poems of Joy, Humor, and Sexuality, Poetry Ireland Review*, and *Tin House*. She lives in Silver Spring, Maryland.

Dymphna Cusack (1902–1981) wrote twelve novels, numerous plays, and children's books and was a founder of the Australian Society of Authors. An antinuclear and peace activist, she willed her estate to the Communist party. *Come in Spinner* was produced as a television series by the Australian Broadcasting Company.

Katy Day is a literary arts administrator and single mother in Washington, DC. Her poetry has appeared in *The Rumpus, [PANK] Magazine, Barrelhouse Magazine, Tinderbox Poetry Journal*, and elsewhere. She was a finalist for the Brett Elizabeth Jenkins Poetry Prize and awarded the Exceptional Manuscript Scholarship from Sierra Nevada College.

Emily DeDakis is a writer, producer, and dramaturg based in Belfast, Northern Ireland, working with Accidental (an artist-led workspace and theatre) and Fighting Words Belfast (a creative writing center for young people). Her writing has appeared in *Dead Housekeeping, Vacuum, Ulster Tatler,* and *Yellow Nib* and on the BBC.

Lynne DeSilva-Johnson is a multimodal creator and scholar, addressing intersections between persons, language, technology, and system change. Recent features include *Big Echo, Matters of Feminist Practice*, and *The Exponential Festival. Sweet and Low* is forthcoming from Lark Books. They teach at Pratt Institute and are founder/creative director of The Operating System.

Diane di Prima's forty books include *Loba, Memoirs of a Beatnik*, and *Recollections of My Life as a Woman: The New York Years.* She co-edited *The Floating Bear* with Amiri Baraka, cofounded Poets Press, New York Poets Theatre, and San Francisco Institute of Magical and Healing Arts, and was San Francisco Poet Laureate.

Sharon Doubiago is the author of *Hard Country, South America Mi Hija*, named the Best Book of the Year by the *LA Weekly*, and *Psyche Drives the Coast,* which won the Oregon Book Award for Poetry. Her prose books include *El Niño* and *The Book of Seeing with One's Eyes.*

Margaret Drabble is the author of nineteen novels. Her third, *The Millstone* (1965), received the John Llewellyn Rhys Memorial Prize. She has also written a screenplay, stories, biographies, and literary history and received the Golden PEN Award for her lifetime's service to literature. She is the sister of novelist A. S. Byatt.

Minerva Earthschild is a Reclaiming-initiated witch, ordained Zen priest, and an attorney, mediator, and children's advocate. She has facilitated workshops and rituals for women healing from abortion, and she has taught magic and yoga. She is a recent widow and is currently doing grief work, which encompasses healing from all forms of loss.

Mariana Enriquez is an Argentine writer. She wrote the novels *Bajar es lo peor* and *Cómo desaparecer completamente* as well as a novella and two story collections. Her work has been anthologized in Spain, Mexico, Chile, Bolivia, and Germany.

Annie Ernaux's most recent work, *The Years*, has received the Françoise-Mauriac Prize, the Marguerite Duras Prize, the Strega European Prize, the French Language Prize, the Télégramme Readers Prize, and the 31st Annual French-American Translation Prize, and is shortlisted for the International Booker Prize. Her next book will be out from Seven Stories in 2020.

Pat Falk is an award-winning author of five books of poetry and prose, most recently *A Common Violence*. Her work has appeared in literary journals including *New York Times Book Review* and *Creative Nonfiction*. A professor at SUNY's Nassau Community College, she maintains a website atpatfalk.net.

Camonghne Felix is a poet, political strategist, media junkie, and cultural worker. Her debut full-length collection of poems, *Build Yourself a Boat* (Haymarket Books, 2019), is longlisted for the National Book Award.

Annie Finch is a poet, writer, teacher, and performer. Her books include *The Ghost of Meter*, *Calendars*, *A Poet's Craft*, *Spells: New and Selected Poems*, and a book-length poem about abortion entitled *Among the Goddesses: An Epic Libretto in Seven Dreams*.

Anne Finger has published several novels, short stories, and a memoir, including *Call Me Ahab* and *Past Due: A Story of Disability, Pregnancy, and Birth*. A polio survivor, she is an activist for the disabled and former president of the Society for Disability Studies and AXIS Dance Company.

Daisy Fried is the author of three books of poetry, most recently *Women's Poetry: Poems and Advice*. She is the poetry editor of the literary resistance journal *Scoundrel Time*, and is a member of the faculty of the Warren Wilson College MFA Program for Writers.

SeSe Geddes lives in Santa Cruz, California, where she teaches belly dance and creative journal writing. She believes abortion needs to be safe, legal, and de-stigmatized. Additionally, she believes in creating a society that offers support for women who choose to have children. Pro-choice and pro-family go hand in hand.

Kristen R. Ghodsee is an award-winning author, ethnographer, and professor of Russian and East European Studies at the University of Pennsylvania. She has written nine books, and her articles have been translated into over a dozen languages and published in *Foreign Affairs*, *Dissent*, *New Republic*, *Washington Post*, and *New York Times*.

Jennifer Goldwasser was born in 1977 in San Francisco. An artist and craftsperson, she works independently with fibers and other mediums, occasionally writing poems, songs, and letters. She is passionate about natural healing, spirituality, and environmental ecology. She is a single parent of two young children.

Valley Haggard is a writer, teacher, and reiki master. The founder of small press and online journal *Lifein10minutes.com*, Valley is the author of *The Halfway House for Writers* and *Surrender Your Weapons: Writing to Heal*. She lives in Richmond, Virginia, with two cats, a bearded dragon, a husband, a son, and a hound.

Jennifer Hanratty is a woman and mother living in Belfast, Northern Ireland. Women and health care providers in Northern Ireland face up to life in prison for ending a pregnancy, even in cases of rape or fatal fetal anomaly.

Farideh Hassanzadeh-Mostafavi is an Iranian poet, translator, and freelance journalist. She has translated editions of selected poems of T. S. Eliot, Federico García Lorca, Marina Tsvetaeva, Iaroslav Seifert, Khalil Gibran, and Blaga Dimitrova. *The Anthology of Contemporary American Poetry* is her newest work.

Deborah Hauser is a poet, feminist, activist, women's health clinic escort, certified ennui therapist, fairy tale revisionist, and author of *Ennui: From the Diagnostic and Statistical Field Guide of Feminine Disorders*. She leads a double life on Long Island, where she works in the insurance industry.

Bobbie Louise Hawkins (1930–2018), author of *One Small Saga* (1984) and *My Own Alphabet* (1989), wrote more than twenty books of fiction, nonfiction, poetry, and performance monologues. She performed her work in New York City and San Francisco, as well as in Canada, England, Germany, Japan, and Holland.

Langston Hughes (1901–1967) was the author of *The Weary Blues*, published in 1926. Among his awards and honors include a Guggenheim Fellowship, a Rosenwald Fellowship, and a grant from the American Academy of Arts and Letters. He was the author of more than thirty-five books, including poetry, short stories, novels, an autobiography, musicals, essays, and plays.

Ulrica Hume is the author of *An Uncertain Age*, a spiritual mystery novel, and *House of Miracles*, a collection of interrelated tales about love, one of which was selected by PEN and broadcast on NPR. Her lyrical flash pieces appear online and in anthologies. She is a labyrinth guide. ulricahume.com

Colette Inez (1931–2018) was the author of ten books of poetry including *The Woman Who Loved Worms*, a memoir, the libretto for an opera on Mary Shelley, and the text of the award-winning song cycle *Miz Inez Sez*. She received Guggenheim and NEA awards and taught widely including at Columbia University.

Florence James (1902–1993) was a New Zealand–born writer, editor, and literary agent. With Dymphna Cusack, she wrote a children's book and the prize-winning novel *Come in Spinner*. She worked for two decades in London and was active as a pacifist and member of the Religious Society of Friends in Australia.

Ruth Prawer Jhabvala (1927–2013) wrote several novels and short stories, and in collaboration with James Ivory and Ismail Merchant, she won two Oscars for Best Adapted Screenplay (for *Howards End* and *A Room with a View*). She won the Booker Prize in 1975 for *Heat and Dust*.

Georgia Douglas Johnson (1880–1966) was an African American poet and playwright. She was the author of a syndicated newspaper column and published four collections of poetry: *The Heart of a Woman*, *Bronze*, *An Autumn Love Cycle*, and *Share My World*.

Leyla Josephine is a poet, performance artist, screenwriter, and theater maker from Glasgow, Scotland. She has been featured on *Guardian*, *BBC*, *Upworthy*, and *BuzzFeed*. She has won many poetry slams including the UK National Poetry Slam. Her first book, *Hopeless*, was published by Speculative Books.

Soniah Kamal's novel, *Unmarriageable: Pride & Prejudice in Pakistan*, is a Financial Times Readers' Best Book of 2019. Her debut novel, *An Isolated Incident*, was a finalist for the Townsend Award for Fiction. Her TEDx Talk is about second chances. Her work has appeared in the *New York Times*, *Guardian*, *Atlantic*, and more.

Paula Kamen, based in Evanston, Illinois, is a playwright and the author of four nonfiction feminist books, including *All in My Head*, about women and chronic pain. Her commentaries and reviews have appeared in the *New York Times*, *McSweeney's*, *Washington Post*, *Salon*, and *Ms.* paulakamen.com

Julie Kane is the co-editor with Grace Bauer of *Nasty Women Poets: An Unapologetic Anthology of Subversive Verse* (Lost Horse Press, 2017). Her latest poetry collection is *Mothers of Ireland* (LSU Press, 2020). She is a former National Poetry Series winner, Fulbright Scholar, and Louisiana Poet Laureate.

Pratibha Kelapure is a real person who lives in an imaginary world of words that she built by founding the online journal *The Literary Nest*. The poem in this collection is inspired by several tragic stories of abortion in cultures where women lack any rights.

Kenyan Teenagers Six hundred fourteen young people in Nairobi spoke with researchers about how unplanned pregnancy was handled among their friends. Their school textbooks and exams teach that abortion is wrong and harmful. Sixty-three percent of them said they attend Christian or Muslim religious services once a week. Their average age is sixteen.

Lauren R. Korn is an MA student of creative writing at the University of New Brunswick and the director of content for *Adroit Journal*. In her poem, "And There Is This Edge," anthologized here, the phrase "there is this edge" is borrowed from Joy Harjo's "Call It Fear."

Myrna Lamb (1935–2017) wrote sixteen plays and five screenplays. Her short plays, including *What Have You Done for Me Lately?* were produced at the *New Feminist Theater*, and Joseph Papp's Public Theater produced her feminist musicals *Mod Donna* (1970) and *Apple Pie*. Her awards include NEA and Guggenheim grants.

Joan Larkin's books include *Blue Hanuman*, *My Body: New and Selected Poems*, and *Cold River*, among others. She has edited several anthologies, including *Gay and Lesbian Poetry in Our Time* with Carl Morse, and has been a lifelong teacher, most recently at Smith College. Her honors include the Shelley Memorial Award and the Academy of American Poets Fellowship.

Jenna Le authored *Six Rivers* (NYQ Books, 2011) and *A History of the Cetacean American Diaspora* (Indolent Books, 2018), which won second place in the Elgin Awards. She was selected by Marilyn Nelson as winner of Poetry by the Sea's inaugural sonnet competition. Her poetry appears in *Los Angeles Review*, *Massachusetts Review*, and *West Branch*. jennalewriting.com

Violette Leduc (1907–1972) was the author of *La Bâtarde*, which was published in 1964 and earned her the acclaim of Simone de Beauvoir, Jean-Paul Sartre, and Albert Camus. A film about her life, *Violette*, was produced in 2013.

Ursula K. Le Guin (1929–2018), author of *The Left Hand of Darkness* (1969) and *The Dispossessed* (1974) among other novels, short stories, essays, children's books, poetry, and translations, was awarded the National Book Foundation Medal for Distinguished Contribution to American Letters in 2014.

Dana Levin's fourth book is *Banana Palace*. Her work has appeared in *Best American Poetry*, *New York Times*, POETRY, and *American Poetry Review*. A grateful recipient of honors from the Rona Jaffe, Whiting, and Guggenheim Foundations, Levin serves as Distinguished Writer in Residence at Maryville University in St. Louis.

Amy Levy (1861–1889) was a British poet, novelist, and essayist. In 1879, she became the second Jewish woman to enroll in Cambridge University and the first Jewish woman to enroll at Newnham College, which she left two years later after publishing her first poetry collection, *Xantippe and Other Verses*. Her other works include two more collections of poetry and three novels.

Shirley Geok-lin Lim's *Crossing the Peninsula* received the Commonwealth Poetry Prize. Awarded the Multiethnic Literatures of the United States Lifetime Achievement Award, she's published ten poetry collections, six books of fiction, and *The Shirley Lim Collection*. Her memoir *Among the White Moon Faces* and anthology *The Forbidden Stitch* received American Book Awards.

Audre Lorde (1934–1992), a Black lesbian feminist poet, writer, essayist, critic, and activist, pioneered Black and lesbian feminism and intersectional theory. Her eighteen books include the poetry collections *Coal* and *The Black Unicorn*, *Sister Outsider: Essays and Speeches*, *The Cancer Journals*, and the memoir *Zami: A New Spelling of My Name*.

Busisiwe Mahlangu is the author of *Surviving Loss*, produced at South African State Theatre, and founder of Lwazilubanzi Project. She's received poetry and slam awards from the National Library of South Africa and Mzansi Poetry Academy. She designs jewelry through Busi Designs and studies creative writing at the University of South Africa.

Deborah Maia worked full-time in microbiological research before changing her focus to herbal medicine and childbirth education. She developed a system of "ritual massage," incorporating ritual with body work, and wrote *Self-Ritual for Invoking Release of Spirit Life in the Womb*, published in 1989 by Mother Spirit Press.

Shikha Malaviya is a South Asian poet and writer. She is a cofounder of The (Great) Indian Poetry Collective, a mentorship-model press publishing voices from India and the Indian diaspora. She has been a TEDx speaker and AWP mentor, and was selected as Poet Laureate of San Ramon, California (2016).

Kate Manning is the author of the novels *Whitegirl* and *My Notorious Life*, which is based on the true story of an infamous Victorian midwife. A former documentary television producer, she has won two Emmy Awards and has written for the *New York Times*, the *Washington Post*, and the *Guardian*.

Angie Masters is a pansexual feminist Guatemalan teacher, sociology student, and poet. She is a founder of the Tz'unun Mobile Library Collective, member of the Atrapados en Azul Collective, and a human rights activist dedicated to the eradication of violence against women and to using art for grassroots social transformation.

Caitlin Grace McDonnell is a poet/writer/teacher/mother who lives in Brooklyn. Her poems and essays have been published widely and she has a book,

Looking for Small Animals (nauset press), and a chapbook, *Dreaming the Tree* (belladonna). She is at work on an autobiographical novel.

Leslie Monsour, author of two poetry collections and recipient of five Pushcart Prize nominations as well as an NEA fellowship, has had poems, essays, and translations appear in numerous publications. She passionately believes reproductive choice is an essential right for women. The choice is not easy, but the freedom to make it is essential.

Yesenia Montilla is an Afro-Latina poet and a daughter of immigrants. Her poetry has appeared in *Gulf Coast*, *Prairie Schooner*, and other publications. She received her MFA from Drew University and is a CantoMundo graduate fellow. Her first collection, *The Pink Box*, was longlisted for a PEN award in 2016.

Mary Morris received the Rita Dove Award and is the author of a book of poems, *Enter Water, Swimmer*. Her work appears in POETRY, *Poetry Daily*, *Arts & Letters*, *Prairie Schooner*, *Massachusetts Review*, and numerous other fine literary journals. She lives in Santa Fe, New Mexico. mary@water400.org

Thylias Moss, sixty-five, has published fourteen books and won a MacArthur Genius Grant and nominations for the National Book Critics Circle Award, but she is most proud of falling in love with spoken-word artist and collaborator Bob Holman, seventy-one.

Carol Muske-Dukes's ninth book of poems is *Blue Rose* (Penguin, 2018), which made the Pulitzer long list. She is a professor at University of Southern California, where she founded the PhD program in creative writing/literature. Former Poet Laureate of California, she is also a novelist, essayist, playwright, and recipient of many awards.

Burleigh Mutén lives in the woods of western Massachusetts, where hawks soar, owls glide, and the moonlight dapples the forest floor. She is the author of the verse novel about Emily Dickinson *Miss Emily* as well as several other children's books.

Zofia Nałkowska (1884–1954) was a Polish feminist and author of thirteen novels and novellas, a memoir, essays, and five plays. She is best known for her books *Granica (Boundary)* (1935), *Węzły Życia* (1948), and the short story collection *Medaliony* (1947). She served as executive member of the Polish Academy of Literature.

Vi Khi Nao is the author of *The Old Philosopher* (winner of the Nightboat Prize), the short story collection *A Brief Alphabet of Torture* (winner of the 2016 FC2's Ronald Sukenick Innovative Fiction Prize), and the novel *Fish in Exile*. She holds an MFA in fiction from Brown University.

Gloria Naylor (1950–2016) was the author of the novels *The Women of Brewster Place*, which won the American Book Award and National Book Award and was adapted for television by Oprah Winfrey, *Linden Hills, Mama Day, Bailey's Cafe*, and *The Men of Brewster Place*, as well as the fictionalized memoir *1996*.

Hanna Neuschwander is a science communicator and essay writer. She lives in Portland, Oregon, with her husband and two living daughters.

Joyce Carol Oates is the author of fifty-eight novels, including *The Gravedigger's Daughter, We Were the Mulvaneys, Them*, and *Blonde*. Her story "Where Are You Going, Where Have You Been?" is the basis for the movie *Smooth Talk*. She has won many awards including the Norman Mailer Prize and the National Book Award.

Frank O'Hara (1926–1966) was an American writer, poet, and art critic. He is considered an original member of the New York School. His first volume of poetry was *A City Winter and Other Poems*, and *The Collected Poems of Frank O'Hara*, the first of several posthumous collections, shared the 1972 National Book Award for Poetry.

Sharon Olds is the author of twelve books of intensely honest and personal poetry. Her books include *Satan Says, The Dead and The Living*, which won the National Book Critics Circle Award, *Stag's Leap*, which received the Pulitzer Prize, and *Odes*. She taught for forty years at New York University.

Ginette Paris is emeritus professor of jungian and archetypal psychology at Pacifica Graduate Institute in Santa Barbara, California. She teaches and lectures in the US, Canada, and Europe. She is a psychologist, therapist, and author of many books, including *The Psychology of Abortion*, originally published as *The Sacrament of Abortion*.

Dorothy Parker (1893–1967) was an American poet, writer, and critic, and a founding member of the famed Algonquin Round Table. Her books include the poetry collections *Enough Rope* and *Sunset Guns* and the books of fiction *Laments for the Living* and *Here Lies*. She was inducted into the American Academy of Arts and Letters in 1959.

Molly Peacock, author of *The Analyst* and six other collections of poetry, co-founded Poetry in Motion on New York City's subways. Also the author of *The Paper Garden: Mrs. Delany Begins Her Life's Work at 72*, Peacock is featured in the documentary about child-free women, *My So-Called Selfish Life*.

Cristina Peri Rossi is a Uruguayan novelist, poet, translator, and author of short stories and more than thirty-seven works including *La nave de los locos*

(1984). Exiled from Uruguay in 1972 and living in Spain, she is known for her outspoken defense of civil liberties and freedom of expression.

Marge Piercy has written nineteen volumes of poetry, including *The Moon Is Always Female*, *The Art of Blessing the Day*, and *Circles on the Water*; seventeen novels, including *Braided Lives* and *Woman on the Edge of Time*; and a memoir, *Sleeping with Cats*. The recipient of four honorary doctorates, she is active in antiwar, feminist, and environmental causes.

Katha Pollitt is an American poet, essayist, and critic whose work focuses on abortion, racism, feminism, and welfare reform, from a left-leaning perspective. Pollitt's writing has appeared in the *New York Times*, *Mother Jones*, *Harper's*, the *Nation*, and the *London Review of Books*. Her latest book is *Pro: Reclaiming Abortion Rights*.

Alexis Quinlan is a writer and teacher in New York City. Her most recent chapbook is titled *an admission, as a warning against the value of our conclusions* (Operating System, 2014).

Sylvia Ramos Cruz's work is rooted in art, women's lives, and everyday injustices, informed by her life in Puerto Rico, New York, and New Mexico. Her award-winning work appears in print and online publications. Her poem here was inspired by a newspaper article that touched her as a surgeon and a feminist.

Susan Rich is the author of four collections of poems, including, most recently, *Cloud Pharmacy*. Her poetry appears in the *Antioch Review*, *Harvard Review*, *New England Review*, and *O Magazine*. Awards include a PEN USA Award and a Times Literary Supplement Award (London). She lives in Seattle.

Ana Gabriela Rivera is a Honduran poet, environmental engineer, feminist, and founder of the Colectiva Matria and La Línea Segura Hn. She is dedicating her life to studying and sharing intersectional feminism, including fighting for the right to abortion without restrictions.

Angelique Imani Rodriguez is a Bronx-Boricua with work in *The James Franco Review*. A three-time VONA fellow, she is currently editing *Fried Eggs and Rice: An Anthology by Writers of Color on Food* and running her online book club, the Boricongo Book Gang. She hopes "Not Yours" will encourage women to stand in their truth.

Alida Rol worked for almost three decades as an obstetrician-gynecologist. Her career was informed by the belief that women should have as much voice in their health care decisions as possible, including the right to terminate a pregnancy safely. She lives and writes in Eugene, Oregon.

Cin Salach has collaborated with musicians, painters, photographers, and most recently chefs and scientists, for over thirty years. Her belief that poetry can change lives has led her to create her business poemgrown, helping people mark the most important occasions in their lives with poetry. And there is no occasion more important to mark than a woman's right to choose.

Saniyya Saleh (1935–1985) was a Syrian poet and the author of *al-Ghobar* (*The Dust*), *al Zaman al-Daiq* (*The Tight Time*), *Hiber al-Idaam* (*The Assassination Ink*), *Qasaed* (*Poems*), and *Zacar al-Ward* (*The Male Rose*).

Jacqueline Saphra is a poet and playwright. Her second full-length collection, *All My Mad Mothers* (Nine Arches Press), was shortlisted for the T. S. Eliot prize 2017. Her collection *Dad, Remember You Are Dead* was also published by Nine Arches.

Anne Sexton (1928–1974) was the author of ten collections of poetry including *To Bedlam and Part Way Back*, *Live or Die,* retellings of fairy tales called *Transformations*, and *The Awful Rowing Towards God*. A pioneer of confessional poetry, she won many awards including the Shelley Memorial Award and the Pulitzer Prize.

Purvi Shah won the inaugural SONY South Asian Social Service Excellence Award for her leadership fighting violence against women. She is the author of *Terrain Tracks* and *Miracle Marks*. Her favorite art practices are her sparkly eyeshadow, raucous laughter, and seeking justice—including reproductive justice. @PurviPoets, purvipoets.net

Ntozake Shange (1948–2018) was a renowned playwright, poet, and novelist. She wrote and performed in the Obie Award–winning *for colored girls who have considered suicide/when the rainbow is enuf,* for which she invented the term "choreopoem" (combination of poetry, dance, and music). Her novels include *Betsey Brown* and *Sassafrass, Cypress & Indigo*.

Manisha Sharma, an Indian, writes across genres about social issues. Her work is a 2019 semifinalist for the American Short(er) Fiction Contest. An AWP mentee in poetry, She has been a resident at the Vermont Studio Center and Bread Loaf Writers' Conference. She is a lecturer of English and teacher of yoga-meditation at New River Community College in Virginia.

Larissa Shmailo is a poet, novelist, translator, editor, and critic. Her most recent novel is *Sly Bang* and collection of poetry is *Medusa's Country*. She is grateful abortion was legal for her and wants to keep it safe, free, and legal for all women forever.

Leslie Marmon Silko is the recipient of a MacArthur Foundation Grant (1981) and the Native Writers' Circle of the Americas Lifetime Achievement Award (1994). Her books include *Almanac of the Dead*, *Storyteller*, *Ceremony*, and *Gardens in the Dunes*.

Agnes Smedley (1892–1950) was an American journalist and writer and an activist for women's rights, birth control, and children's welfare. She is believed to have been a spy for communists in India, Russia, and China. Her six published works include books about Chinese communism and the influential novel *Daughter of Earth*.

Ellen McGrath Smith teaches at the University of Pittsburgh. Her books include *The Dog Makes His Rounds*; *Scatter, Feed*; and *Nobody's Jackknife* (West End Press, 2015). Her work has won Orlando and Rainmaker awards, and has appeared in the *New York Times, American Poetry Review*, and other journals. ellenmcgrathsmith.com.

Edith Södergran (1892–1923) was a Swedish-speaking Finnish poet. She released four volumes of poetry during her lifetime. *Landet som icke är* (*The Land Which Is Not*) was published after her death.

Starhawk is an author, activist, permaculture designer and teacher, and a prominent voice in modern earth-based spirituality and ecofeminism. She is the author or coauthor of thirteen books, including *The Spiral Dance: A Rebirth of the Ancient Religion of the Great Goddess* and the ecotopian novels *The Fifth Sacred Thing* and *City of Refuge*.

Alina Stefanescu was born in Romania and lives in Alabama. She is the author of the poetry collection *Stories to Read Aloud to Your Fetus* (Finishing Line Press, 2017). Her fiction collection, *Every Mask I Tried On*, won the Brighthorse Books Prize. She is president of the Alabama State Poetry Society.

Gloria Steinem is a feminist activist and author of several bestselling books, including *Revolution from Within* and the memoir *My Life on the Road*. A founder of The National Women's Political Caucus and The Women's Media Center and founding editor of *Ms. Magazine*, she was awarded the Presidential Medal of Freedom in 2013.

Ellen Stone is the author of *The Solid Living World* (Michigan Writers' Cooperative Press, 2013). Stone writes about abortion for her younger self, her three daughters, and the strong women in her family.

Amy Tan's novels include *The Joy Luck Club*, which spent forty weeks on the *New York Times* bestsellers list, and five other *New York Times* bestsellers. She has also written a memoir, screenplays, and two children's books. Her essays and stories have appeared in numerous magazines and anthologies, and her work has been translated into thirty-five languages.

Ann Townsend is the author of three collections of poetry, *Dear Delinquent* (2019), *The Coronary Garden* (2005), and *Dime Store Erotics* (1998), and co-editor (with David Baker) of *Radiant Lyre: Essays on Lyric Poetry* (2007). Professor of English at Denison University in Granville, Ohio, she is the cofounder of VIDA: Women in Literary Arts.

Joanna C. Valente is a human who lives in Brooklyn. They are the author of *Sirs & Madams*, *The Gods Are Dead*, *Marys of the Sea*, *Sexting Ghosts*, *Xenos*, *No(body)* (forthcoming, Madhouse Press, 2019), and the editor of *A Shadow Map: Writing by Survivors of Sexual Assault*.

Jean Valentine is author of over a dozen collections of poetry including *Door in the Mountain: New and Collected Poems*, which won the National Book Award. She has received the Shelley Memorial Award, Bollingen Prize, and numerous other awards and served as State Poet of New York 2008–2010.

Nicole Walker is the author of the collections *The After-Normal: Brief, Alphabetical Essays on a Changing Planet* from Rose Metal Press and *Sustainability: A Love Story* from Mad Creek Books. Her previous books include *Where the Tiny Things Are*, *Egg*, *Micrograms*, *Quench Your Thirst with Salt*, and *This Noisy Egg*.

Hilde Weisert's 2015 poetry collection, *The Scheme of Things*, was published by David Robert Books. Her awards include the 2017 Gretchen Warren Award, 2016 Tiferet Journal Poetry Award, and 2008 Lois Cranston Poetry Award. She's copresident of the Sandisfield Arts Center in western Massachusetts, and lives in Sandisfield and Chapel Hill, North Carolina. hildeweisert.com

Lindy West is an American writer, comedian, and activist who publishes in *Jezebel*, *GQ*, and *Guardian*. Her books include *Shrill: Notes from a Loud Woman* (now a show on Hulu) and *The Witches Are Coming*. She is the cofounder of #ShoutYour-Abortion and received the Women's Media Center Social Media Award.

Laura Wetherington's first book, *A Map Predetermined and Chance* (Fence Books), was selected by C. S. Giscombe for the National Poetry Series. She is the poetry editor for Baobab Press and currently teaches creative writing at Amsterdam University College and in SNC Tahoe's low-residency MFA program.

Lesley Wheeler's forthcoming books include *Unbecoming*, her first novel; *The State She's In*, her fifth poetry collection; and *Poetry's Possible Worlds*, a suite of hybrid essays. Poetry editor of *Shenandoah*, she lives in Virginia, where she votes on the side of reproductive freedom.

Arisa White is the author of *You're the Most Beautiful Thing That Happened*, *A Penny Saved*, and *Hurrah's Nest*. She coauthored *Biddy Mason Speaks Up*, the second book in the Fighting for Justice series for young readers. White is an assistant professor of creative writing at Colby College. arisawhite.com

Vibra Willow is a longtime priestess, teacher, and ritualist in the Reclaiming tradition who has led many public and private rituals and contributed pieces to various publications on feminist witchcraft and paganism over the years. She is a retired lawyer and teaches human rights, English, and legal English to international lawyers.

Mary Wollstonecraft (1759–1797) was an English writer and philosopher. She was the author of novels, a history of the French Revolution, an etiquette book, and *A Vindication of the Rights of Woman* (1792). She died after birthing her second child (Mary Shelley, author of *Frankenstein*). *Maria: or, The Wrongs of Woman* was published posthumously.

Sholeh Wolpé is an Iranian-born writer. She is the author of several plays and twelve collections of translations, anthologies, and poetry, including *Keeping Time with Blue Hyacinths* and *The Conference of the Birds*. She has lived in the UK and Trinidad and is presently based in Los Angeles. sholehwolpe.com

Mo Yan is the author of *The Garlic Ballads*, *The Republic of Wine*, *Shifu, You'll Do Anything for a Laugh*, *Big Breasts and Wide Hips*, *Life and Death Are Wearing Me Out*, *Red Sorghum*, and *Pow!* In 2012, he was awarded the Nobel Prize in Literature.

Galina Yudovich works as a program specialist in the Office of Global Women's Health at the American College of Obstetricians and Gynecologists. She is enrolled in the MSW program at San Francisco State University, where she is a Status of Women Policy Fellow.

TIMELINE OF PRE-TWENTY-FIRST-CENTURY WORKS

Anonymous Balladeers, "Tam Lin" (c. 1549)

Mary Wollstonecraft, from *Maria: or, The Wrongs of Woman* (1798)

Amy Levy, "Magdalen" (1884)

Edith Södergran, "We Women" (c. 1918)

Georgia Douglas Johnson, "Motherhood" (1922)

Dorothy Parker, "Lady with a Lamp" (1932)

Langston Hughes, "Cora, Unashamed" (1934)

Agnes Smedley, *Daughter of Earth* (1935)

Zofia Nałkowska, *Granica (Boundary)* (1935)

Gwendolyn Brooks, "the mother" (1945)

Frank O'Hara, "An Abortion" (1952)

Anne Sexton, "The Abortion" (1962)

Violette Leduc, *La Bâtarde* (1964)

Margaret Drabble, *The Millstone* (1965)

Myrna Lamb, *What Have You Done for Me Lately?* (1968)

Saniyya Saleh, "A Million Women Are Your Mother" (c. 1970)

Margaret Atwood, *Surfacing* (1972)

Rita Mae Brown, *Rubyfruit Jungle* (1973)

Ruth Prawer Jhabvala, *Heat and Dust* (1975)

Diane di Prima, "Brass Furnace Going Out: Song, After an Abortion" (1975)

Ntozake Shange, *for colored girls who have considered suicide when the rainbow is enuf* (1976)

Colette Inez, "Nicolette" (1977)

Marge Piercy, "Right to Life" (1980)

Margaret Atwood, "Christmas Carols" (1981)

Gloria Naylor, *The Women of Brewster Place* (1982)

Audre Lorde, *Zami: A New Spelling of My Name* (1982)

ABOUT HAYMARKET BOOKS

Haymarket Books is a radical, independent, nonprofit book publisher based in Chicago. Our mission is to publish books that contribute to struggles for social and economic justice. We strive to make our books a vibrant and organic part of social movements and the education and development of a critical, engaged, international left.

We take inspiration and courage from our namesakes, the Haymarket martyrs, who gave their lives fighting for a better world. Their 1886 struggle for the eight-hour day—which gave us May Day, the international workers' holiday—reminds workers around the world that ordinary people can organize and struggle for their own liberation. These struggles continue today across the globe—struggles against oppression, exploitation, poverty, and war.

Since our founding in 2001, Haymarket Books has published more than five hundred titles. Radically independent, we seek to drive a wedge into the risk-averse world of corporate book publishing. Our authors include Noam Chomsky, Arundhati Roy, Rebecca Solnit, Angela Y. Davis, Howard Zinn, Amy Goodman, Wallace Shawn, Mike Davis, Winona LaDuke, Ilan Pappé, Richard Wolff, Dave Zirin, Keeanga-Yamahtta Taylor, Nick Turse, Dahr Jamail, David Barsamian, Elizabeth Laird, Amira Hass, Mark Steel, Avi Lewis, Naomi Klein, and Neil Davidson. We are also the trade publishers of the acclaimed Historical Materialism Book Series and of Dispatch Books.